God of Liberty

GOD OF
LIBERTY

*A Religious History of the
American Revolution*

THOMAS S. KIDD

BASIC BOOKS
A Member of the Perseus Books Group
New York

Books published by Basic Books are available at special discounts for bulk purchases
in the United States by corporations, institutions, and other organizations. For more
information, please contact the Special Markets Department at the Perseus Books
Group, 2300 Chestnut Street, Suite 200, Philadelphia, PA 19103, or call (800) 810-
4145, ext. 5000, or e-mail special.markets@perseusbooks.com.

Designed by Brent Wilcox

Library of Congress Cataloging-in-Publication Data

Kidd, Thomas S.
    God of liberty : a religious history of the american revolution / Thomas S. Kidd.
        p.   cm.
    Includes bibliographical references and index.
    ISBN 978-0-465-00235-1 (alk. paper)
    1. United States—Church history—18th century.   2. United States—History—
Revolution, 1775-1783—Religious aspects.   3. Christianity and politics—United
States—History—18th century.   I. Title.
    BR520.K53 2010
    277.3'07—dc22
                                                                    2010013629

10 9 8 7 6 5 4 3 2 1

CONTENTS

CONTENTS

"Rebellion to Tyrants Is Obedience to God"

Religion and the American Revolution

T HE EVANGELICAL CHAPLAIN David Avery of Franklin, Connecticut, saw his first action of the Revolutionary War at the Battle of Bunker Hill. That June in 1775, minutemen from New England seized Bunker Hill and Breed's Hill in Charlestown, Massachusetts, just to the north of British-occupied Boston. Under the cover of darkness, the colonial troops hastily built fortifications atop Breed's Hill that would allow them to bombard the British army across the river. The sight of the fort so provoked the British that they decided to assault the insolent militiamen and drive them from the Charlestown heights. The British navy barraged Charlestown, setting the small town's wooden buildings ablaze, while 2,300 British infantrymen crossed the narrow Charles River to attack the 1,500 colonists occupying the hill.

As the redcoats began to ascend Breed's Hill, Avery stood on nearby Bunker Hill and raised his arms toward heaven, praying for God to bless the American forces. For a time, his prayers seemed to work: The first American volleys unleashed terrible destruction on the British, who retreated. They regrouped and assaulted the hill once more, only to be repulsed by a volley that to one of the surviving British soldiers sounded like an "uninterrupted peal of thunder." As the British surged forward for a third assault, the American commander reportedly shouted for the Americans not to "fire until you can see the whites of their eyes." The militiamen began shooting only at close range—but they had begun to run out of ammunition. Some drew back from the charging British, while others tried firing nails or pieces of scrap metal from their guns or bludgeoning the redcoats with their muskets. But in hand-to-hand combat, the militiamen were overwhelmed by British swords and bayonets, and the Americans called for a general retreat. Avery lost a close friend, Dr. Joseph Warren, the young physician and leader of the Massachusetts Provincial Congress, shot dead during the withdrawal. The colonial troops took severe losses in the battle, but the British losses were even greater: With over 1,000 casualties, it was the bloodiest clash for the redcoats during the war.[1]

Avery found the battle to be truly horrific. "To us infantile Americans, unused to the thunder and carnage of battle, the flames of Charlestown before our eyes—the incessant play of cannon from their shipping . . . all heightened the majestic terrors of the field, exhibiting a scene most awful and tremendous." Yet Avery came to see the British army's costly victory at Bunker Hill as a sign of divine favor for the Patriots. God, Avery averred, "was our Rock and fortress: he covered our heads with an helmet of salvation." For this evangelical chaplain, it was God who had broken up the formidable British army, who had covered the Americans' retreat, and who had turned what should have been a rout of the Patriots into a brave defense by the Americans. Through counseling, preaching, and praying, Avery helped troops understand that God remained with them, even in defeat.[2]

As a young man, Avery had experienced salvation under the ministry of the celebrated evangelical preacher George Whitefield; he had gone on to be tutored by the pastor and founder of Dartmouth College, Eleazar Wheelock, and had graduated from Yale and served for a time as a missionary to the Oneida Indians. In the years leading up to the American Revolution, he had himself become a luminary among evangelicals, preaching in the emotional style of Whitefield while embracing the Calvinist theology of Jonathan Edwards, the brilliant pastor and theologian of Northampton, Massachusetts.[3]

The news of the opening of the war at Lexington and Concord, Massachusetts, in April 1775 compelled Avery to leave his congregation in Vermont to serve the Patriot cause. Fellow evangelical chaplain Thomas Allen had exhorted him to "appear valiantly on God's side and your country's side, against sin and against American foes. Oh pity the souls of your fellow soldiers, many of whom no doubt remain under the dominion of spiritual death."[4] In the army Avery spent most of his days praying with sick and dying soldiers, who were facing the threat of mortal disease more often than enemy fire. He occasionally served on reconnaissance and sentry duty, too. He was one of more than a hundred chaplains in the Continental Army, where faith played a vital role.

After the battle of Bunker Hill, Avery fled with General George Washington through New York and New Jersey during the bleak fall of 1776. Washington had evacuated New York City, just barely escaping capture by the British that August. Following defeats at White Plains and Fort Washington in New York, Washington's army retreated into New Jersey and Pennsylvania. It was the darkest time of the war, and many began to wonder whether Washington had what it took to lead the Americans to victory. And some Americans might have wondered whether God did indeed see the justice of their cause.

On Christmas night of 1776, Avery crossed the Delaware River with Washington and witnessed the surprise attack on the Hessians—mercenaries hired by the British army—at Trenton, New Jersey. The unexpected victory was Washington's great moment of redemption. Although Americans would later remember the terrible weather on the night of the crossing before the attack, Avery and other American soldiers struggled much more with the conditions of the return trip back across the Delaware on December 26. The second crossing was so rough Avery feared he might die. "We were greatly distressed with a very cold storm of rain, hail, and snow, which blew with great violence. . . . I was extremely chilled, and came near perishing before I could get to a fire." Avery also saw Washington's critical victory at Trenton as orchestrated by God. Adverse weather and fierce British troops could not ultimately stop what Avery saw as a holy struggle for freedom.[5]

Avery was present, too, when British general John Burgoyne surrendered his great army to the Americans at Saratoga, New York, in October

1777. Burgoyne had hoped to invade upstate New York and cut New England off from the rest of the colonies—a move that Avery and others feared would allow the British to unleash French Catholic and Native American forces from the north to overrun the colonists. The French Catholics of Canada remained an ominous presence to many Protestant Americans throughout the war, even though in 1778 France would ally with the Americans and enter the war against Britain. Burgoyne's humiliating defeat led Avery to call for "the highest thanks of all Americans to the God of armies."[6] Such victories buttressed the beliefs held by Avery and legions of Americans of all denominations that the Revolutionary War was not simply about unfair taxes and colonial politics. The conflict summoned Americans to support God's sacred cause of liberty.

It was not only the most traditional, evangelical believers who found religious meaning in the American Revolution and in the founding of the American nation. Nor would their faith in the spiritual significance of the nascent country abate when the war was over.

After the final victory at Yorktown, after the framing of the U.S. Constitution, and after the presidency of George Washington, Thomas Jefferson, in America's third nationwide election, would defeat the sitting president, John Adams, in what Jefferson called the "Revolution of 1800." Jefferson's election was the final event of the revolutionary era, because it represented the Constitution's first peaceful transfer of presidential power from one party to another.

Nine months after the new president's inauguration, on New Year's Day, 1802, the Baptist evangelist John Leland delivered a prodigious gift to Jefferson: a 1,235-pound block of cheese. What newspapers rightfully declared to be a "mammoth" cheese came from the preacher's own farming community in Cheshire, Massachusetts, which seems to have voted unanimously for the deist Jefferson in the 1800 presidential election. The cheese's red crust was adorned with the motto "Rebellion to tyrants is obedience to God."[7]

Two days after the presentation of the cheese, on Sunday, January 3, Leland delivered an effusive sermon before the president and a joint session of Congress. Not all in attendance were impressed with the clergyman. A Federalist congressman hostile both to Jefferson and to Leland's evangelicals, writing in his journal, called Leland a "cheesemonger" and a "poor, ignorant, illiterate, clownish preacher." Leland spoke on the text "Behold a greater [one] than Solomon is here," a not-too-subtle glorification of his beloved president. The embarrassed Federalist congressman groaned that "such a farrago, bawled with stunning voice, horrid tone, frightful grimaces, and extravagant gestures . . . was never heard by any decent auditory before."[8]

To say that Jefferson and Leland made religious odd fellows is an understatement. Leland had devoted his life to saving souls and would estimate at the end of his career that he had preached about 8,000 sermons. An evangelical, Leland simply confessed, "My only hope of acceptance with God is in the blood and righteousness of Jesus Christ." Jefferson, on the other hand, did not believe that the blood of Jesus would save him or anyone else, although he attended church regularly as president. He always professed to be "sincerely attached" to the teachings of Jesus, but he did not believe that Jesus ever claimed to be the Son of God. He similarly thought the doctrine of the Trinity was nonsense, the "mere Abracadabra of . . . the priests of Jesus." What, then, led Leland to admire Jefferson so much that he would think to give him that big cheese?[9]

The answer to this question goes a long way toward explaining how religion, both during the Revolution and afterward, provided essential moral and political principles to the revolutionaries and forged the new American nation. Although Jefferson and Leland could not have been more opposed in their personal religious views, they shared the view that the state should assure religious liberty for all its citizens. Indeed, the Baptists of New England saw Jefferson as something of a political savior. Religious dissenters like the Baptists had long suffered persecution in Congregationalist New England, even after they and their fellow New Englanders had fought for liberty in the Revolution. Jefferson had championed religious freedom in Virginia, where Leland, as a traveling preacher, had come to know and love the future president. Jefferson the skeptical deist and Leland the fervent evangelical both believed that government should afford liberty of conscience to its citizens and should not privilege one Christian denomination over another. Their shared beliefs about the unfettered place of religion in public life made fast friends of men from theologically opposite religious traditions. To modern American eyes, this public friendship seems a most improbable alliance.

Not all conservative Christians liked Jefferson, to be sure. Many hated him because they saw him as an infidel. One even called him a "howling atheist."[10] But these critics did not represent America's emerging model of church-state relations. Jefferson and Leland did.

The link between Jefferson and Leland indicates that at the time of the founding of the United States, deists and evangelicals (and the range of believers in between) united around principles of religious freedom that were key to the success of the Revolution and that aided in the institution of a nation. The alliance of evangelicals and deists was fragile and hardly unanimous, but it proved strong enough to allow Americans to "begin the world over again," as Tom Paine put it.[11]

Only public religious beliefs—that is, religious beliefs that had public, political implications—united revolutionaries, because the personal faiths of the colonists were too diverse to unify them. In 1776 America was already a nation of many religious persuasions, and just like today, differing personal beliefs divided people. In the public realm, however, five religious ideas connected far-flung and widely varied Americans. The first idea is represented in the alliance of Leland and Jefferson: the disestablishment of state churches. All across America during the Revolution, it would be evangelicals who led the charge against state-supported religious establishments, but they often gained critical assistance from liberal Christians or deists like Jefferson who shared their goals. From the Baptists of New England to the Presbyterians of South Carolina, dissenters against the state-sponsored churches sought to prevent governments from preferring or officially establishing any Christian denomination and from taking notice of religion in law.

Jefferson was also an architect of the second major point of agreement between deists and evangelicals: the idea of a creator God as the guarantor of fundamental human rights. In European traditions, kings and their defenders had often used Christian doctrine to uphold the political hierarchy. But in America, revolutionaries began to appropriate the idea of common creation as the primary basis for the political liberties of all humanity. Of course, the most famous articulation of this idea came in Jefferson's Declaration of Independence, which proclaimed that "all men are created equal" and that "they are endowed by their Creator with certain unalienable rights."[12] This principle of rights by creation was critical to the Patriots' efforts to liberate themselves from the British government.

The doctrine of the common creation of all people would also prove to be one of the most cogent arguments against slavery. At the time of the Revolution, and for tragic decades thereafter, many American leaders tried to restrict the concept of God-given equality to white men. However, from 1776 onward, some Americans would take Jefferson's language of equal rights and use it for more politically challenging ends than the founders intended. If, as the Bible taught, all humans descended from a single, God-initiated origin, then what principle could justify racial slavery? Sadly, such logic remained a minority position among white American Christians, especially in the South, through the Civil War. Nevertheless, the doctrine of rights guaranteed by creation, widely shared among deists and evangelicals, would set American slavery on a path to extinction.

Beyond the principles of disestablishment and rights by creation propounded by both deists and evangelicals, a wide spectrum of Americans in the revolutionary era also believed in a third precept: the threat to the polity posed by human sinfulness. Because of their doubts about the goodness of human nature, they saw centralized government power as dangerous. This conviction heavily influenced both the decision to revolt against the British state and the nature of a new American government. Although most of the founders did not share the Calvinist conviction that humans were entirely depraved creatures, most revolutionary Americans did believe that the best kind of government divided the powers of government so that no one state entity possessed too much power. Older European political theory held that God vouchsafed political sovereignty in a monarch, a notion that Patriots rejected. Americans of this era shunned any central consolidation of power because, as James Madison put it in Federalist No. 51, men were not angels.

The belief in human sinfulness was a staple of both Calvinism and classical republican ideology—a political tradition that was identified with the republics of ancient Greece and Rome and that emphasized the importance of checks and balances in political power and the need for a virtuous people to preserve liberty. Most historians see the founders' belief in classical republicanism as a primary driver of the Revolution. Although republican ideology emphasized the virtuousness of landed, independent men, it also highlighted the ever-present danger of corruption among people because of their craving for domination over others.

The confluence of republican and Calvinist doubts about human nature took full force in the framing of the Constitution. Madison, having attended Calvinist-leaning Princeton, knew well the doctrines of original sin and human depravity. Although he believed that humans had a natural capacity for good, he nevertheless came to the Constitutional Convention in 1787 with a plan of government that would account for human sinfulness while also creating a government that could act effectively against threats to the national interest.

A fourth and related moral principle of many and various revolutionary Americans held that a republic needed to be sustained by virtue. Americans were convinced that political integrity had crumbled in England in the 1760s and 1770s, which led the British to assault the colonists' liberties. In a republican system, if sovereignty was given over to "the people," then those people must be willing to act benevolently, always keeping in mind the public good. Centralized government power might prevent people from running wild, but such political authority risked becoming tyrannical. If the people of the Republic acted selfishly, then anarchy would ensue, opening the door for the rise of an autocrat who would deprive people of their liberty.

During the Revolution, a new blend of Christian and republican ideology led religious traditionalists to embrace wholesale the concept of republican virtue. Conservative Protestants had traditionally been uneasy with the ideal of republican virtue, because its defenders often held a high view of the human potential for goodness independent of the practice of Christianity. But by the 1770s, even Calvinists and other conservative believers agreed with Samuel Adams when he declared that if they remained virtuous, Americans could create a "Christian Sparta," a unique amalgamation of the Christian and classical republican traditions.[13]

The fifth and final salient point of agreement between deists and evangelicals in the Revolution was the belief that God—or Providence, as deists and others might prefer to deem it—moved in and through nations. This long-held view had flourished in Britain during its seventeenth- and eighteenth-century conflicts with Europe's Catholic powers, especially France. As recently as the end of the Seven Years' War with France in 1763, most British American colonists believed that God had shown particular favor to the British Empire, of which they were then still a vital part, and many of them considered the Catholic French to be aligned with Antichrist.

With the onset of the revolutionary crisis, a major conceptual shift convinced Americans across the theological spectrum that God was raising up America for some special purpose. Britain, they believed, had abandoned its providential role, descending into corruption and evil. This change of heart hearkened back to the earlier Puritan notion that America could be what John Winthrop called a "city on a hill," a witness of virtue and Christian probity to the rest of the world.

Starting with the war's opening shots at Lexington and Concord in 1775, Americans like Avery infused the unfolding Revolution with prophetic and providential significance. Baptist leaders Isaac Backus and James Manning believed that the Revolution was an "important step towards bringing in the glory of the latter day" that would inaugurate the Kingdom of God on earth. Although the Episcopalian Washington would not go as far as Backus and Manning, he nevertheless insisted that all Americans should see the hand of God in the war: "The great author of the universe," as he put it, had intervened to ensure America's victory. There exists quite a difference in faith and emphasis between associating the war with general Providence and seeing it as the fulfillment of Christian prophecy, but such assertions reflected the new civil spirituality developing in America. During and after the Revolution, many people conflated America's political affairs with divine purposes, which lent an aura of redemptiveness to the war and to the agenda of a fledgling nation.

This civil spirituality served as a transcendent framework in which to define, justify, and fight a war and establish the new American nation. It united the continuum of American believers around the proposition that "the cause of America" had become "the cause of Christ"—or at least of Providence. Civil spirituality could also mask morally complicated or questionable matters with the veil of divine approval. Americans did, of course, define civil spirituality in very different ways, which would lead to an enduring conflict about the place, role, and definition of God in the nation's identity and affairs. Some founders envisioned America as a specifically Christian nation, while others embraced a more general American religiosity. Even in the early years of the Republic, these differing specifics would threaten to divide Americans irreparably, such as during the ratification of the Constitution and the presidential election of 1800.[14]

Yet the five religious principles on which the revolutionaries agreed were not mere slogans. They provided inspiration to both prominent political leaders like Jefferson and preachers like Avery. They vitally bound together Americans of widely differing religious opinions. If not for their common view of the relation of church and state, Leland and Jefferson might have despised one another. But their union, and the joining of countless other Americans of contradictory private beliefs, forged an unusually free nation in which the exercise of religion could flourish. Common public religious values also gave ballast to a new country that badly needed stability.

In our own time, more than two centuries after the revolutionary era and even in the midst of today's intense conflict over the definitions of morality and values, propositions based on faith actually undergird many of America's greatest political tenets. Many Americans now see religion as something that only divides us and that perhaps should be excluded from public conversation. Others call for a return to the sectarian Christian nation that supposedly existed at America's founding, a time when they believe most leaders were devout, evangelical Christians. But a closer examination shows that at the nation's founding, American religion was both diverse and thriving. In its nascent and most vulnerable moments, from the conflicts on Avery's Massachusetts battlefields to the framing of the new government that Jefferson would later lead, public spirituality united revolutionary America. The public spirituality shared by the revolutionary era's evangelicals, mainstream Christians, liberal rationalists, and deists established many of America's most cherished freedoms. *God of Liberty* will explore those principles of public spirituality and their essential connection to the success of American civil society.

CHAPTER 1

"No King but King Jesus"

The Great Awakening and the
First American Revolution

I N 1765, AS THE AMERICAN colonies erupted into controversy over the
Stamp Act, a law imposed by Parliament to generate more tax revenue
from the colonists, perhaps no one was more indignant at British perfidy
than twenty-nine-year-old John Adams of Braintree, Massachusetts. The
young lawyer was finding the rhetoric he needed to advance the cause
that would define his life: the liberty of the American people. Meeting
regularly with other agitators against the Stamp Act, including his cousin
Samuel Adams, John emerged as one of the key intellectual and political
defenders of resistance when he penned the Braintree Instructions in
September 1765. These directives to the legislative representative from
Adams's hometown insisted that the colonists should not be taxed by
Parliament because they were not represented there. Read publicly at
Braintree's town council, which was assembled at the Middle Parish Congregationalist Church, the instructions called on the Massachusetts colonial leaders to stand against British tyranny. Adams wrote that the people
of Massachusetts should allow "the most clear and explicit assertion and
vindication of our rights and liberties to be entered on the public records,
that the world may know, in the present and all future generations, that
we have a clear knowledge and a just sense of them, and, with submission
to Divine Providence, that we never can be slaves."[1]

The Braintree Instructions crystallized the Massachusetts colonists' growing anger against Parliament. Forty towns endorsed Adams's protest. The young lawyer was exhilarated by his first taste of political resistance, writing in his diary that "the Year 1765 has been the most remarkable year of my life. That enormous engine, fabricated by the British Parliament, for battering down all the rights and liberties of America, I mean the Stamp Act, has raised and spread, through the whole continent, a spirit that will be recorded to our honour, with all future generations."[2]

But Adams warned Americans that the threat posed by British power and its minions was not simply political. It was also religious. In *A Dissertation on the Canon and Feudal Law* (1765) he told colonists that the Stamp Act revealed a conspiracy within the British government to destroy the colonists' precious liberties. Adams declared that attacks on liberty came in both political and religious forms. He anticipated that the British would use not only the power of taxation but the might of the Anglican Church (the Church of England) to subdue the colonists.

Such an assertion spoke to the very core of the motives that had led so many of his fellow Americans to the shores of this continent. More than a century earlier, the first colonial Americans, especially the Puritans, had fled from the persecutions of an earlier oppressive king, Charles I, and his state-established Anglican Church to found free, godly societies in the New World. Adams's estimation of the value of human liberty was explicitly theological: "Liberty must at all hazards be supported," he avowed, because all people had "a right to it, derived from our Maker."[3]

Adams's words were fueled by philosophical and political animosity. He personally loathed the Massachusetts clergymen, mostly ministers of the Church of England, who were trying to consolidate and advance the authority of the British government by telling colonists to obey the new tax law. He called these parsons "devout religious slaves," averring that "a religious bigot is the worst sort of men." These deceivers would manipulate the Christian obligation of obedience to authority by using it to foist oppressive laws upon people, he believed; they aided and abetted the rise of tyranny.[4]

Adams himself was raised in a conservative Congregationalist family, descendants of the founding Puritan colonists. His father longed for John to become a minister himself. Adams, however, believed that the law suited him better than the church, and even as a young man he questioned a number of points of the traditional Calvinist Christianity of his upbringing. Nevertheless, Adams believed that his decision to practice law did not diminish his responsibilities as a Christian layperson. The very weekend that he signed to become a legal apprentice, he wrote in his diary about his pastor's Sunday sermon, in which the minister pointed to the ways in which God's love and power was displayed in nature. Adams wrote of entering a kind of spiritual ecstasy when contemplating the "amazing concave of heaven sprinkled and glittering with stars." The thought of God's abiding presence stirred deep emotions in him.[5]

Although Adams would by the time of the Revolution personally embrace the liberal theology of the Unitarians, he still lived in the essentially conservative political and religious milieu formed by New England's Puritan fathers. Religion and politics were not strictly separated realms, for the best kind of government enabled people to live good, godly lives in orderly freedom. Such a theology held that rulers—including kings—deserved respect and obedience unless they promoted immorality or tyranny. When that happened, the people had the right to resist. Or even rebel.

By 1765, although the political domination of Puritanism had ended because of growing religious toleration and diversity in the colonies, many of the Puritans' ideas about politics and resistance persisted. American colonists knew well those times in English history, in the 1640s and 1680s, when kings they felt to be ungodly had oppressed the people. Charles I had been deposed and then beheaded in 1649. Less than forty years later, in 1688, in what Protestants called the Glorious Revolution, King James II, a Catholic, was dethroned and replaced by Protestant King William and Queen Mary. According to Adams, the "spirit of liberty" had brought down Charles I and James II, and he believed history might be repeating itself with the colonists' resistance to the Stamp Act. It was too early to tell, he realized, but perhaps this crisis would bring down George III, too. As for the Stamp Act, Adams worried that if Americans did not remain vigilant, a corrupt few in the British government would push through similar laws levying oppressive taxes and then use spurious religious notions of unconditional obedience to justify them. To Adams, that kind of unrestrained power suggested the mysterious spirit of Antichrist at work. (In the eighteenth century, people usually just spoke of "Antichrist" rather than "the Antichrist.") Without the monitory oversight of popular authority, political and religious tyranny would become (in the language of the Scriptures) "the man of sin, the whore of Babylon, [and] the mystery of iniquity," he wrote.[6]

Educated people had the best chance of resisting the creeping coercion of the state and church. Adams pointed to the colonial colleges, especially Harvard and Yale, as key bulwarks that preserved the people's ability to combat dictatorial rule. Yet the Stamp Act, which required a tax on all kinds of printed goods, seemed designed to deprive the reading public of books and newspapers, leave the populace ignorant and servile. Malevolent forces within the British government and church intended "to enslave all America," Adams warned. Only the vigilance of an educated Christian people could preserve their liberty.[7]

Over the last two centuries, Adams has become recognized as one of the most fascinating and venerated of early America's leaders. Yet despite all his recent renewed celebrity, we typically do not recognize him as a religious thinker. His passion for Christian liberty helped place him in the first rank of the founding fathers.

The Americans' conflict with Britain was not predestined to occur. It would take leaders like Adams, leaders of exceptional political vision and religious insight, to transform the indignities and oppression of the colonists into a crusade for liberty and independence. As late as two years before the Stamp Act, Americans were firmly on the side of the British kingdom. In 1763, at the end of the Seven Years' War, colonists had celebrated the British defeat of the French in North America. Bitter rivalry between the British and French had exploded in the mid-1750s into a war to determine which European nation would control eastern North America. British colonists in America fought alongside the British regular army to secure the victory. Many Americans predicted in 1763 that the British Empire would enter an unprecedented era of peace and prosperity, with an increasingly important role for the American colonies. One Massachusetts pastor anticipated that American colonists would immediately witness the "era of our quiet enjoyment of those liberties, which our fathers purchased with the toil of their whole lives, their treasure, their blood. . . . Here shall be the late founded seat of peace and freedom. Here shall our indulgent mother [Britain], who has most generously rescued and protected us, be served and honored by growing numbers, with all duty, love, and gratitude, till time shall be no more."[8]

Yet in 1765, the relationship between the British and their American colonists began to fall apart. The key to the disagreement was the British government's desire to generate tax revenue from the colonies to help pay off the massive debt incurred during the Seven Years' War. Accordingly, Parliament passed the Stamp Act, which stipulated that goods from newspapers to playing cards had to be printed on paper bearing a royal stamp, reflecting the tax paid.

Colonists were instantly indignant at the new tax and began to devise means to resist it. Led by Patrick Henry and the Virginia legislature, Americans argued that Parliament did not have the right to tax them to raise revenue. In October 1765, delegates from nine colonies met in New York and passed an unprecedented resolution decrying the Stamp Act and demanding its repeal. In the cities, colonists harassed British stamp agents so mercilessly that by the end of the year, the new law had become unenforceable.

John Adams interpreted the controversy with Britain as a contest between spiritual tyranny and spiritual liberty. Many colonists shared his views. At a 1766 meeting of the Sons of Liberty in Boston, for instance, an anonymous speaker compared the Earl of Bute and Lord Grenville, two of the Stamp Act's chief proponents in England, to the monstrous beasts of the book of Revelation. By accepting paper with the royal stamp, he warned, colonists would "receive the mark of the beast." Although the speaker seemed not to interpret the Stamp Act as a literal fulfillment of prophecy, he and like-minded colonists used biblical rhetoric to set the imperial struggle in stark moral terms.

To John Adams and the American colonists, political and religious liberty were intertwined and inseparable. History had shown Americans that good rulers preserved the sacred trust of political and religious freedom, Adams believed, whereas evil rulers used political power and religious rationalizations to destroy a people's freedom. The colonists' worldview had prepared them to interpret the Stamp Act as an early warning signal that the spirit of tyranny might be afoot again in the British government.

To understand the ideological impetus motivating many colonists during the American Revolution, we need to look at the deeper religious, political, and military background of colonial American history. The Seven Years' War, following immediately upon the massive Christian revivals of the Great Awakening in the 1740s, prepared many Americans to interpret the American Revolution as the next great contest in the course of prophetic history as revealed in the Bible. The Great Awakening and the Seven Years' War forged a visceral bond among Protestantism, anti-Catholicism, and liberty. To many Americans who were Congregationalists or Anglicans, as well as those belonging to other denominations not sanctioned by the state, the overall Protestant faith represented spiritual and political freedom, whereas Catholicism, or what was called the spirit of popery, represented tyranny and bondage. And by 1765, "popery" meant not just Catholicism but any form of oppression.[9]

From a worldwide geopolitical standpoint, the Seven Years' War (known in America as the French and Indian War) may have actually been more significant than the American Revolution. Whereas the Revolution represented a vicious secessionist squabble within the British Empire, the Seven Years' War sent the major powers of Europe into a contest for control of colonies across the world. It was the first truly global war in human history.

American colonists had no difficulty appreciating the significance of the Seven Years' War (which actually lasted from 1754 to 1763—the "seven years" refers to the time between the official declarations of war and peace). For centuries, European Catholics and Protestants had fought bitter wars of religion and politics. Beginning in 1689, religion, politics, and geography had again incited intermittent war between the Catholics and Protestants. Protestant Britain and Catholic France (which was sometimes joined by Catholic Spain) battled in a series of imperial contests rooted in European politics and often fought on colonial soil. British Protestants and French Catholics had faced off in North America over French settlements running along the St. Lawrence River in Canada and in a thin line down the Mississippi River valley to New Orleans. To some British colonists, that string of settlements seemed like a noose encircling the British Atlantic seaboard—and a noose that was bound to tighten. The French enjoyed better relationships with Native Americans than did the British, mostly because the comparatively small number of French colonists displayed less interest in taking the Indians' land. French Catholic missionaries, the Jesuits, traditionally had more success at converting Native Americans to their faith than did English missionaries, partly because the Jesuits did more than the English Protestants to learn native languages and understand native cultures. The French also successfully recruited a number of Native Americans to go to war against the British colonists.

In the 1750s, the long-standing conflict between the French and British finally erupted in a major war over control of the Ohio River valley, the rich, arable land that lay directly between the British and French territories in North America. As British settlements pushed rapidly west into the Ohio River valley in the early 1750s, France responded by building a new chain of forts to secure the region for itself. The English colonies, especially Virginia, organized efforts to combat the French presence in the valley, which precipitated the Seven Years' War.

War often fosters speculation about the advent of end times—the days prior to coming of the Kingdom of God on earth—and the Seven Years' War was no different. Many colonists hoped that the Seven Years' War would finally end what they perceived as an apocalyptic struggle between Catholics and Protestants. The Seven Years' War was essentially a European war, yet its battles raged across the world, from Calcutta to the Caribbean, and from Quiberon Bay to Quebec. A conflict of this scale led some people to speculate that such a worldwide war might herald the coming of the last days before Jesus Christ returned to deliver his people from their enemies. The American chaplain Theodorus Frelinghuysen told his troops that though the war might be difficult, divine history was on their side: "Antichrist must fall before the end comes. . . . The French now adhere and belong to Antichrist, wherefore it is to be hoped, that when Antichrist falls, they shall fall with him."[10]

The anti-Catholicism of eighteenth-century British Protestants (which was shared by many key figures in the American Revolution) shocks modern sensibilities. Colonial-era Protestants often associated Catholicism, or "popery," with the evil figures of the Bible's book of Revelation, including the mysterious "beast." Thus, Pastor John Burt of Bristol, Rhode Island, would have surprised no one in his audience when in 1759 he described the French as children of the "Scarlet Whore, that Mother of Harlots, who is justly the abomination of the earth." New Englanders like Burt seemed to indulge a particularly virulent anti-Catholicism, largely because they had experienced a generation of local but inhumanly violent combat on their borders with New France (that is, Canada). But it was not only New Englanders who expressed this sort of anti-Catholicism. Samuel Davies, a Presbyterian pastor in Virginia (where the fighting in the Seven Years' War originated), proclaimed that the military contest represented nothing less than the "grand decisive conflict between the Lamb and the beast." He warned a Virginia military company that if they wanted to escape the "infernal horrors of Popery," they should turn to God for help.[11]

The small Catholic community in North America, outside of Quebec, would come to support the American Revolution, despite the bitter anti-Catholicism of the Patriot movement. Catholics saw the war as a possible way to alleviate the widespread discrimination against them in America. Supporting the American cause of liberty might help win liberty for themselves. Catholics played significant roles in the Revolution, especially in Maryland. In the early 1600s, the Calvert family had founded Maryland as a Catholic refuge, but the colony had fallen under Protestant domination a century later. Catholic politician Charles Carroll of Carrollton achieved popularity in Maryland in the 1770s by his staunch defense of American resistance against Britain. When he was elected to the Annapolis Convention in 1774, he became the first Catholic to hold political office in Maryland since the seventeenth century. In 1776, he served as a member of the Continental Congress and signed the Declaration of Independence—the only Catholic to do so.

Although American Catholics were ready and willing to fit into the emerging American political order, they faced intense and enduring prejudice. From where did this raging anti-Catholicism arise? Part of the answer points back to the European past and the conflicts associated with the Protestant Reformation that began in the early sixteenth century. Once the German monk Martin Luther started protesting against the abuses of the Catholic Church and Europe split between Protestant and Catholic powers, European countries had to decide which side to support. Because all countries had state-sponsored churches, the splintering effects of the Reformation had both religious and political repercussions.

In England, the government came to support the Protestant Church of England under King Henry VIII in the 1530s, but that new allegiance hardly settled the question of England's official faith. England occasionally returned to the rule of a Catholic king or queen. Catholic monarchs in Britain caused trouble for the American colonists, and not just for religious reasons. Many northern colonial governments had briefly lost their political charters, and much of their independence, in the mid-1680s under Charles II and James II, adding to the colonists' hatred of these Catholic sympathizers. Massachusetts regained a measure of independence from the Crown after the Glorious Revolution of 1688–1689, but until the American Revolution the colony would remain much more closely aligned politically with England than it ever had been in the seventeenth century. New Englanders would always look back on the dark days under James II as a reminder of what could happen if the throne of England fell under the control of oppressive forces.

In Britain, fears about Catholic political power came to a head in the 1680s and 1690s. Just as James II took the throne in England, King Louis XIV of France, a Catholic, revoked the protections given French Protestants under the Edict of Nantes and began trying to root out the Protestants, known as Huguenots. Because of this traumatic history, English Protestants came to identify their faith with liberty, while associating the forces of Catholicism with slavery and the loss of religious freedom. In their view, religion and government could not be separated, because all rulers supported the spirit of either Protestantism or Catholicism. On both sides of the Atlantic, many British Protestants paired what they called "popery and arbitrary government" as the greatest threats to the liberty of their people.

Many of the original colonists had come to America to escape the threat of Catholicism or any religious traditions that smacked of it—which included the Church of England. The Puritans of Massachusetts and Connecticut went to America because they feared that England and its official state church remained too "popish," or tainted by Catholic practices. The Puritans wanted a "purer," simpler church model, free from elaborate church hierarchy and based on their interpretation of the New Testament. Because they publicly criticized the established Church of England, many fell under persecution, and some decided in the 1630s to leave England and make a new start in America. There they could establish what Governor John Winthrop of Massachusetts called a "city upon a hill," a godly example that England would hopefully come to emulate.

Although many American colonists wanted freedom from Catholicism and freedom for a vibrant and flourishing Protestantism, they came to realize that maintaining their religious purity was a spiritual challenge. The second and third generations of Puritans in New England struggled to maintain the pious fervor of the original immigrants. Preachers lambasted the colonists for greed and immorality and warned that the judgment of God was near. For these Protestants, the wrath of God seemed often to come in the form of Indian wars.

Conflict with Native Americans started almost as soon as the first colonies were settled. At various times, it threatened to wipe out entire Native American groups, the English colonists, or both. Even worse for many Protestant settlers, some of the Indian attackers found allies among the Catholics. In the 1720s, for instance, a French Jesuit named Sebastien Rale, headquartered at a missionary station in Norridgewock, Maine, began telling local Wabanakis that they should fight against the English to maintain their land rights. The subsequent brutal war on the frontier of northern New England solved nothing, and it ended with Father Rale getting shot through the head and scalped by the Massachusetts militia. Indians were not the only ones who took scalps in the colonial wars.

What the Americans saw as their sinfulness, and the relentless threat of war that plagued New England (and to an extent, colonies further south), seemed to demand dramatic intervention by God. Pastors told their churches that their troubles with the Indians and Catholics would end only when the colonists repented. By the 1720s, many pastors had begun to pray for "revivals," or outpourings of the divine Holy Spirit, who would precipitate religious renewal and perhaps bring about the salvation of many souls. The Puritans and many other Protestants believed that every person needed personally to accept God's offer of salvation in order to be forgiven of their sins and enter heaven when they died. As the revivalist movement began to emerge, many church leaders put increasing focus on the individual's experience of salvation, or being "born again," a transaction that Jesus had taught must happen for anyone to see the Kingdom of God. Zealous new church leaders such as the British Anglican revivalist George Whitefield and Jonathan Edwards of Northampton, Massachusetts, focused intensely on the idea of a new birth—for them, the only spiritual question that mattered. The preaching of the new birth led to the Great Awakening.

The Great Awakening of the 1730s and 1740s was the most profound social upheaval in the history of colonial America. Shaking American Christianity to its core and revitalizing religious commitment even as it threatened colonial America's institutional churches, this first American revolution would herald the political revolution of 1776. The Great Awakening shattered the staid world of religious hierarchy, upending formal religious practice, which tended to be very hierarchical and clergy-centered, with church attendance often required by law and seating in church determined according to social status. The ministers who preached long, rhetorical, and theologically sophisticated sermons were challenged by new figures like Whitefield, the electrifying young preacher from England, who began dramatically changing people's expectations of what churchgoing meant. He took his controversial, emotional preaching style out of the church buildings (from which he was often banned) and into the fields, where in his compelling perorations he directly told assembled throngs that they needed to be born again. In the colonies, Whitefield caused an unprecedented sensation, which was fueled by newspaper advertisements about his travels and by the widespread publication of his personal journals. He and his fellow "evangelicals" (literally, those who delivered the "good news" about Jesus) broached the possibility that some established ministers might not actually be born again, converted Christians. Their accusations unleashed a flood of popular criticisms against ministers, who had previously wielded nearly unquestioned authority over their congregations.

The Great Awakening introduced common people to an exhilarating new world of spiritual possibilities. Never before had so many people had a chance to speak for themselves. Laypeople with no religious training often "exhorted" in the revival meetings, rousing their listeners to accept the new birth in Jesus. Critics complained that the evangelicals were too "noisy," because in their most frenzied assemblies everyone had an opportunity to testify. Women, children, African Americans, Native Americans, and the poor—all were suddenly free to speak out about their apprehension of the Lord's grace. Educated white men listened to these usually silent or silenced folks and concluded that they were filled with the Spirit. The most radical of the evangelical movements ordained uneducated men, including African Americans and Native Americans, into the ministry. Even women found leadership roles in certain evangelical churches as "deaconesses" or "eldresses." A new era of spiritual democracy had begun.

All this excitement proved too much for some established ministers and colonial authorities. In New England, they decided to make an example of one particularly outrageous itinerant preacher, James Davenport. In his early life, Davenport had given no sign of breaking with the tradition of his staid Puritan family; he graduated from Yale in 1738 and found work at a Congregationalist church in Southold, Long Island. But the example of Whitefield stirred him to become an itinerant preacher. Leaving his home congregation to preach in New Jersey, Connecticut, and Massachusetts, Davenport had no qualms about publicly questioning the salvation of established ministers—sometimes naming those he deemed unconverted and publicly praying for them to experience the new birth. His deeply emotional sermons evoked the agonies of hell and the joys of heaven, and on at least one occasion he spoke for twenty-four hours straight. He also led crowds of poor people, African Americans, and Native Americans singing through the streets of New England towns. His critics were horrified. One hostile account suggested that Davenport was crazy and claimed that "in any sober country in the world, he would be confined; and yet, in [Connecticut], he is attended with crowds, and looked upon by numbers as an angel of God. In a hot day, he strips to his shirt, mounts a cart, or any eminence upon the street, and roars and bellows, and flings about his arms, till he is ready to drop down with the violence of the action."[12] To some colonists, Davenport's ministry seemed nothing less than a spiritual insurrection.

Connecticut officials arrested Davenport in 1742, banning him from the colony under a new anti-itinerancy law. His supporters rioted outside the Hartford courthouse as Davenport called for God to pour judgment on the arresting officials, and the tumult did not subside until the Hartford militia was called in. Not dissuaded, Davenport made his way to Boston, where he publicly proclaimed the names of well-regarded ministers whom he considered unconverted. He was arrested again, but a jury declared him mentally incompetent and released him.

Davenport, by his own admission, went too far in 1743 when he returned, illegally, to Connecticut and, preaching on a pier in New London, called on his adherents to burn all books written by unconverted Christian authors, as well as their own fine clothing, which he believed had become barriers to their full commitment to God. Davenport himself contributed his plush breeches to the growing pile, but a female supporter plucked the pants out, threw them in his face, and told him to come to his senses. Her defiance broke the crowd's support for Davenport. One skeptical observer thought the conflagration had ended not a moment too soon, because "had fire been put to the pile, [Davenport] would have been obliged to strut about bare-arsed."[13]

As comical as Davenport's book and clothes burning might have been, he and other less theatrical but equally captivating evangelicals helped pioneer a formidable new religious movement. The birth of American evangelical Christianity in the 1740s resulted in the first widespread popular uprising against established authority in the history of British colonial America, and it heavily influenced many of those who would fill the rank and file of the Patriot movement in the American Revolution.

The evangelical defiance of religious establishments continued well after the major revival fires had begun to smolder. In the 1740s and 1750s, a number of the most radical evangelicals started unauthorized new congregations that were faithful to the principles of revivalism. They were flouting Massachusetts and Connecticut colonial laws that did not allow people to open new congregations without official approval. That prohibition meant that members of these "Separate" churches could face fines and various punishments, especially for tax evasion if they refused to pay tithes that would support the established churches from which they had fled.

The Separate movement of illegal evangelical meetings also produced new, aggressive Baptist churches. Baptist churches had existed in America before the Great Awakening, but they were small and had almost no connection to these new, more militant Baptists. Although almost all Reformed (or Protestant) churches, including Puritan churches, baptized infants—a practice that continued in most of the churches of the Great Awakening—some of the Separates became convinced that the way to maintain a truly pure church was to baptize only converted adult believers. This theological precept flowed directly from the revivalist focus on the new birth. For Baptists, baptizing unconverted babies made no sense; they believed people should experience the new birth of conversion and then receive baptism by immersion in water, which symbolized their spiritual transformation from sin and death to new life in Christ. The new Baptist churches faced intense persecution from colonial governments, not only in New England but also in the South, and especially in Virginia. To those who believed that infant baptism put children under the protective covering of the church, withholding baptism from babies seemed cruel. The Baptists also often refused to apply for preaching licenses or to pay taxes meant to support the established churches.

After some decades of state persecution for their religious beliefs, a number of Separate and Baptist evangelical leaders became convinced that the union of church and state led to the corruption of both. Thus, in the era of the Revolution, evangelicals, liberal Christians, and deists would find themselves cooperating in the cause of disestablishment, or the separation of church and state.

The Great Awakening's regional effects were uneven, and many of the most recognizable of the founding fathers, especially Thomas Jefferson, had little patience for evangelical piety. But the Awakening's influences on the culture of revolutionary America were deep. Revivalist preachers pioneered a new style of rhetoric in which leaders appealed directly to the people in a homespun style filled with biblical allusions. Revolutionary writers and orators like Patrick Henry and even religious skeptics like Tom Paine self-consciously employed an evangelical style to motivate their audiences.

The Great Awakening also stoked the belief of many Americans that religious signs portended major changes, including massive numbers of conversions, transformative political events, or both. When Whitefield appeared, his leading American supporters wondered what the spiritual fervor might portend for the world at large. Whitefield's chief defender in Charleston, South Carolina, the Reverend Josiah Smith, proclaimed in 1740, "Behold! . . . Some great things seem to be upon the anvil, some big prophecy at the birth; God give it strength to bring forth!" From the 1740s to the 1780s, Americans were expecting great upheavals in the spiritual and political order.[14]

Although the Great Awakening changed much in colonial America, it did not lessen the pervasive animosity toward Catholicism. If anything, the sense of apocalyptic possibilities created by the Great Awakening reenergized British Americans' sense that world events were hurtling toward the end of days. British evangelical leader Isaac Watts wrote to a Boston pastor in 1740 and told him that if a new war with the French broke out, it might further the coming of God's kingdom: "it is by the convulsion of nations that Antichrist must be destroyed, and the glorious kingdom of Christ appear," Watts said. Key figures in the Great Awakening naturally lent their support when Britain clashed with France again starting in the mid-1740s. Combat against Catholic infidels was one of the few issues on which they agreed with their antirevivalist opponents.[15]

In 1765, the legacy of revivalism was one element of the religious zeal fueling the controversy with Britain over the Stamp Act. War was another—especially providential interpretations of war by many different Protestant denominations. American colonists saw the series of wars from the 1740s to the 1770s, leading up to the American Revolution, as divinely designed to vindicate both liberty and Protestantism. They perceived God's power behind every success and puzzled at God's mysterious purposes behind every failure.

In the mid-1740s, long-term tension and sporadic violence between New England and New France had finally turned into war. The British and French both sought to control Nova Scotia, a province to the northeast of New England with strategic military significance and bountiful fisheries. Nova Scotia technically belonged to the British, but between 1720 and 1740 the French had built a formidable fortress at Louisbourg on Cape Breton Island, just to the north of Nova Scotia at the entrance to the Gulf of St. Lawrence. The fortress stood behind massive stone walls protected by heavy cannons and a garrison of 1,500 soldiers. After France initiated attacks on Nova Scotia's settlements in 1744, New Englanders resolved to conquer Louisbourg.

New Englanders brought intense religious zeal to the campaign against Louisbourg. William Pepperrell of Maine, a close friend of George Whitefield, was chosen to command the expedition. Whitefield himself, who had returned to America in 1744, preached to Pepperrell's troops before they sailed, and he also provided them with the campaign's Latin motto, "*Nil desperandum Christo duce*" (No need to fear with Christ as our leader). Although the British colonists faced steep odds in the mission, it seemed as if God was on their side. When the New Englanders captured an abandoned French artillery battery outside the fortress and discovered that the French had spiked, but not destroyed, the cannons, they repaired the disabled cannons and quickly turned them against the great citadel. The British colonists also captured French ships carrying much-needed supplies and munitions. They laid siege to Louisbourg and ultimately came away with a stunning victory in June 1745.[16]

Many colonists celebrated the Louisbourg triumph as providentially given by God. Evangelical luminary Jonathan Edwards counted the victory as evidence "of its being a day of great things, and of the wonderful works of God in this part of the world." Edwards attributed the success at Louisbourg to the prayers of the colonists. A more skeptical Benjamin Franklin, living in Philadelphia, calculated that perhaps 45 million prayers had been offered by New Englanders, which theoretically gave them a huge advantage against the handful of Catholic Frenchmen's prayers to the Virgin Mary. If the colonists' prayers did not work, he told his brother, he would have an "indifferent opinion" of prayer from then on. He concluded, however, that when it came to making war, he preferred works to faith.[17]

Despite the eye-rolling by skeptics like Franklin, the British colonists' response to Louisbourg typified Americans' attitudes toward war before the Revolution. Many colonists, both evangelicals and nonevangelicals, shared a tendency to see God's hand in any military victory, but especially in those that featured auspicious circumstances such as unusually favorable weather. Although not uniquely evangelical in its sources, the American disposition toward providentialism seems only to have been encouraged by the excitement of the Great Awakening. From Louisbourg to the American Revolution, colonists like Pepperrell would seek to employ the spirit of Whitefield as a means to secure God's favor in their battles. When God seemed to intervene on their behalf, as at Louisbourg, Americans (especially New Englanders) effusively discovered great spiritual significance in the victory. Thomas Prince of Boston thought the conquest of Louisbourg could be the "dawning earnest" of the millennium—the thousand-year reign of the Kingdom of God—and prayed that the British might now hold the island fortress forever. Some in Boston grumbled in 1748 when, after diplomatic negotiations, Britain returned Louisbourg to the French without consulting the American colonists. For the colonists, it was an early omen that British officials seemed too willing to make concessions to the feared power of Catholicism.[18]

Tension between the British and French ignited once again in 1754, when the fight over French forts along the Ohio River escalated into the Seven Years' War. The French constructed their new forts in the Ohio River valley in 1753–1754, including most significantly a major citadel, Fort Duquesne, at the forks of the Ohio in western Pennsylvania (at present-day Pittsburgh). In 1754, the governor of Virginia sent a regiment, led by twenty-two-year-old Lieutenant Colonel George Washington, to oust the French from Fort Duquesne. The campaign went badly: Washington attacked a small French patrol, drew the ire of the much larger French and Indian forces, and sought shelter in the aptly named Fort Necessity, erected in a swamp surrounded by hills. Surrounded and awash in rising rainwater, Washington's regiment surrendered on July 4, 1754. Facing demotion, the young colonel resigned from active service and returned to his Virginia farm, expecting never to serve again.

When officials in London and Paris heard of Washington's defeat in Pennsylvania, they began mobilizing for war in North America and around the globe. The British sent General Edward Braddock on a massive expedition against Fort Duquesne in 1755, but that ended in a disaster even greater than Washington's. Braddock did not take the allied French and Native American threat seriously; he walked his 2,000-man army into an ambush just outside of Fort Duquesne. Almost half his army was killed or wounded, and Braddock himself lay among the dead.

Americans worried that Braddock's defeat showed that God was holding against them some sin they had committed. Virginia's Samuel Davies thought that the colonists were lazy and complacent and that they failed to understand the horrible moral implications of French victory. He warned that the "imprecation of the Prophet will fall upon the mean, sneaking coward. 'Cursed be the man that keepeth back his sword from blood.' [Jeremiah 48:10] Shall we tamely resign such a flourishing, wide-extended country into the merciless hands of barbarity, arbitrary power, and popish superstition?" He demanded that the colonists' fight like men for their liberty.[19]

The colonists—or more accurately, the British regular army—did keep fighting, and in North America the tide of the war began to turn toward the British by 1758. A huge British force reconquered Louisbourg in 1758, clearing a route for the British to sail up the St. Lawrence River and assault Quebec, which had long enticed the Crown. The walled city was the capital of French Canada, and its defeat would signal the end of the official French presence in North America and the immediate threat of Catholicism in the New World. A pastor from Worcester, Massachusetts, quoting the words of Moses to the nation of Israel, assured Massachusetts militiamen going to Canada that God would fight for them in the campaign: "The Lord your God is he that goeth with you, to fight for you against your enemies, and to save you."[20]

Conquering Quebec would prove difficult. The town had repelled earlier British attacks with its stout defenses and strategic position high on cliffs above the river. The British dispatched a massive army of 9,000 soldiers, transported on 141 warships, up the river to Quebec, led by British General James Wolfe, who was suffering terribly from "the gravel," or kidney stones, which gave him severe fevers and convulsions and led him to fear an imminent demise. Time was running out, however, as the British camped to the southeast of the city, puzzled at how to attack it. Finally, the British decided on a risky plan to slip upriver by night, past the city's artillery batteries, and make their way up 150-foot cliffs to an open area west of the city known as the Plains of Abraham. They unexpectedly pulled off the maneuver and had assembled half of Wolfe's army just outside the western walls of Quebec by daybreak.

The French, waking up to the unexpected sight of Wolfe's vast army, panicked. They left the security of the citadel and engaged the British, only to suffer a terrible defeat. Wolfe was killed by a French marksman in the battle, but he had vanquished the French and won lasting renown in the annals of British military history. The French officially surrendered Quebec on September 18, 1759.

British colonists in America reacted predictably to the wondrous triumph at Quebec. Pastor Samuel Langdon of Portsmouth, New Hampshire, proclaimed that God was "manifesting his wrath against the antichristian powers," and he predicted that shortly the enemies of Antichrist would shout "Babylon the great is fallen!" A celebratory ditty printed on broadside predicted:

The Time will come, when Pope and Friar,
Shall both be roasted in the Fire;
When the proud Antichristian Whore
Will sink, and never rise more.

In the providential victory of the British over the French, many Americans believed God was delivering the "Protestant interest" from the Catholic menace.[21]

Later in the Seven Years' War, the British colonists turned their attention to the Caribbean, where they fought France and Spain for control of the lucrative sugar islands there. In 1762, Britain set its sights on Havana, Cuba, which many called the "key to the New World" because of its military and mercantile value to Spain's Atlantic empire. Colonists eagerly joined in the British siege of the heavily fortified city that summer, but heat, disease, and poor supplies diminished their strength. The British commander, the Earl of Albermarle, decided on a bold but costly plan to tunnel under the city's key fortress and blow it up from below. The audacious strategy worked, leaving Havana vulnerable to British assault. Within weeks the city, along with its millions of pounds in gold and silver, as well as most of the Spanish Caribbean fleet, lay in British hands.

Colonists celebrated the fall of Havana—a terrible loss for Catholic Spain—with fireworks and days of thanksgiving. Evangelical pastor Joseph Sewall of the Old South Church in Boston rejoiced that the "great supporters of Antichrist" had been dealt such a grievous blow. The governor of North Carolina, Arthur Dobbs, similarly saw the conquest of Havana as a sign of "Divine Providence in favor of the Protestant apostolic religion and the cause of liberty."[22]

In early 1763, the European powers signed the Treaty of Paris, formally ending the war. In North America, the treaty eliminated the official French presence in Canada and the Ohio River valley. The Spanish received what would turn out to be temporary custody of New Orleans and the Louisiana Territory, west of the Mississippi River. The Spanish gave Florida to the British, meaning that the British controlled the North American mainland east of the Mississippi. But although the British had vanquished their European foes, their control really existed only on paper. Soon they would find it very difficult to keep their own colonists in check.

For their part, American colonists emerged from the Seven Years' War with enormously optimistic expectations about their material and spiritual prospects. The defeat of the French and the Spanish meant that colonists were safe from the threat of popery and arbitrary foreign government. Colonists had long seen Catholicism as the primary threat to their liberty and economic fortunes. Now, with the French gone and the Spanish sequestered beyond the Mississippi, all signs seemed to point to a prosperous future for the British Empire in America. Boston Congregationalist minister Jonathan Mayhew reflected the high hopes for a British Protestant future in America in 1759, after the conquest of Quebec. The continued blessings of God would in due time make America into a "mighty empire," a proposition to which he immediately added the caveat, "I do not mean an independent one." Why not an independent one? Because for Mayhew and most of his fellow colonists, as long as Protestant Britain defended civil and religious liberty, Americans would remain safe under its care. He foresaw "mighty cities rising on every hill," filled with Americans professing pure biblical religion. "O happy country! happy kingdom!" Mayhew exulted. If the British government remained committed to the principles of liberty (and in the glow of the victory in the Seven Years' War, there seemed no reason to doubt that it would), then Americans could expect a future that might herald the millennium.[23]

Such high expectations are easily disappointed. Even though the British government had just saved the colonists from the despised Catholics, the period immediately after the Seven Years' War was primed for frustration and conflict. The Americans anticipated more freedom and prosperity, while the British wanted effective control of North America and tax revenue to pay off debts from the war. In 1763, two years before the Stamp Act, the colonists were delighted to be British, but they also recognized that the empire had not always acted on their behalf, or even on behalf of Protestant Christianity. Americans knew well that seventy-five years earlier the despotic kings Charles II and James II had shut down the legitimate governments of New England and forced the colonists to live under what they called the "cruel oppressions of arbitrary government" until the Glorious Revolution saved them. All colonists would have admitted that, as a nation run by mere men, Britain could quickly be subverted by malevolent interests and abandon the spirit of Protestant liberty.[24]

By 1763, Americans viewed infringements on their liberty as having wicked origins. As British politician Edmund Burke would later put it, the colonists could "snuff the approach of tyranny in every tainted breeze." Immediately after the war, rumors began to emerge that the colonists would soon face a dire threat to their civil and religious liberties. No less an authority than evangelist George Whitefield reportedly warned New Hampshire ministers in 1764 that there was a "deep plot laid" in England against the Americans' freedom, and that their "golden days were at an end."[25]

The colonists realized that the postwar years were not going to be the paradise they had expected. Parliament soon introduced a new system of taxes that would require the colonists to share the burden of the war deficit. The Sugar Act of 1764 imposed new duties on a range of consumer goods imported into the colonies, including (besides sugar) cloth, coffee, and wine. The new law also sought to alleviate the major problem of tax evasion in the colonies by reducing the duty on imported molasses but rigorously enforcing its collection.

Some colonists murmured against the Sugar Act, primarily merchants and politicians directly affected by it. A few leaders began to piece together an argument against taxation without representation: Parliament had no right to pass tax laws on the colonists, because tax laws should only be passed by a people's elected representatives. If Parliament could pass laws like the Sugar Act, asked the Massachusetts legislature, "are we not reduced from the character of free subjects to the miserable state of tributary slaves?"[26]

Massachusetts legislator James Otis penned the most aggressive response to the Sugar Act in his tract *The Rights of the British Colonies Asserted and Proved* (1764). According to Otis, Parliament had supreme authority in imperial affairs but did not possess the right to tax the colonists. He argued that the governmental principles put forth by William and Mary in the Glorious Revolution protected British citizens from such laws. Otis believed that God had chosen William as the "glorious instrument of delivering this kingdom from popery and arbitrary power." Unjust laws like the Sugar Act flouted the spirit of the Glorious Revolution, he insisted.[27]

Although Otis and several legislatures registered disapproval of the Sugar Act, the British government could not have envisioned the firestorm that the passage of the Stamp Act in 1765 would ignite. Part of the reason for the widespread unrest was that the relatively mild protests against the Sugar Act had come to nothing, and frustration with Parliament began to compound. And whereas the Sugar Act had only indirectly affected most Americans, the Stamp Act touched almost everyone.

There existed as well a religious aspect to resistance against the Stamp Act. British officials commented that non-Anglican Christians seemed particularly outraged by the stamp tax. Governor William Franklin of New Jersey wrote to his famous father Benjamin that "Presbyterians" in New England had tried to spread the unrest to all the colonies. An angry stamp distributor in Philadelphia, John Hughes, similarly reported that Presbyterians there had begun to question the authority of the king, declaring that they would honor "No King but King Jesus." Parliament decided to repeal the Stamp Act, realizing that there was no point in risking civil war over the issue. But to the colonists, the repeal offered only a reminder to be vigilant in their defense of Christian liberty against the tyrannical spirit of this new manifestation of Antichrist. The *Boston Gazette* blamed an "Infernal, atheistical, Popish" cohort for passing the Stamp Act, but rejoiced that their "DIABOLICAL Purposes" had been frustrated.[28]

One Connecticut account of the repeal shows how deeply the colonists had come to associate political tyranny with the spirit of Antichrist. When word arrived of the repeal in 1766, a crowd composed largely of evangelicals celebrated, saying "that victory was gained over the beast, and over his mark . . . [and] we can yet buy and sell without the mark, or the name of the beast, or the number of his name." They called the king's supporters "papists." Pastor Joseph Emerson of Pepperell, Massachusetts, speaking at a thanksgiving service celebrating the repeal, noted that the protesters believed that their "civil and religious privileges" were both jeopardized by the act. If the Parliament was not bound to respect the colonists' rights in the matter of taxation, then what would become of their religious liberty?[29]

In the years after 1763, Americans were embracing a new kind of civil spirituality, that is, a spirituality that put a heavy emphasis on political values. Civil spirituality needs saints, and for many Americans, no one deserved more praise in the cause of civil and religious liberty than George Whitefield, who died during his last visit to America in 1770. In a eulogy for Whitefield, Pastor Nathaniel Whitaker of Salem, Massachusetts, declared that Whitefield was "greatly concerned for the liberties of America, and under God it was in no small measure owing to him, that the Stamp Act, that first attack upon our liberties in these colonies, was repealed." Whitaker gave no evidence for this extravagant claim—though perhaps he remembered Whitefield's warnings to colonists about the act in 1764. But in a larger sense, Whitaker undoubtedly meant that Whitefield had revived evangelical faith in America, and by definition, reviving Protestantism meant reviving liberty.[30]

Most Americans seemed to sigh in relief at the repeal of the Stamp Act in 1766, but they also reminded themselves that the threat of unchecked power in human hands required constant vigilance by a virtuous people. Even a liberal pastor like Jonathan Mayhew, who had abandoned traditional Congregationalism for Unitarianism, maintained a dim view of human nature. "Power is of a grasping, encroaching nature," he declared; it was always sliding toward oppression when wielded in churchly or political offices. Only God himself could wield absolute power and maintain his benevolence. Many, like evangelical minister Benjamin Throop, believed that Americans had staved off, for the time being, the fatal loss of all liberty. "We could not long expect to enjoy our religious liberties, when once our civil liberties were gone," Throop warned.[31]

Evangelical Presbyterian pastor John Zubly of Savannah, Georgia, struck a slightly more reserved note than Mayhew or Throop. While expressing thanks to God for rescuing the colonists, Zubly reminded his audience that good laws did not ensure ultimate liberty. A people's sins actually brought the judgment of God in the form of tyrannical government, he said, adding that the wisest course of action in the face of crises like the Stamp Act was for people to examine their hearts and see if they had accepted the liberty from sin that was offered by Christ. "We can never be said to be free while we are the servants of sin," he cautioned, placing a certain theological gap between spiritual and political liberty.[32]

Most American Protestants in the revolutionary era failed to make such fine distinctions. The long tradition of anti-Catholicism and the fervor of the Great Awakening had reenergized British Americans' tendency to conflate the civil and spiritual spheres. The colonists saw the outcome of the Seven Years' War as a great providential victory for Protestant liberty, but the passage of the Stamp Act harshly reminded them of the tenuousness of their freedoms. The French and Spanish had been beaten, but the Antichristian spirit of tyranny remained at large.

John Adams wrote in 1767 that liberty's friends must always be vigilant to protect it, for malevolent forces always sought to destroy political and religious freedom. In a historical sense, Adams was not surprised to find liberty assaulted in Britain and America. He recognized that from the ancient republics of Greece and Rome, to eighteenth-century Britain, history had always recorded the fragility of liberty. There was an eternal struggle between freedom and the evils of tyranny that Adams expected to continue until the end of days: "The world, the flesh, and the devil, have always maintained a confederacy against [liberty], from the fall of Adam to this hour, and will, probably, continue so till the fall of Antichrist."[33] Americans must fight against this devilish plot to destroy their liberty, Adams believed, no matter what the costs.

The religious and military experiences of the decades before the American Revolution primed colonists to employ apocalyptic ideas to understand the crisis with Britain. John Adams's talk of the "man of sin, the whore of Babylon, [and] the mystery of iniquity" might be startling today, but it arose naturally out of the context of the Great Awakening, the Seven Years' War, and the Stamp Act. Tyranny was not just political; it was religious, Americans understood. However they manifested themselves, threats against the colonists' liberties all grew from the same malignant root: the spirit of popery and arbitrary power.

CHAPTER 2

"The Sacred Property of Every Man"

Radical Christians and the Struggle for Religious Liberty in America

J OHN WALLER, known to friends as "Swearing Jack," was a typical Virginia gentleman—brawling and vulgar—until he encountered the Baptists. At first Waller despised the radical evangelical sect because it stood against the profanity and violence that characterized Virginia's elite society. As a lawyer, Waller had actually participated in the prosecution of one of these annoying preachers, Lewis Craig. But when he encountered the evangelical itinerant in court, something about Craig caught Waller off guard. The minister possessed a quiet strength and fortitude that Waller had never beheld. His curiosity stoked, Swearing Jack began attending the Baptists' meetings, and after seven or eight months he became convinced that God loved him and would save him from an eternity in hell. Accepting Christ's offer of forgiveness, he was publicly baptized by immersion in water, foreswearing the Anglicanism of his birth for a faith that cast him out of the colonial gentry.

After paying off his gambling debts, Waller began preaching. But in Virginia, preaching was illegal without a state license. The onetime gentleman lawyer was arrested for the first time in 1768 for disturbing the peace, thanks to his habit of confronting people with passages from the

Bible. Now known as a troublemaker by the authorities he had once represented, Waller finally incurred the full wrath of Virginia's establishment in 1771, when he was preaching at an outdoor meeting in Caroline County. The sheriff confronted Waller in the company of the local Anglican minister, who reportedly jammed the end of a horsewhip in Waller's mouth, after which the sheriff's posse hauled Waller out of the meeting and brutally whipped him. They left him covered with blood, but Waller cleaned himself off, returned to the stage, and continued preaching. He counted himself blessed to suffer for the cause of Christ, and Christian liberty, in an unfree place like colonial Virginia.

James Madison, a bookish and idealistic twenty-two-year-old graduate of the College of New Jersey in Princeton, watched and worried as the persecution of Baptists like Waller unfolded in Virginia. He wrote to a friend in Pennsylvania in 1774 asking him to pray that liberty of religious conscience would be given to all citizens of the colonies. Madison had grown up in a traditional Anglican family, and in the early 1770s he seemed still to accept and practice the faith of his birth. He did not, however, approve of the Anglican church's treatment of evangelicals like Waller, which he saw as a "diabolical, hell-conceived principle of persecution."[1]

Madison embraced notions about church-state relations that had emerged from the Enlightenment, with its emphasis on toleration and pluralism, but his theories about religious freedom were put to a practical test as he monitored the persecution of Virginia's evangelicals. On the issues of church and state, Madison and many other founders of the American Republic were profoundly influenced by the seventeenth-century English philosopher John Locke, who argued that civil authorities should never try to coerce people into holding uniform religious opinions and should only regulate religious practices in the interest of the state's wellbeing. Madison believed that Virginia's civil authorities had trespassed from their proper jurisdiction by policing the private beliefs of the evangelicals. He reported in disgust to his Pennsylvania friend that five or six Baptist pastors remained in local jails, simply for unlicensed preaching of essentially orthodox Christianity. Madison wrote that wild stories promulgating the "monstrous effects" of evangelical dissent were derailing efforts to promote religious freedom. The colonial Virginia government supported the clerics and parishes of the Anglican Church with tax funds and legal protection, and the established church's defenders did not look kindly on the evangelical interlopers. Madison lamented that many of the legislators were so devoted to the Anglican establishment that they would not "hear of the toleration of dissentients."[2]

James Madison and Thomas Jefferson were the best-known advocates for religious freedom in the revolutionary period, but their views on religious freedom were formed well before the conflict with Britain, when they were young men reacting to the persecution of the Baptists. Enlightenment writers such as Locke played a major role in framing the ideal of religious liberty for these famous founders, but it was mainly the evangelical dissenters from the established churches who fought on the front lines of the struggle for freedom to worship God in their own way. They were the ones who suffered humiliation, fines, and imprisonment, and their tribulations helped Jefferson and Madison solidify their convictions against religious oppression.

The revolutionary era, then, saw an unlikely alliance of evangelicals, Enlightenment liberals, and deists working together to win religious freedom. In this coalition, Jefferson and Madison were the best political advocates, but to give weight to their cause they relied on the masses of evangelical believers in Virginia. As the revolutionary crisis began to unfold, Madison, Jefferson, and the evangelicals all speculated that it might represent their opportunity to establish unequivocal religious freedom in Virginia. Madison anticipated harsh opposition from the forces of the established state church. "The clergy are a numerous and powerful body, and have great influence at home [in England] by reason of their connection with and dependence on the bishops and crown," he wrote, "and will naturally employ all their art and interest to depress their rising adversaries; for such they must consider dissenters who rob them of the good will of the people and may in time endanger their livings and security."[3] The leaders of the state church would not give up their long-held privileges easily.

In the medieval period, Europeans had simply assumed that a union between church and state, and the persecution of those who challenged it, was a natural, even God-sanctioned state of affairs. The law changed somewhat in 1689, when Britain adopted the celebrated Act of Toleration, a law that should have freed dissenters from state persecution, allowing them to be "tolerated," if not completely free. The law offered them only second-class status in English society and politics. Dissenters in the colonies also remained under a variety of legal restrictions; they also often had to pay taxes to support the established church, even though they did not attend it. Now, in the years leading up to the American Revolution, Enlightenment liberals and dissenters were clamoring for full religious liberty—which meant the elimination of official state churches, religious taxes, and religious tests for service in public office. But the dissenting evangelicals, and most of their liberal allies, hardly imagined that separation of church and state meant that religion should be only private, personal, and apolitical. That concept would only appear more recently, in the twentieth century.

Protestants in colonial America normally did not believe in religious liberty. They believed that the state should support a particular Christian denomination—either Anglican or Congregationalist—and should ban non-Christians and heretics from holding public office. Some colonies, like Pennsylvania, did provide religious freedom in a sense that we would recognize today, as Quaker leader William Penn refused to make Quakerism the official church of the colony and freely allowed all kinds of Christians, as well as Jews, to settle in the colony. Maryland, too, practiced an early kind of religious liberty. Its founder, the Catholic Lord Baltimore, mandated that the proprietary colony offer religious liberty to Protestants, in order not to offend the prevailing English sentiment of anti-Catholicism. But America's original founders did not typically come to the continent's shores to establish religious liberty in the modern sense. Given their background of persecution in England, one might imagine that the Puritans of New England would look more favorably on religious freedom, but in Massachusetts the Puritans' idea of religious liberty extended only to the freedom given non-Puritans to leave the colony. All who stayed were expected to attend church and conform to Puritan standards of public morality.

Traditionally, European Christians believed that nations needed to honor institutional Christianity by law, or else risk the health of society and invite the judgment of God. Most European immigrants to America believed that the Bible clearly outlined not only the essentials of Christianity, but which denomination was most faithful to the biblical model—usually the one to which those particular immigrants adhered. Thus, Massachusetts and Connecticut established the Congregationalist (Puritan) Church by law, whereas many of the mid-Atlantic and southern colonies made the Anglican Church their official denomination.

With the institutionalization of a particular denomination, many of the colonies' legislatures banned religious outsiders. Early Virginians, for instance, outlawed Quakers, who were perceived as dangerous, heretical visionaries by many English Protestants. Virginia also barred Catholics from holding office and forbade "popish priests" from entering the colony. As a result, Maryland became a land of exile for a variety of Christian groups, many of whom had left Virginia because of the colony's attempts to enforce conformity to the Church of England. No one outpaced the Puritan colonies in trying to maintain a religiously orthodox population. Anglicans, Baptists, Quakers, and Catholics—all were unwelcome in seventeenth-century Massachusetts or Connecticut. Neighboring Rhode Island became a stew of sectarianism, full of outcasts and refugees fleeing Puritan justice, and it was so notorious for its dissension that for the Puritans the term "Rhode Islandism" became synonymous with religious disorder.[4]

The colonies' attempts to maintain religious conformity did not wholly succeed, even among the Puritans. Some critics, such as Anne Hutchinson, rose from the Puritans' own ranks. Hutchinson, a charming English woman who worked as a midwife, pushed her husband William to move the family to Massachusetts in 1634, following their beloved pastor, John Cotton, who had left their native Lincolnshire for Boston. The Hutchinsons anticipated that Puritan Massachusetts would be a welcoming refuge for them, and Anne, talented and devout, began hosting spiritual weekday meetings at the Hutchinsons' home in the spring of 1635. The meetings began as opportunities for Anne to reprise Cotton's sermons for women unable to attend on Sundays, but they quickly evolved into something more. Men began attending too, and some who had attended Sunday also joined Hutchinson's weekday meetings. Attendees asked Anne to clarify difficult points of theology and to comment on the sermons of both Cotton and his copastor John Wilson.

Anne Hutchinson deeply valued Cotton's strong emphasis on salvation by God's grace alone, even as she worried about Wilson's relentless demands for Christians to practice good works. Wilson would have readily conceded that salvation came by grace alone, but he believed that grace did not negate the requirement that Christians perform godly deeds. Soon Hutchinson began chastising Wilson and other Boston ministers for implying that godly deeds somehow contributed to one's salvation. Hutchinson, like many radical Puritans, believed that conversion occurred in a sudden, unpredictable encounter with the Holy Spirit. Her downplaying of external morality earned her the epithet of "antinomian" ("against God's law") from contemptuous Puritan authorities. Put on trial before the General Court of Massachusetts, she indiscreetly testified that she had received her views by the immediate revelation of the Spirit. To her judges, such revelation sounded like the stuff of Quakerism, and she was banished in 1637 to the outer darkness of Rhode Island.

After Hutchinson's husband died in 1642, she and her children made their way south to the Dutch colony of New Netherlands. While she was living on Long Island, her family fell under attack from Native Americans, who killed her and five of her children. She may have been burned alive. Her Puritan adversaries took the circumstances of her death as a vindication of their cause. One of her most bitter antagonists, Thomas Weld, wrote that her death was a

> most heavy stroke upon herself and hers. . . . Some write that the Indians did burn her to death with fire, her house and all the rest named that belonged to her. . . . I never heard that the Indians in those parts did ever before this, commit the like outrage upon any one family, or families; and therefore God's hand is the more apparently seen herein, to pick out this woeful woman, to make her, and those belonging to her, an unheard of heavy example of their cruelty above others. Thus the Lord heard our groans to Heaven, and freed us from this great and sore affliction.[5]

To Weld, Hutchinson's dissenting ways had finally incurred the wrath of God.

Like Hutchinson, the celebrated dissenter Roger Williams emerged from the Puritan community. He came to Massachusetts as a Puritan pastor, but the mercurial Williams soon began to criticize the Puritans for not formally separating from the Church of England and for compelling all residents to attend Congregationalist churches. Banished from Massachusetts, Williams founded Providence, Rhode Island, in 1636; there he crafted that colony's famously expansive policy on religious freedom. In Rhode Island, all denominations, and even non-Christians, could practice their faith freely. Williams himself soon became a Baptist, influenced by the testimony of English Baptists in favor of the separation of church and state. Although Williams, seemingly incapable of maintaining a denominational identity, soon gave up on organized religion altogether, he set the example of Baptist dissent against the colonial establishments of religion.

Williams established himself as a pioneering advocate for the separation of church and state because he feared that the state's meddling would corrupt the church. More than a century and a half before Jefferson penned the phrase, Williams spoke of a wall separating the church from the world. Whereas many Puritans envisioned their colony as a nascent Christian nation (or commonwealth) similar to Israel of the Old Testament, Williams argued that the coming of Christ had rendered all nations "merely civil" in nature, not spiritual. Thus, according to Williams, God instituted civil governments to protect people's lives and liberty, but not to police the affairs of the soul. In his vision of church and state, Williams made a strong distinction between converted and unconverted people: The two groups shared common interests in civil society, but a pure church could not allow any unregenerate persons into its membership or expect civil rulers to shepherd the church. Williams viewed the very existence of state churches as signs of the wrath of God against disobedient Christians.[6]

The Puritans disagreed with every element of Williams's theology of the public role of religion. To Williams, the church was so sacred that state support would soil it. To the Puritans, religion was so important that it demanded state support. They did not doubt that God's expectations of righteousness extended beyond the realm of individuals and families and into the sphere of societies. Godly governments would publicly promote truth and purity. The Puritan colonies, accordingly, sought to prevent the incursions of religious outsiders, sometimes using the most severe tactics to do so. Between 1659 and 1661, for instance, the Massachusetts Bay Colony's authorities hanged four Quakers whom they had earlier banished and who had ventured back into the colony's borders. The colonies typically only exiled dissenters, however; death sentences were infrequent and came after failed attempts to exile the unwanted evangelists and make them stay away.

By any estimation, most of the early colonies did not embrace religious freedom. In the late seventeenth century, however, established churches in both Britain and America faced growing pressure to tolerate other Christians. In 1660, Charles II assumed the vacant English throne, his father Charles I having been deposed and executed by Puritan revolutionaries in the 1640s. Charles II was not sympathetic to Puritans, including those in New England, and in the 1680s he tried to consolidate all New England under one royal authority. James II succeeded his brother Charles II in 1685 and proved even more hostile toward the Puritan colonies. The Glorious Revolution of 1688–1689, in which James II was ousted in favor of William and Mary, relieved much of the royal threat against the Puritan colonies—but it also signaled a major step toward liberty for Christian minorities. Although the 1689 English Act of Toleration mandated the right of private religious conscience for Protestant dissenters, the status of official church-state relations under the Toleration Act remained uncertain. In Massachusetts, the government was forced by a new charter of 1692 to tolerate the presence of all Protestants, including Anglicans, Quakers, and Baptists. With this change, the age of exclusionary Puritanism had come to an end.

Nevertheless, Massachusetts maintained a state-supported Congregationalist establishment for another 140 years. After 1692, dissenters were free to believe what they wanted, but Massachusetts and most other colonial governments still insisted they support an official church through taxes paid by all citizens, regardless of their denomination. Church establishments, whether Congregationalist or Anglican, persisted in most of the colonies after the Glorious Revolution, although the tax burden of supporting those establishments could be fairly light in colonies like New York and South Carolina.

The Great Awakening of the mid-eighteenth century fundamentally challenged the concept of state-supported churches and ministers, with the revivalist revolt bringing into question the spiritual legitimacy of those churches and their pastors. To be sure, some moderate evangelicals had no intention of subverting the established order, for they themselves were supported by it. Some radicals, however, came to believe that essential to Christian liberty was the freedom to preach openly in any parish and to be able to financially support a church and pastor of one's choice, instead of being forced to pay a state-sanctioned minister's salary and fund his church. In New England, many of these radicals became "Separates" and started their own churches, which endorsed and promoted the revivals. Under the terms of the state establishments of religion, these churches were illegal: No one could found a church without state approval. The major season of imprisonments and fines against Separate churches in New England would not last beyond the late 1740s, but the issue of unfair taxation would remain the primary grievance of the dissident evangelicals.

The radical Separates also agitated for the right of laypeople to preach. College-educated men had traditionally monopolized the Protestant ministry, but the revivalist surge of the 1740s brought their dominance under fire. If the most important spiritual credential was conversion, the radicals reasoned, then why could a Spirit-filled layperson not preach? He (or she) might even preach better than an educated, ordained minister, especially if that minister had not personally experienced the new birth they believed salvation required.

One of the earliest instances of separation in Connecticut demonstrated the radical evangelists' agenda. In Canterbury, Connecticut, in 1741, at the height of the Great Awakening, the Congregationalist church dismissed its pastor, leaving the pulpit open for both radical itinerants and Spirit-filled laymen to do their work. By the next year, the Canterbury church was burning with revivalist fire. A critical observer scoffed that the church was "in worse confusion than ever" and that "many were exhorting and making a great hubbub."[7]

Leading the Canterbury movement were the brothers Elisha and Solomon Paine, who resisted the state church authorities at every turn. Although they had both attained prominent positions in law and politics, they lacked the education usually possessed by clerics; nevertheless, they claimed the right to preach. Angry Massachusetts authorities threw Elisha in jail in 1743 for violating anti-itinerancy laws there; the evangelist refused to pay bail because he believed he had done nothing wrong. Hardly chastened by his imprisonment, he continued to preach throughout New England upon his release.

Back in Canterbury, the local Windham Ministerial Association forced on the church a new antirevivalist pastor, James Cogswell. Elisha Paine ended up in jail again when he wrote a letter publicly rebuking the local ministers for their choice. Many in the local association were moderate evangelicals, but they could not countenance the disorderly behavior of laypeople like the Paines. Pastor Cogswell complained that Elisha had cornered him after service one Sunday and told him that he would rather be physically tortured than sit through Cogswell's sermons. Elisha was not just complaining about the pastor's preaching style; in his estimation, Cogswell taught that people could be saved through good works, neglecting the role of the Holy Spirit in conversion. In sum, Cogswell "talked like the Papists," Elisha declared. The crisis between the Paines and the Windham Association came to a head in 1745 when fifty-seven of the Paines' supporters withdrew from the established church and signed a new church covenant, thus opening an unauthorized congregation.[8]

In the face of fierce opposition in towns like Canterbury and colonies such as Connecticut and Massachusetts, the Separates continued building the American case for religious liberty. Solomon Paine, the pastor of Canterbury's new Separate church, became one of the key advocates for the rights of religious dissenters in New England, leading more than three hundred Separates in presenting a petition for religious liberty to the Connecticut legislature in 1748. Anticipating Jefferson's phrase in the Declaration of Independence, they called freedom of conscience in matters of religion an "unalienable right" given by God, and they asked the Connecticut legislature to enact "universal liberty" and to stop persecuting the evangelical dissenters. The legislators refused them. Nevertheless, Solomon Paine and the Separates had put the legislature on notice that it could not fairly claim to defend the colonists' freedoms as long as it did not respect the Separates' liberty of worship.[9]

Evangelical Baptists drew the most ire from colonial religious authorities. These radicals saw baptism for adult converts as the biblical solution to preserving the pure church they sought. Infant baptism, the practice of the Congregationalist and Anglican established churches, brought many people into the church as children who never experienced the life-transforming event of conversion—experiencing God's grace personally—as adults. In some Congregationalist churches, these baptized but unconverted adults were accepted as "halfway" members who had the right to baptize their children but not take the Lord's Supper (communion). Other churches allowed unconverted people of good morals all the privileges of normal church members. Baptists came to believe that membership in the church required clear evidence of conversion, or being born again, which would be recognized by public baptism, often in a local pond or river. Although no one could ever hope to have a church made up only of the truly saved (no one but God knew a person's heart and whether he or she had truly accepted Christ as savior), Baptists anticipated that making membership conditional on conversion and adult baptism would maintain as pure a church as humanly possible.

Baptist pastor Isaac Backus became one of the eighteenth century's greatest champions of religious liberty. His spiritual development illustrates the trajectory followed by many from Congregationalist to Baptist. Backus, a farmer from Norwich, Connecticut, had experienced the new birth during the Great Awakening, partly through the influence of the radical itinerant James Davenport. Norwich's pastor, Benjamin Lord, supported the Great Awakening but worried about the role of lay preachers who ranted about the power of the Holy Spirit. In 1744, as the fervor of the revivals began to subside, Norwich's congregation began to feud about the proper standards for church membership. Lord sought to deemphasize the role of personal testimonies of conversion, while Backus and his radical followers began to believe that Lord did not desire a pure congregation of saints. By mid-1745, thirteen members, including Backus, had stopped coming to the church, telling Lord that they no longer wished to be a part of a corrupt congregation. One woman simply explained that she did not have to attend the church "any longer than I am edified." The Separates went on to form their own congregation in the western part of Norwich.[10]

Backus had no college degree, but he began traveling widely and preaching to radical evangelical audiences. When he visited Titicut, Massachusetts, he generated such a warm response that people asked him to stay and start a new church, which he did. Solomon Paine and others came to ordain Backus to the ministry, for none of the established ministers would participate. Paine himself had received ordination from his Separate congregation in Canterbury. As was the case elsewhere, the Titicut Separates faced fines and the threat of imprisonment for their refusal to attend or support the colony's established church. Backus ran into his own divisive issue: the proper role of baptism in the church. Some within his congregation converted to Baptist principles, but Backus wavered until finally coming out in favor of what came to be called believer's baptism, that is, receiving rebaptism by immersion. Through forming Baptist associations and clamoring for religious liberty, Backus would help launch the Baptists into a religious phenomenon that by the time of the Civil War would make them, along with the Methodists, one of the two largest Protestant denominations in America. In the years leading up to the American Revolution, as the denomination grew in numbers and presented an increasing threat to state-sponsored religious power, the Baptists would increasingly decry the demands of the religious establishment.

The Baptist movement expanded well beyond New England, too, as northeastern Baptists soon began to send missionaries to the South. As hard as it may be to imagine today, in the colonial period New England was the most heavily churched area of the country, and the South was the least. The paucity of congregations in the South had long bothered many religious leaders in the North, and evangelicals emerging from the Great Awakening felt obliged to send missionaries to the benighted region. No evangelical group was more effective at evangelizing the eighteenth-century South than the Baptists.

A preacher named Shubal Stearns would become New England's primary missionary set on redeeming the South. Stearns followed a religious path similar to the one Isaac Backus had trodden. He had been converted during the revivals of the early 1740s, and he had helped lead a separation from the Congregationalist church in his hometown of Tolland, Connecticut. Attracted by the promise of church purity, Stearns accepted Baptist principles and received believer's baptism in 1751, the same year as Backus. Stearns soon became the minister of Tolland's new Baptist church, but because he felt the southern colonies desperately needed the Baptists' gospel, he and his family moved to Sandy Creek, North Carolina, in 1755.

Stearns developed a reputation as a captivating evangelist with mystical powers. One of his converts, Tiden Lane, first encountered Stearns at an outdoor revival meeting where Stearns was preaching under a peach tree. The preacher locked his gaze upon Lane, leading the other man to think that Stearns might have an "evil eye." As Stearns was exhorting the crowd, Lane began to swoon, and he fell down, unable to move. Another convert, Elnathan Davis, went to a baptismal service with his roughneck friends, presumably to mock the Baptists. His cohorts became too frightened to draw close, but Davis ventured forward and marveled at the sight of so many people trembling and crying. He tried to run away, but Stearns's voice charmed him. Soon he began to shake, too, and he fell over, immobile, terrified that he would be damned to hell. Through the Baptists' counsel he came to believe that he too could be saved. Stearns baptized Davis, who immediately began preaching as a Baptist minister. Although Stearns's Sandy Creek Baptists remained a minority among the South's settlers, they had begun the long process of making the southern backcountry into the Bible Belt it is today.[11]

The Baptists and other growing evangelical denominations threatened the religious establishments of the South, just as they had those of the North. To some, radical evangelical faith seemed to foster political democracy. A cranky Anglican parson, Charles Woodmason, who traveled widely in the southern backcountry in the 1760s, wrote that the evangelicals poisoned the minds of North Carolinians, instilling "democratical" notions in them, making them hostile to the Anglican establishment, and telling them that "they owe no subjection to Great Britain." The evangelical dissenters in North Carolina did seek exemption from taxes to support Anglican parishes, but the colonial government rejected the bid and actually increased taxes for Anglican support in the 1760s. The growing anger of North Carolina evangelicals fed into the "Regulator revolt" of 1766–1771, when backcountry farmers rose up against financial and judicial abuses of the provincial government. Herman Husband, a key leader of the Regulation, had been converted under evangelist George Whitefield's ministry and later became a Quaker. He loathed the civil and ecclesiastical oppression he saw in the British Empire and in the North Carolina government, and he anticipated the day when the people could bring about proper reform in church and state, which would bring on the millennium and the "utter downfall of Mystery Babylon." Like other Protestants of different stripes, Husband associated tyranny with the spirit of Antichrist.[12]

Nowhere did the clash between evangelical dissenters and the Anglican establishment become as acute as it did in the colonial Virginia that young James Madison would inhabit. Evangelical Presbyterians from Pennsylvania and New Jersey began preaching in Virginia in 1743, generating emotional revival meetings and inciting a number of defections from Anglican congregations. Patrick Henry, the Anglican rector of St. Paul's Parish in Hanover, Virginia, and the uncle of the Patriot leader Patrick Henry, angrily denounced the Presbyterians' work. Henry heard reports that the evangelicals questioned the salvation of Virginia's Anglican parsons, including that of Henry himself. Unlike the somber Parson Henry, the evangelicals screamed in their meetings, calling the unconverted "Damn'd double damn'd . . . Lumps of hellfire, incarnate Devils, 1000 times worse than Devils." People fell into convulsions under these verbal assaults, exhibiting the kind of extravagant behavior that ministers like Henry would never tolerate in Anglican services.[13]

Virginia's Anglican authorities particularly resented the way roving itinerants entered their parishes without permission. One such itinerant was Samuel Davies, an evangelical Presbyterian from Pennsylvania who came to Hanover, Virginia, in 1748 and went on to lead the Virginia dissenters' fight to preach freely. Like other dissenters, Davies pointed to the freedom guaranteed by the 1689 Act of Toleration in England as the grounds for evangelical rights in Virginia. Davies tried to comply with the regulations imposed by the Virginia establishment by securing licenses to preach at various meetinghouses in Hanover County. Davies envisioned an alternative parish system of Presbyterian churches that would be recognized by law in the colony. People had the right to choose their own doctor, Davies reasoned, and they were "entitled to the same liberty in choosing a physician for their souls."[14]

The Presbyterians' challenge to the Anglicans' dominance was only one sign of growing hostility toward Virginia's established clergy. Some elite Anglican vestrymen (the church's lay officers, who also filled most of the key political posts in the colony) had also begun to clash with their parsons. Debates over the Anglican clergy's salaries had led the Virginia legislature to pass the Two Penny Act in 1758, which authorized cash payments to replace allowances of tobacco—the means by which most ministers had previously been paid—at the rate of two cents per pound, well below the current market price of tobacco. Functionally, this resulted in a reduction of pay for the clergy, some of whom protested to the Privy Council in London, which then invalidated the Two Penny Act, leading several parsons to sue to recoup their losses. Hanover County officials recruited the young lawyer Patrick Henry to defend the parish's interests against the ministers' lawsuit. Henry was an Anglican like his uncle, but he stood against the clergy in this case and fumed against the Privy Council's heavy-handed ruling. In his brief against the clergy, Henry characteristically raised the stakes of the issue when he proclaimed that the king, by invalidating a reasonable colonial statute, had degenerated into a "tyrant." Like other Patriots, such as John Adams, Henry feared that the British government would use the power of the church to dominate the colonists politically, and he employed this local issue to address larger concerns about American liberty.[15]

The Anglican establishment in the colonies, nervous about the loss of power, grew vindictive toward dissenting competitors. Although the Anglicans reduced their active persecution of Presbyterians in the early 1760s, reluctantly accepting their presence, ecclesiastical violence returned with a vengeance later in that decade, when Shubal Stearns's Baptists began to make serious inroads among Virginia's populations. Baptist preachers like John Waller routinely endured beatings and insults and occasionally suffered imprisonment. The Presbyterians had followed Davies's example by trying to fulfill every legal requirement while advocating fuller freedom—but the Baptists refused to comply with license and tax regulations and seemed to flourish in the face of oppression by the provincial government.

Baptists affiliated with Stearns's Sandy Creek, North Carolina, network of churches had begun to infiltrate Virginia in the late 1750s. By the late 1760s, they had begun to pick off key converts like Waller, who himself faced severe persecution from civil and ecclesiastical authorities. The Baptist itinerants remained steadfast despite the threats against them, and many developed reputations for having mystical powers. Waller, for instance, not only possessed a mesmerizing preaching style but was also reputed to have once miraculously healed a woman by prayer and anointing with oil. Other Baptist pastors had portentous dreams that foretold of their persecution in Virginia. James Ireland, like Waller another former rake converted by the Baptists, was warned in a dream of coming trials sometime before he was arrested and imprisoned in Culpeper, Virginia, where he continued to preach to his followers through a grate in the wall. His opponents, enraged, beat and whipped his friends. Some hooligans even urinated on him as he exhorted. Others attempted to suffocate him by burning "brimstone and Indian pepper" at the cell window. Ireland was one of about thirty-four Baptist itinerants imprisoned in Virginia in the 1760s and 1770s; their ill treatment only cemented the Baptists' resolve to seek full liberty to preach their gospel.[16]

James Madison and Thomas Jefferson were two of the Enlightenment liberals who rallied to the cause of the harshly persecuted Baptists. Even skeptics like Jefferson joined evangelicals and rationalist Christians to support disestablishment; they could all agree that their colony's treatment of religious dissenters was deplorable. Protests by Anglicans against the persecution of evangelicals appeared as early as 1771. A writer calling himself "Timoleon" (the name of a general and statesman of ancient Greece) argued in the *Virginia Gazette* that the dissenters should enjoy protection under English law. It was insufficient cause, he wrote, to imprison the evangelicals simply because some saw them as "a pack of ignorant enthusiasts." Timoleon argued instead that multiple denominations made Virginia society healthier. "Liberty of conscience," he concluded, "is the sacred property of every man." No politician or clergyman could take it away without becoming a tyrant.[17]

In early 1776, as the move toward American independence grew in urgency, Jefferson and Madison began to collaborate with the evangelical dissenters. During the months before the July Declaration of Independence, Virginia and other American colonies began to organize governments free of the British aegis. The new governments needed statements of basic liberties, and Madison helped craft Virginia's that May. The Virginia Declaration of Rights became the basis for a governmentally sanctioned effort in Virginia to shed its establishment and abandon its tradition of persecution. Although delegate George Mason had proposed that the Declaration of Rights should provide full toleration of dissenters, Madison persuaded the convention to approve an even more expansive statement of the "free exercise of religion" for all. Mason's "toleration" implied that the government still wielded authority over the conscience, but Madison's "free exercise" implied a natural right to religious liberty that was not subject to changing political winds. This same language would be adopted fifteen years later in Madison's First Amendment to the U.S. Constitution.[18]

Madison also tried to insert language in the Declaration of Rights that would have prevented anyone from receiving any "peculiar emoluments or privileges" on the basis of religion, but the clause was rejected. Patrick Henry, who introduced Madison's proposal, was asked directly whether it meant to disestablish the church, and he denied that it would have done so. At this point in the revolutionary era, most of Virginia's political leaders still wanted to foster the coexistence of an Anglican establishment and the free exercise of religion, which in practice meant a halt to the active persecution of the Baptists.[19]

Baptists and Enlightenment liberals would not be satisfied until they ended the state's establishment of religion. In late 1776 Jefferson and Madison worked on a committee that addressed petitions for religious freedom from Baptists and others, which flooded the Virginia legislature after the adoption of the Declaration of Rights earlier in that eventful year. Jefferson, recognizing the profound effect of the evangelical movement in his home state, would recall that

> by the time of the revolution, a majority of the inhabitants had become dissenters from the established church, but were still obliged to pay contributions to support the pastors of the minority. This unrighteous compulsion to maintain teachers of what they deemed religious errors was grievously felt during the regal government, and without a hope of relief. But the first republican legislature which met in '76 was crowded with petitions to abolish this spiritual tyranny. These brought on the severest contests in which I have ever been engaged.

Jefferson and Madison helped end legal penalties against dissenters and temporarily stop state funding for the Church of England (which would be called the Episcopal Church after independence was achieved). But Jefferson's, Madison's, and the evangelicals' greatest victory for religious freedom lay in the future. Support for some kind of religious establishment remained strong in Virginia, and the moment for establishing full religious freedom in the state did not come until ten years later, in 1786, when Madison and the Baptists won approval for the Bill for Establishing Religious Freedom.[20]

The movement for religious liberty would succeed in America because evangelicals, rationalists, and deists fought for it together. The settlers of the American colonies, with few exceptions, did not hold a modern view of religious freedom. That principle had to be crafted in the era of the Revolution. Even though Jefferson and Madison eagerly cooperated with evangelicals in the name of religious freedom, no one should mistake either of the two founders for an evangelical. Although Madison was quite serious about his Anglican faith during the early years of the Revolution, he drifted toward deism or Unitarianism later in life. Jefferson would also make clear his skepticism about the Bible and traditional doc-trines such as that of the Trinity. Nevertheless, these two religious ratio-nalists were so appalled by Virginia's persecution of dissenters that they mobilized on their behalf to advocate for religious liberty in their state and nationwide.

Even before the advent of the American Revolution and the Virginia Declaration of Rights, the stage had been set for the cooperation of evan-gelicals and more liberal Christians, not only in the Patriot cause but also in the struggle to disestablish the state churches. The evangelicals wanted disestablishment so they could freely preach the gospel; the rationalists and deists wanted disestablishment because they felt an enlightened gov-ernment should not punish people for their religious views. The combi-nation of the two agendas would transform America, helping make it both intensely religious and religiously free.

CHAPTER 3

"The Pope, the Devil, and All Their Emissaries"

The Bishop Controversy and Quebec Act

I N 1767 THE BRITISH Parliament imposed another round of taxes, the Townshend Duties—levied on imported tea, glass, paper, and paint—and the colonies erupted with new appeals for resistance, including refusal to import the taxed goods. Unrest in the colonial towns, especially Boston, convinced the British to send four regiments of British troops to America. The colonists were apoplectic, believing that the presence of a "standing" army in peacetime signified the next stage of the assault on their freedom.

John Dickinson's *Letters from a Farmer in Pennsylvania* (1767) articulated the colonists' grievances against the Townshend Duties. Dickinson was no farmer, or at least, not a common farmer; he studied law at the Middle Temple in London in the 1750s, became a wealthy lawyer in Philadelphia, served in both the Delaware and Pennsylvania assemblies, and established himself as one of the largest landholders in Delaware, his plantation worked by dozens of slaves. Like many Americans, Dickinson had a great deal to lose, politically and financially, if the British successfully enforced the collection of the new taxes. Dickinson's *Letters* argued that Parliament had no right to impose taxes for the purpose of raising revenue (as opposed to taxes meant to regulate the flow of commercial goods). His compelling polemic against parliamentary taxation made his *Letters* the most influential American pamphlet before Thomas Paine's *Common Sense*.

Dickinson's tone was direct but measured—befitting his pacifist Quaker family background—but Samuel Adams of Boston believed that Dickinson had not fully plumbed the depths of the British threat to liberty. Adams was raised as a Calvinist in Boston, and unlike his second cousin John, he would maintain that faith throughout his life. Samuel graduated with an M.A. from Harvard in 1743, writing affirmatively on the question "Whether it be lawful to resist the supreme magistrate if the common-wealth cannot be otherwise preserved." After making a mess of his business affairs, including the malt house he inherited from his father, he entered Boston politics in the 1750s and embraced his true calling: promoting American liberty and virtue and fighting political and religious tyranny.

Adams thought it was unfortunate that Dickinson would give so much attention to the financial and political issues of taxation without representation but largely ignore the threat against Americans' religious liberty. "What we have above everything else to fear," Adams declared in the *Boston Gazette*, "is POPERY." Adams identified those who supported the royal government in Massachusetts as potential proselytes for the Catholic Church. He also believed that the Stamp Act and the Town-shend Duties were intended to soften Americans' resolve and to prepare them for the ultimate tyranny of religious oppression. These acts were "contrived with a design only to inure the people to the habit of contem-plating themselves as the slaves of men; and the transition from thence to a subjection to Satan, is mighty easy."[1]

As the revolutionary crisis developed, many colonists like Samuel Adams applied their longtime aversion to the Catholic Church to a new enemy, perceiving the dark forces of Roman Catholicism behind the po-litical actions of the British and believing that their freedom as Protes-tants was in jeopardy. Their fears gave added fuel to the revolutionary cause, as Americans took the warnings to heart and prepared themselves to take whatever actions were necessary to defend themselves.

Dickinson and Adams both correctly identified the issues that divided Britain and America. Strife over political and economic concerns certainly caused much of the controversy between Britain and the American colonies, but religion also played a major role in precipitating the Revolution. Between 1761 and 1775, matters of religious power arose around two key questions that would spark the tinderbox of British-American relations: the potential appointment of an Anglican bishop for America, and the welcoming British policy toward Catholics in Canada that was reflected in the 1774 Quebec Act.

These two issues raised fears among many American Protestants that Britain would take away their religious liberty and replace their churches with new Anglican state establishments or, worse, the kind of Catholic rule that Britain had experienced in earlier centuries. To Americans, the prospect of the loss of religious liberty was intimately connected to the loss of civil liberty. As John Adams recalled in 1815, "The apprehension of episcopacy contributed . . . as much as any cause" to the undermining of Britain's political authority. Because it corroded Americans' loyalty to the empire, the fear of the loss of religious liberty led directly to the Revolution.[2]

The aggrandizement of the Anglican Church in America particularly worried New Englanders. Many Congregationalists believed that "high-church" Anglicans would commandeer their New England churches if they could. (High-church Anglicans, characterized by their exclusive faith and emphasis on hierarchy, were different from many of their "low-church," or more broad-minded, brethren in that they considered non-Anglicans' churches to be totally illegitimate as Christian institutions.) The Congregationalists' Puritan forefathers had functionally left the Anglican Church when they migrated to New England in the 1630s, a time when the Puritans tightly controlled the Connecticut and Massachusetts churches. The Puritans despised the "popish" ceremonies of formal Anglican church practice and its elaborate church hierarchy, believing that these features of Anglicanism were not grounded in the Bible or in anything but wrong-headed tradition. Until the 1680s, New Englanders did not have to tolerate the public meetings of Anglicans or any other non-Puritan churches. As part of the toleration forced upon them following the Glorious Revolution (1688–1689), Puritans had to accept Anglican churches and missionaries in New England. The Anglicans' Society for the Propagation of the Gospel evangelized Congregationalists as if they were non-Christians without Christian churches or preachers, winning a few notable converts. In 1722, Congregationalists were shocked when the rector and two tutors at Yale College became Anglicans—"Yale apostates" snatched from one of Congregationalism's citadels.

In the decades after those conversions, Congregationalists feared the Anglican Church's incursions in America. They worried especially about possible attempts by the Church of England to foist an Anglican bishop on the colonies, which they viewed as the critical step in forcing an Anglican establishment on New England. Their fear of a bishop provided New Englanders with more opportunities to articulate the limits of submission to authorities seeking to deprive Christian citizens of their religious and civil liberties. The Sunday following January 30, 1750, the anniversary of King Charles I's execution during the English Civil War, Pastor Jonathan Mayhew of the West Church in Boston addressed the simmering tension between Congregationalists and Anglicans in his explosive sermon *A Discourse Concerning Unlimited Submission*. Mayhew warned against the dangers of civil and ecclesiastical tyranny, which he said could easily overwhelm nations if unchecked. He insisted that if Americans were to keep from becoming "priest-ridden" they must keep all "imperious bishops" out of their land. The aggressive Anglicans represented the "kingdom of Antichrist," he declared, and must be opposed by every friend of Christian liberty.[3]

Mayhew's sermon electrified Boston. John Adams recalled that it was "read by everybody." It established the tone and justification for opposition to an Anglican bishop and resistance to British religious and political power. High-church Anglicans might lament the removal and execution of Charles I, but Mayhew viewed the episode as a perfect example of godly resistance to a tyrannical king: Britons deposed Charles I, a king who Mayhew said favored Catholicism and disparaged the authority of Parliament, to save the country from "slavery, misery, and ruin." Just as Britons proved they "will not be slaves," the British colonists in America would not submit unconditionally to the authority of corrupt politicians and priests.[4]

In the following years, clumsy moves by Anglican authorities exacerbated New England's religious conflict. In 1761 the Anglican missionary

East Apthorp moved into a lavish new mansion near Harvard Yard, which did not endear him to the ascetic residents of Massachusetts—and their irritation was aggravated by a pro-Anglican letter to the *Boston Gazette* proclaiming that the Anglicans were in Cambridge to free the people from the "shackles of bigotry, which their fathers brought into this land." Apthorp defended the Society for the Propagation of the Gospel in 1763, avowing that it only meant to promote the health of Christianity in a land once dominated by Puritan "superstition" and "fanaticism." Such words did not win him friends among the Congregationalist pastors of Massachusetts—especially the combative Jonathan Mayhew. Mayhew's *Observations on the Charter and Conduct of the Society* (1763) ridiculed Apthorp and his mansion as evidence of the "grand design of episcopiz-ing . . . all New England." (Churches labeled "episcopal" are those, like the Church of England, that are led by bishops.) Mayhew called the man-sion a "palace" designed for a successor of the apostles, meaning a bishop. The house's name stuck, as Apthorp's home subsequently became noto-rious in Boston as the "Bishop's palace." Mayhew argued that the society, instead of trying to evangelize non-Christians, as it claimed was its mis-sion, was seeking to destroy the churches of New England. He reminded New Englanders that it was Anglican tyranny that had led the Puritan fa-thers to flee England, and he called on his fellow Congregationalists never to submit again to the "yoke of episcopal bondage."[5]

When the archbishop of Canterbury—the head of the Church of England himself—weighed in against Mayhew, the pastor returned fire by directly accusing the Anglicans of planning to place a bishop in Apthorp's "sumptuous dwelling-house." He saw the prospect of a resi-dent bishop as a pretext to begin depriving Americans of their religious liberties. Even though Mayhew still saw George III as a friend of Amer-icans' rights (the British army had just delivered the Americans in the Seven Years' War, after all), he believed that London could easily reverse itself. If one bishop were sent to America, more could easily follow, in a scheme to supplant the established churches of New England and force the region's dissenters to pay taxes to support the Anglican clergy, as was the case in the colonies to the south. "People are not usually deprived of their liberties all at once," Mayhew warned, "but gradually."[6]

The dispute between Mayhew and Apthorp helped crystallize colonists' fears about the imposition of Anglican authority by parliamentary fiat. As John Adams recalled it, the debate "spread a universal alarm against the authority of Parliament" among Bostonians just as the Stamp Act crisis was about to begin. If Parliament could tax the colonists without consent, so also could it force on them a tyrannical religion.[7]

Some Anglicans in America tried to calm the colonists' fears. Thomas Bradbury Chandler, rector of St. John's Church in Elizabethtown, New Jersey, insisted in 1767 that any resident bishop would wield no civil authority and would only support the Anglican Church by confirming church members and ordaining new ministers, which at that point required Americans to take an impractical trip across the Atlantic. But the moderate Anglicans' argument was not helped by an incendiary sermon by John Ewer, bishop of Llandaff, Wales, who spoke in London before the Society for the Propagation of the Gospel in 1767. Generalizing wildly and inaccurately about the colonists, Ewer argued that their forefathers had not gone to America for religious purposes and that in the American wilderness they had lost faith and morality, living like "infidels and barbarians." The growth of the Anglican Church in America, and the arrival of an Anglican bishop, would, he said, restore the continent's religious fortunes. Ewer even suggested that all Americans ought to be made to pay for the benefit of Anglican clergy and a bishop.[8]

Ewer's sermon provoked outrage from colonists, renewing non-Anglicans' resolve not to allow a bishop in their midst. The veteran Congregationalist pastor Charles Chauncy of Boston exclaimed that though the colonists had known for many years that the aim of the Anglicans was to "episcopise the colonies," no one had ever stated that goal as explicitly as Ewer. The Presbyterian polemicist William Livingston of New York claimed, contrary to Ewer's aspersions, that the colonists were in fact among the most virtuous and religious people on earth. Livingston's pastor, the evangelical John Rodgers of New York's First Presbyterian Church, circulated antiepiscopacy writings widely, praying that God would save the Americans from "that worse than Egyptian bondage, diocesan episcopacy." By 1770 Rodgers was confident that the massive opposition to a bishop had thwarted the prospect indefinitely. But others like Boston pastor Andrew Eliot still feared that the efforts to promote a bishop in the colonies revealed "secret influences" in London who favored not only high-church Anglicanism but Roman Catholicism.[9]

Fears about the imposition of Catholicism may have been ludicrous, given that the Church of England had been Britain's established church for three-quarters of a century. Nonetheless, many Anglican clergymen really did desire to send a bishop to America, in order to strengthen the church and to provide a ready means for confirmation and ordination. It had become clear that in order for Anglicans to compete for adherents, they needed to develop a more robust infrastructure in the colonies, and that required a bishop. But even to many Anglican laypeople, the quest for a bishop seemed designed to aggrandize Britain's religious and political power in America. The fear of the loss of religious liberty by the imposition of a bishop was one of the most sensitive issues among Americans, including evangelicals and Anglican laypeople, in both the North and the South. To many, attacks on political liberty—such as the Stamp Act and the Townshend Duties—were just the secular version of the threats they faced against their right to worship God as their Bibles instructed them to do.

Hostility toward the Anglican clergy was also brewing in the South, even though most of the southern colonies afforded official status to the Anglican Church. One example of the growing tension in the South was the controversy over the 1759 repeal of Virginia's Two Penny Act. That act was intended to help relieve inflation in the price of tobacco, which had shot up dramatically because of debilitating drought. Many debts in Virginia were paid in tobacco, including the salaries of Anglican parsons. But when Virginia's legislature allowed debts to be paid in cash instead, which functionally represented a pay cut for the ministers, a few Anglican clergy complained about the act to the British Privy Council, which was responsible for reviewing colonial laws. The council struck down the act, and some clergy sued to collect the full value of their wages in tobacco.

The repeal engendered hostility among many Virginians, including the young lawyer Patrick Henry. The self-taught Henry had only recently passed the bar exam and was eager to make a name for himself. In 1763 he defended Hanover County against one of the ministers' lawsuits, and he turned his argument into an assault on the clergy and British government generally. "A King, by disallowing acts of this salutary nature, from being the father of his people, degenerates into a tyrant, and forfeits all right to his subjects' obedience," Henry proclaimed. The judge (who was Henry's father) and the jury were convinced, and the exasperated parson was awarded the insulting sum of one penny in damages. Henry, although an Anglican himself, had burst onto the political stage by denouncing the clergy and their royal backers.[10]

By the early 1770s, many Anglicans, dismayed by the futility of their attempts in the North, were putting their efforts into getting the southern colonies to formally invite a resident bishop—a proposal that caused almost as much controversy in the South as in the North. The shared protests of Americans from different colonies helps explain why a range of Christians, from southern Anglicans to northern dissenters, who seemingly had little in common religiously, would cooperate so well during the Revolution. Patriot Anglicans and dissenters both saw the imposition of a bishop as part of the broader threat against their civil and religious liberties. High-church Anglicans, especially among the northern clergy, pushed hardest for a resident bishop and were among the Americans most likely to oppose the Revolution.

High-church Anglicans in the South also pressed the issue of an American bishop. A lightly attended meeting of Anglican ministers in Virginia in 1771 passed a resolution requesting a bishop from Canterbury, but their entreaty produced outrage, not only among dissenters but among many Virginia Anglicans. Two Anglican professors at the College of William and Mary, Thomas Gwatkin and Samuel Henley, protested the resolution, saying that establishing an American bishop would weaken the civil bonds between the colonies and the empire, raise the same sorts of fears as the Stamp Act had, frighten American dissenters, and encourage those who wanted to "endanger the very existence of the British Empire in America." Gwatkin and Henley accused the parsons of circumventing Virginia's authorities, arguing that the clergy had no right to file such a resolution without going through the legislature and governor. To ignore the elected officials of the colony represented a presumptuous exercise of power "repugnant to the rights of mankind." Other protesters warned that given the escalating conflict between Britain and the colonies, it was a particularly poor time to give more religious or political authority to the king and his ministers.[11]

Richard Bland, a longtime member of the Virginia House of Burgesses, reflected the ambivalence of Virginia Anglicans who opposed the strengthening of the Anglican hierarchy. He despised the 1771 resolution to invite a resident bishop and celebrated when the House of Burgesses formally commended Gwatkin, Henley, and the other protesters who resisted the convention's "pernicious project" of introducing a bishop. Bland saw a bishop as a threat to Virginia's traditional vestry system, in which a parish's lay council—its vestry—controlled church affairs, and he warned that the appointment of a bishop would surpass any other controversies (including the Stamp Act) that had arisen in North America, because religious disputes were the most "fierce and destructive" that a government could face. Bland remained deeply attached to the Anglican faith, but he avowed that he could "embrace her doctrines without approving of her hierarchy." That hierarchy, Bland asserted, was only a "relic" left over from the pre-Reformation Catholic Church in England, which made it anathema to American Protestants.[12]

High-church Anglicans had no better luck in promoting a resident bishop among North and South Carolinians than they did elsewhere. Although the Anglican Church had been established in North Carolina in the mid-1760s, the church had never had much of a hold on the colony except in its eastern coastal towns. In the colony's backcountry, Baptist and Presbyterian dissenters deeply resented the tax support given to Anglican ministers. The Anglican parson Charles Woodmason irritably reported that northern evangelical missionaries had poisoned rural settlers against all things Anglican, "instilling democratical and commonwealth principles into their minds—embittering them against the very name of bishops, and all episcopal government." He believed that these same preachers were questioning the whole notion of America's subjection to the British government as early as the mid-1760s.[13]

In 1774, Charleston pastor William Tennent III wrote that the Anglicans of South Carolina had a similar response to the idea of a resident bishop as their Virginia brethren, saying that they were angry at northern Anglicans for promoting the notion. Some South Carolina Anglicans had told him that they would abandon the Church of England if Parliament even offered to send a bishop to America. At first glance, the South seemed the most likely region to welcome an Anglican bishop, because the Anglican Church was established there, but the fear of British power and the tradition of local control of churches ultimately made southerners just as resistant as northerners to increased Anglican power.[14]

In 1773 the conflict between America and its mother country grew even more fiery, when Parliament infuriated the colonists by passing the Tea Act, granting the East India Company a monopoly to sell tea in the colonies. The controversy reached a flash point in Boston, where East India Company ships arrived in December, and Bostonians refused to allow the ships to unload their cargo. Under the cover of night, a group of white colonists thinly disguised as Native Americans boarded the ships and tossed about £10,000 worth of tea into Boston Harbor. This incident, the Boston Tea Party, escalated tension between Britain and the colonies to unprecedented heights. After the destruction of the tea, British authorities decided they had to get the raucous Patriots under control; in 1774, Parliament passed what became known as the Intolerable Acts, which closed Boston to commercial ships, reorganized the Massachusetts government under British authority, and allowed royal troops to be forcibly housed in private buildings.

Where would this crisis end? With conflict growing on all fronts, the colonists merged their fear of an Anglican bishop with broader concerns about the loss of all political and religious liberty through absolute tyranny that portended the advent of Catholicism. In conjunction with the looming crisis over the Intolerable Acts, the years 1773 and 1774 saw a spate of publications featuring intense, apocalyptic anti-Catholicism. Samuel Cooper, the rationalist Congregationalist pastor of Boston's wealthy Brattle Street Church, proclaimed in a Harvard lecture titled *A Discourse on the Man of Sin* that "popery is incompatible with the safety of a free government." He noted worriedly the presence of the predominantly Catholic colony of Quebec to the north, and he cautioned his audience to be vigilant against any attempts to impose Catholicism in the other colonies. Similarly, Samuel Langdon, soon to become president of Harvard, published a 1774 tract in which he systematically claimed that

Roman Catholicism represented one of the mystical beasts of the book of Revelation. Newspaper advertisements for the 1773 reprinting of an anti-Catholic book, Antonio Gavin's *A Master Key to Popery*, recommended the volume in light of recent attempts by powers within the British government to foster Catholicism in parts of North America. The publisher warned that tortures of the Spanish Inquisition such as "wooden shoes, fetters, chains, racks, [and] burning to death" would accompany the establishment of Catholicism in America.[15]

Given their extreme sensitivity to what they saw as the specter of Catholicism, it was no surprise that the colonists exploded with outrage against the Quebec Act of 1774. The Quebec Act was the latest in a long string of misunderstandings between the colonists and the British government. After capturing the region from the French in the Seven Years' War, the British needed to make clear the legal status of Quebec. In an attempt to pacify the conquered Quebecois, the act reinstated the principles of the French legal system, and most critically, granted French Canadian Catholics the freedom to practice their religion openly. Even more ominously, the act also moved Quebec's border down to the Ohio River, encroaching upon territory claimed by Connecticut, Massachusetts, and Virginia.

The Quebec Act would have angered most Americans with any proprietary interest in the boundaries of their settlements and claims, but because it came in the aftermath of the Intolerable Acts of 1774, many colonists became convinced that the long-feared European plan to destroy Christian liberty had finally been revealed. The *Connecticut Courant* proclaimed that "the mask is at length thrown off," with "Popery" to be established in Canada and "slavery" in Massachusetts.[16]

The colonists' response to the Quebec Act was venomous, painting it as the most abominable violation of English law yet put forth by Parliament. The *Massachusetts Spy* newspaper suggested that the act heralded unprecedented cooperation between Rome and London and went on to predict that the Catholic religion would become established in England within five years. The newspaper reported that the pope was mobilizing French Catholics to destroy the people of Boston, who were "bitter enemies to the Romish religion and monarchical power." To the *Massachusetts Spy*'s editors, the Quebec Act surpassed all previous tax laws in abhorrence: Whereas the Stamp Act and other measures had threatened the colonists' financial security, the Quebec Act simultaneously threatened the colonists' strategic security and their most precious liberty—religious freedom. The newspaper's writer recalled how Britain's Glorious Revolution had removed James II and replaced him with William and Mary because of James's embrace of Catholicism; now, less than a hundred years later, the British government had established Catholicism in a large part of its dominion.[17]

A number of American writers began to insist that if George III had been ensnared by Catholicism like his predecessor James II, then he should meet James's fate: removal from power. Pastor Joseph Lyman of Hatfield, Massachusetts, reminded his congregation that James II had revoked the revered Massachusetts charter in the 1680s in order to "set up Popery and arbitrary power." The Glorious Revolution had saved New Englanders, and all the British Empire, from enslavement to the "Man of Sin," by which he meant the power of Catholicism, but recent events, including the passage of the Quebec Act, suggested a renewed attack by the forces of spiritual evil. Lyman postulated that God would frustrate the plot against their liberty because Catholicism was a religion "in a peculiar manner accursed by him."[18]

The prospect of an established, aggressive Catholic Church in Quebec impelled many colonists, especially in New England, to adopt a bellicose, defensive posture. No doubt some speculations about the impending horrors of the Quebec Act were meant only for rhetorical effect, but the controversy reflected how badly the British government misapprehended the temperament of American Protestants. By mid-1774, fears about the intentions of the British government had been raised to a feverish level. The celebrated Suffolk Resolves, adopted by delegates to the Suffolk County (Massachusetts) Convention in 1774 and endorsed by the intercolonial Continental Congress then in session, insisted that the Quebec Act was dangerous to the interests of the Protestant faith and the civil liberties of Americans. "As men and Protestant Christians," the delegates declared they must take all necessary measures against the British government for the safety of Americans.[19]

The Quebec Act generated deep concern across America. South Carolina Baptist pastor Richard Furman averred that the act was secretly intended to place a hostile Catholic force at the colonies' northern doorstep. Should the colonists continue to resist parliamentary actions, a Catholic army would swoop down to destroy them. In such an event, nothing would stop the plotters from establishing "the Popish religion" in all the colonies. Similarly, Savannah, Georgia, pastor John Zubly speculated in 1775 that the British conspirators meant to deprive Americans of their religious freedom and establish a hierarchy over them similar to that of the Roman Church in Canada.[20]

The young New Yorker Alexander Hamilton, then a student at King's College (now Columbia University), composed some of his earliest newspaper editorials in response to the Quebec Act. Hamilton had been born on the Caribbean island of Nevis in inauspicious circumstances: He was conceived out of wedlock, abandoned by his father, and, when his mother died in 1768, orphaned. Patrons, including his beloved Presbyterian pastor, arranged for the bright young man to go to the mainland colonies for education. He entered King's College in late 1773, only to be swept up in the furor over the Intolerable Acts and the Quebec Act.

Hamilton insisted that the Quebec Act had enshrined "arbitrary power, and its great engine the Popish religion," in Canada. The language of the act implied to him that Catholic priests could expect guaranteed financial support from the provincial government, whereas the Protestant clergy would receive assistance only at the discretion of the king. Hamilton decried this system as an "atrocious infraction" on Christian liberty and the rights of Englishmen. No serious Protestant would allow the free exercise of his religion to depend on the good will of a ruler, he wrote. Hamilton agreed that the Quebec Act revealed the "dark designs" of the British administration more than any previous transgression. He viewed it as the first step toward encircling the colonists with hostile Catholics, warning that if the British could establish Catholicism in Quebec, they could just as easily do it in New York or any other American colony. Hamilton soon joined a volunteer militia company to prepare for the defense of New York.[21]

To the colonists, the Quebec Act seemed like outright betrayal. It heavily eroded George III's authority in America. A widely circulated article by "Scipio," writing in the *Pennsylvania Journal*, promised the king that American Protestants would fight against the violation of their civil and religious liberties and resist "the Pope, the Devil, and ALL their emissaries." Colonists widely asserted that in approving the act, the king had broken his coronation oath to defend the Protestant faith. Some argued that in violating that oath, the king had dissolved the compact that bound him to the English people, including the English in America. An article reprinted in Connecticut (it originally appeared in London) proposed that when the king broke his coronation oath, all his subjects were absolved from their allegiance to him. That writer went so far as to propose a reenactment of Charles I's beheading: "Off with the head that pays no regard to the sacredness of an oath!" With this rhetoric of indignation and fear, it seemed extremely unlikely that the king's reputation could be repaired among Patriot Americans.[22]

Confidence in the king suffered even more with the outbreak of war at Lexington and Concord on April 19, 1775. The British, led by General Thomas Gage, resolved to put down the insurrection in Massachusetts. On the night of April 18, Gage sent royal troops into the countryside, headed for the town of Concord, where a cache of Patriot arms was stored. Patriot spies, including the silversmith Paul Revere, rode in advance of the redcoat army and roused the local militia, the "minutemen." The two sides met at Lexington, where the first shot of the war was fired. Then the colonists put up a fierce defense of Concord, forcing the royal troops into a bloody retreat back to Boston.

Immediately after those battles, Baptist pastor Isaac Backus of Middleborough, Massachusetts, compared the British Empire's circumstances to those in the 1680s when James II threatened to reduce England to what Backus called "popery and slavery." Backus believed that the British government had begun acting contrary to the colonists' fundamental rights by taxing them without representation and insisting on parliamentary sovereignty in the colonies; he told his congregation that the king had violated his coronation oath by signing the Quebec Act and that the time might have come for his removal.[23]

The furor over the Quebec Act allowed radical Patriots to take command of the escalating momentum for independence. It is important to remember that the path to nationhood was not assured in 1774, nor was the collapse of confidence in King George. Many Americans in mid-1774 still believed that the king would realize that corrupt officials had forced oppressive measures on the colonists, and that he would yet prove to be the colonists' political savior. The loss of religious liberty threatened by the Quebec Act, apparently passed and enforced with the blessing of the king, so offended and disturbed many American Christians that the king and the British administration could never recover the trust they had once held. General Gage, who had become the martial-law governor of Massachusetts in May 1774, wrote that the Quebec Act unfortunately ended hope of limiting the crisis to Boston. In the hinterlands of the province, where "sedition flows copiously from the pulpits," a patriotic "flame blazed out in all parts at once beyond the conception of every body," Gage remarked. Once the colonists perceived the British government to be an agent of Antichrist, no expression of goodwill toward Protestant liberty could calm their fears.[24]

In *The Church's Flight into the Wilderness* (1776), the Reverend Samuel Sherwood of Fairfield, Connecticut, made the most elaborate case for the American Revolution as a fight against Catholicism, which he equated with Antichrist. Sherwood, speaking on a text from the book of Revelation, argued that all of human history revealed a great contest between God's true church and the forces of "Popery." Popery was rooted in the Roman Catholic Church, but any forces of tyranny and oppression were also connected to this Antichristian spirit. Sherwood believed that the legislative actions of Britain against America arose from a system of corruption that ultimately sought to force Roman Catholicism on Protestant America. He singled out the Quebec Act as an "open attempt to propagate and establish Popery, that exotic plant, in these northern regions." He also accused the British government of recruiting Roman Catholic armies in Canada to enslave and destroy the American colonists. In the Quebec Act, Sherwood said, the mystical "flood of the dragon has been poured forth," but he did not believe that true Christianity would be swamped by that deluge of Antichristian power. Instead, he saw the Quebec Act as the death throes of what he, like Pastor Samuel Cooper and Pastor Joseph Lyman, called the "Man of Sin." Sherwood hoped the crisis would lead to the downfall of the power of Antichrist and the coming of the millennium.[25]

Evangelical minister Henry Cumings also used the language of apocalypse to interpret the Quebec Act in a sermon to his congregation in

Billerica, Massachusetts. Pointing to the act as evidence of a government conspiracy to destroy the religious and civil liberties of the colonists, in one vivid passage, he predicted that, "should the present schemes of arbitrary power succeed, the Scarlet Whore would soon get mounted on her horned Beast in America, and, with the CUP OF ABOMINATIONS in her hand, ride triumphant over the heads of true Protestants, making multitudes DRUNK WITH THE WINE OF HER FORNICATIONS." His imagery came from the book of Revelation, chapters 17 and 18. For Cumings and many other civil and religious patriot leaders, placing the British government's poorly planned legislation into an apocalyptic framework helped motivate biblically minded colonists to resist, while assuring them that God had foreseen the troubles with Britain and that their fight against this oppression was part of God's ordained plan. Instead of focusing on political and diplomatic appeals to the British, Cumings recommended that American Patriots look to God to vindicate their cause, because it was God who alone decided between right and wrong. Citing the Glorious Revolution and the defeat of the French at Louisbourg in 1745 as historical evidence, Cumings expressed confidence that God would again come to the aid of his children in America. "The cause of liberty," he assured his church, is "the cause of God."[26]

By 1775, colonists not only in New England but up and down the Atlantic coast were decrying what a great many saw as the plot to establish Roman Catholicism in America. In New York City, a broadside by Philip Livingston reminded the town's residents that James II had attempted to force Catholicism and absolute government on the English, but that they had "refused to bow their necks, to him or to Antichrist," and it urged Americans to refuse to submit this time, too. In Virginia, Arthur Lee wrote a widely circulated pamphlet that also pointed to the memory of the Glorious Revolution, exclaiming, "Spirit of the Stuarts, look down and wonder! This single transaction will put all your merits to the blush!" A Salem, Massachusetts, broadside containing a fictional address to the redcoat army by an "old soldier" warned them that they were being called to attack Americans and force them to submit to the rule of popery and slavery. Colonists had run afoul of the British government, the old soldier declared, because they resisted the establishment of Catholicism and arbitrary power in Quebec.[27]

The uses of anti-Catholicism were limited, as cooler heads would recognize. Once resistance transformed into civil war at Lexington and Concord, the Patriot leaders of the Revolution pragmatically toned down public expressions of anti-Catholicism. The Patriots sought the allegiance of Canadian Catholics disaffected from the British government, as well as of the sizable Catholic populations of colonies like Pennsylvania and Maryland. George Washington took the lead in quashing anti-Catholic displays by the Continental Army in late 1775; he wrote scalding general orders forbidding the observation of Pope's Day, an old English anti-Catholic festival celebrated on November 5 that usually involved the burning of the pope in effigy. Washington would have none of it, calling the practice "ridiculous and childish" and wondering how anyone could be "so void of common sense, as not to see the impropriety of such a step at this juncture."[28]

Yet despite the toning down of anti-Catholicism, writers such as the Patriot essayist Thomas Paine still exploited the apprehensions raised by the Quebec Act and used them to promote independence. In one of the first essays Paine penned after he immigrated to Philadelphia, he declared that the Quebec Act was designed to impose despotic rule on all of America. Then, in one of the most damning indictments of the king in his wildly popular *Common Sense*, Paine asserted that "Monarchy in every instance is the Popery of government."[29]

In 1778, with enormous irony, anti-Catholic American Patriots entered into an alliance with Catholic France, a diplomatic victory that was essential to America's success in the Revolution. Although the French initially balked at backing the revolutionary cause, American diplomats like Benjamin Franklin were persistent. The French were not sure the Americans could win the war, so they waited for a clear sign of hope for the American effort. This sign came in 1777, when the Patriots won a stunning victory over British general John Burgoyne at Saratoga, New York. Just four months later, in February 1778, the Americans and French signed the treaty of friendship and commerce committing France to securing the independence of the United States.

Only fifteen years earlier, at the end of the Seven Years' War, Americans had seen France as one of the chief political agents of Antichrist. Now the French were their indispensable allies. To pragmatic leaders like Washington and Franklin, there was no questioning the wisdom of allying with erstwhile enemies. A few Patriots grumbled about the treaty with France, but it was Loyalists who trumpeted the hypocrisy of the union of Catholics and Protestants. "The Congress have wonderfully altered their tone of late," mocked the *Pennsylvania Ledger*. They "are very willing to make us the instruments of weakening the best friends, and of strengthening the most powerful and ambitious enemies of the reformation, to such a degree as must do more than all the world besides could do, towards the universal re-establishment of Popery through all Christendom."[30]

Patriot Christians interpreted the alliance as a providential action on behalf of America. Even the most conservative Patriot Christians came to believe that if French Catholics supported Americans' liberty, then Americans could cooperate with them. Some thought that their friendliness toward liberty showed that the French were not very serious Catholics any longer. Others postulated that the alliance would lead to the downfall of Catholicism in France by exposing it to godly Protestantism. Presbyterian pastor John Murray compared the French king, Louis XVI, to the Good Samaritan of Jesus's parable: a traditional enemy raised up by God to help his people. "Does the bigot give credit to the Tory's tale, and dream it unlawful to accept such aid?" Murray asked impatiently.[31]

American anti-Catholicism would fade somewhat during the Revolution (only to reappear in force in the early nineteenth century), but in all its calumny it had done its work in preparing many Americans to break with Britain and the king. The opposition to an Anglican bishop and the controversy over the Quebec Act highlighted Americans' fear of the loss of their religious liberty. Americans' reactions to both issues help make comprehensible Samuel Adams's 1768 claim that the colonists should fear popery more than anything else. Their visceral dread of Catholicism spiritualized the meaning of the political conflict over parliamentary sovereignty, and it undermined the fondness colonists once held for George III.

CHAPTER 4

"Victory over the Beast"

The Evangelical Roots of Revolution

O N MARCH 22, 1775, as Britain and the colonies teetered at the edge of war, the great orator Edmund Burke took the floor of the British Parliament to explain why his country should seek reconciliation with the Americans. The colonists' resistance would be very difficult to break, he warned, because of their passionate devotion to liberty. It was not hard to understand why they valued their liberty so much, because many of the colonists were freedom-loving Englishmen themselves. Burke asserted that the American colonists fundamentally derived their ideas about freedom and resistance from their religion, namely Protestant Christianity. Not only were they Protestants, but many of them—Congregationalists, Presbyterians, and Baptists, among others—were dissenters from the Anglican Church. They were Protestants "of that kind, which is most adverse to all implicit submission of mind and opinion," Burke declared. Their brand of Protestantism not only favored liberty, it was "built upon it."[1]

Burke located the roots of the dissenters' love of liberty in their beliefs and in their history. For centuries, dissenters fought against the political and religious establishments of Europe and America. To do so effectively, they had to justify their resistance by appeals to God-given rights of conscience. Especially in the northern colonies, the Americans' religion was "a refinement on the principle of resistance." Be warned, Burke told his fellow members of Parliament: The Americans represented "the

Protestantism of the Protestant religion." The colonists had much experience with resisting established powers, and they would do so again, even to the point of shedding blood.[2]

As if to prove Burke's point from across the sea, Patrick Henry rose the next day at the Virginia Convention to expound upon the reasons why Americans must fight Britain to defend their liberty. When Henry and other radicals advocated for the formation of a defensive state militia (several British warships were already anchored nearby in the James River), some delegates offered cautious opposition. In response, Henry delivered what would become his most famous speech. Calling the struggle against Britain a "holy cause of liberty," Henry assured the convention that God would fight on their behalf. "Is life so dear, or peace so sweet," he asked, "as to be purchased at the price of chains and slavery? Forbid it, Almighty God!" Then in the thundering last line of the speech, Henry extended his arms and proclaimed, "as for me, give me liberty, or give me death!" In language resounding with Christian themes, Henry painted a compelling picture of resistance.[3]

The great speaker's verbal mastery evinced all the signs of the evangelical preaching that he had often heard as a young man in Virginia. He had become fascinated with the popular rhetoric of Virginia's newly arrived Presbyterians and reportedly pronounced Samuel Davies, the most influential Presbyterian preacher of the Great Awakening in Virginia, to be the greatest orator he had ever heard. Though he would remain a traditional Anglican, he was shaped as a speaker by the evangelical rhetorical style. The power of Henry's speeches lay in his emotional style and simple language, which was the sermonic mode of the evangelical preachers. Just as one cannot fully fathom from the page the declamatory brilliance of evangelist George Whitefield, much of the force of Henry's speeches cannot be discerned simply by reading them. His texts relied little on political theory, but they abounded in references to the Bible.

Not only Henry's verbal style but also his beliefs about liberty arose from the Great Awakening. He and other Patriots absorbed Protestant ideas of resistance that would directly influence the American Revolution. One key idea was that Christian doctrine favored limited government power, especially over the individual conscience. God had instituted government, but the fallible people in public office could easily become tyrants if given too much power. To many Protestants, the long history of religious oppression, from the ancient Roman Empire to the eighteenth-century Catholic monarchies of Europe, indicated how easily a strong government could violate religious liberty.

Another salient idea was the evangelical appeal to God, as opposed to rulers or human laws, as the ultimate arbiter of all matters religious and political. Common people could understand the will of God in religion and politics. This religious individualism bred a kind of evangelical populism. From the Separates of the Great Awakening to the Patriots of the American Revolution, common men and women decided for themselves when government had violated the will of God and should be resisted. Evangelists and Patriots both went over the heads of leaders to the people themselves, exhorting them to obey God and not men. The evangelical view of limited government and its style of rhetoric colored America's wars from the siege of Louisbourg in 1745 to the American Revolution. The evangelicals' challenge to authority from the Great Awakening to the Revolution helped forge an American style of resistance that propelled many into independence in 1776.

Patriot clergymen made almost indistinguishable arguments for religious and political liberty. Israel Holly, the evangelical pastor of Suffield, Connecticut, had become a Separate during the Great Awakening and learned to resent the intrusion of political authority into the realm of religious conscience. As he wrote in 1765, civil authorities had a very simple mandate: to defend people's lives, liberty, and property. One of the chief privileges government was bound to defend was religious liberty, which Holly called an "unalienable" right. Such views of government did not only originate with the "late religious commotion in the land" (the Great Awakening), Holly maintained. They were bound up in God's design for government and church. Holly asserted that the liberties he defended were the "essential rights of Protestants."[4]

By 1773, Holly adapted these views about the legitimate bounds of government to the crisis between the colonists and the British government. Like all New Englanders, Holly read with fascination the accounts of Bostonians boarding East India Company ships in December and throwing overboard their cargo of tea. Casting aside any reservations he might have had as a clergyman about this destruction of property, Holly delivered a sermon eleven days after the Tea Party, summoning the colonies to unite in the struggle for their liberties and calling for individuals to give up their private commercial interests for the public good, even if it meant boycotting goods like tea. If the colonists meekly submitted to the encroaching power of the British government, Holly warned, they could lose everything. Cowardice would open the door not only to arbitrary power over their property but also to the loss of their religious liberty. Holly cautioned that the conspirators plotting against the colonists might intend to commandeer their religious liberty next, possibly replacing their own Protestantism with tyrannical Catholicism. He posited an inextricable link among "despotic power . . . , arbitrary government, and Popery." If the secret Catholic power behind the British bureaucracy took control, then "away must go our bibles," and the tyrants would force them to "pray to the Virgin Mary, worship images, [and] believe the doctrine of Purgatory, and the Pope's infallibility." Certainly, Holly's scenario was preposterous—there existed no real plot in Britain or anywhere else to impose Catholicism on the colonies. But many like Holly suspected that the ultimate end of political tyranny would be the forced adoption of Catholicism.[5]

The responsibility for the looming prospect of spiritual despotism began at home, Holly declared. To him, America's trouble with the British government was the judgment of God on the colonies for denying religious liberty to their own evangelical dissenters. He asserted that God threatened lawmakers who oppressed their own people with "arbitrary laws of the same nature." If New England's leaders would repent of their own oppressive spirit, Holly told his congregation, then God would provide a way out of the imperial crisis.[6]

The groundbreaking notions of limited government, the sacred right of conscience, and the people's duty to resist ungodly laws and governments had sprung up among evangelicals thirty years earlier during the revivals. One radical aspect of the Great Awakening was the practice of itinerant preaching, the evangelicals' notion that they could speak to audiences whenever and wherever they liked. Itinerants like George Whitefield, Gilbert Tennent, and especially James Davenport barged into towns and churches uninvited and spoke directly to the people in an emotional language. These preachers and their listeners implicitly asserted that the individual right to hear edifying preaching supplanted traditional Christian veneration for religious order and organization. Itinerants made many political and religious officials angry, and several colonies tried to restrict the evangelicals' movements. Nowhere was this better exemplified than in Connecticut, where a 1742 law prohibited ministers from intruding uninvited into other pastors' parishes and churches—the law that forced the banishment of James Davenport from Connecticut.

Evangelical pastor Elisha Williams of Wethersfield, Connecticut, saw the anti-itinerancy law as a violation of religious liberty. In *The Essential Rights and Liberties of Protestants* (1744), Williams borrowed heavily from English philosopher John Locke ("the celebrated Lock," as Williams called him) to show that government had limited civil purposes: preserving people's lives, freedoms, and property. When the power of government was applied to any other end, it became tyrannical. Although Williams supported state religious establishments for the overall betterment of Christianity, he could not countenance any law that punished people simply for their religious beliefs or practices; Christ alone dictated the doctrines and rituals of faith, so any civil magistrate who doled out punishments in the sphere of religion intruded on the kingdom of Christ. Christians had an "unalienable right" to search the Scriptures for themselves and to respond to God's call on their lives, Williams insisted.

According to Williams, governments that claimed or sought to have binding religious authority smacked of a "spice of Antichristianism" that the Wethersfield pastor associated with Catholicism. Williams adhered to the deep anti-Catholic sensibilities of the time, defining Protestant liberty against the ostensible tyranny of Catholicism. Indeed, he did not believe that Catholics should be afforded liberty of conscience in Protestant societies, because properly speaking, Catholics had no religion; their pseudo-faith was to him a conspiracy against the rights of mankind, and any law that punished people for religious transgressions dallied with the Catholics' Antichristian spirit. According to Williams, Christians had the right to hear any minister preach that they wanted to. Statutes like the

1742 anti-itinerancy law reflected the illegitimate mingling of the civil arena with the Kingdom of God, and Williams warned his readers that such convergence might only be a first step. Christian liberty was usually "lost by little and little." Protestants who did not guard their liberty could easily fall prey to Antichristian tyranny, whether it was explicitly Catholic or not.[7]

Many of the revivalists' opponents also feared that evangelicals bred disrespect for the established authorities. Antievangelical pastor William Hooper of Boston lamented in 1742 that the evangelical zealots despised "all rule and authority." Another minister worried that the radical evangelicals would reject all earthly powers, with the justification that "CHRIST hath made all people kings."[8] It was still common among Christians in eighteenth-century England and America to emphasize a subject's duty to obey God and honor the king. But in some colonists' minds, the influence of Enlightenment thought (such as that of Locke), combined with the experience of the revivals, started to undermine the sacred authority of political power. A large number of colonists also revered moments in English history when the people had risen up against tyrannical political power. During the English Civil War and the Glorious Revolution, one English king had been deposed and another even executed in the name of Protestant Christian liberty. Several colonies, including Massachusetts, had thrown out their royal governments in the aftermath of the Glorious Revolution. This history taught colonists that Christian subjects should obey good kings and authorities, but once officials became corrupt, subjects could only obey for so long.

According to the dissenting evangelicals of the Great Awakening, the worst kind of political corruption led to the persecution of true Christians. When evangelicals felt that government policy contradicted Christian principle (as in the case of Connecticut's anti-itinerancy law), they appealed to their followers to obey God's laws rather than men's arbitrary edicts. Separate leader Solomon Paine wrote in a 1752 tract on religious freedom that Christians should respond to God's call in their choice of a church, even if that contradicted the ruling establishment's dictum; God would ultimately settle the quarrel between his people and illegitimate government. Paine did not believe that he was showing contempt for legitimate political authority, because authority that was "a terror to good works" was not of God. His indictment of the New England religious establishments was so powerful that he was unable to secure a Connecticut publisher; Paine printed his treatise with James Franklin, Ben's older brother, in the relatively free atmosphere of Newport, Rhode Island.[9]

In the revolutionary period itself, starting in 1763, new evangelical awakenings were shaking American churches. These revivals also boosted the spirit of resistance as the colonies moved toward direct confrontation with Britain. John Cleaveland, a prominent Separate evangelical leader as well as an ardent Patriot, led what was among the most dramatic awakenings of the 1760s and made explicit connections between the cause of revival and resistance to Britain. Cleaveland had been expelled from Yale in the early 1740s for attending Separate meetings, and in 1747 he became pastor of a Separate congregation in Ipswich, Massachusetts. In 1763 a major new revival broke out in his church, attracting people away from established churches and infuriating their pastors. Some of Cleaveland's opponents tried to deny the straying members access to communion at their home churches, and one called them "deluded followers of the Beast." In response, Cleaveland asserted the right of religious liberty as a freedom upon which the government could not justly intrude, maintaining that the evangelicals' cause was no different from that of the Sons of Liberty who resisted the Stamp Act of 1765. Both groups defended civil and sacred rights against oppressive governments. Using terminology that had become increasingly common among evangelicals, Cleaveland called a person's liberty to pursue spiritual edification an "unalienable right." Like Elisha Williams before him, he appealed to both evangelical faith and John Locke's philosophy as the basis for his argument against government power over religious conscience. Cleaveland's ideas show the folly of trying to separate the sources of revolutionary ideology into "secular" or "religious" categories: Patriots drew on religious sources as well as Enlightenment philosophers like Locke and saw no contradiction between them.[10]

Beginning in 1768, Cleaveland turned his evangelical ideas of resistance against the British government. Reacting to the furor over the

Townshend Duties, the British sent troops to Boston. The Boston town meeting denounced the soldiers' impending arrival as setting a dangerous precedent; once again, the British had forced a government policy on Americans without their consent. Yet the army came anyway, disembarking on October 1, 1768, under the cover of the guns of British warships. By early 1769, Boston was teeming with redcoats: 4,000 soldiers in a town of 15,000 colonists. From nearby Ipswich, Cleaveland watched with growing apprehension and anger. He warned that some in the British government meant to make the colonists "slaves," by which he meant people under the absolute sway of government power. Although Cleaveland insisted that the colonists did not intend to rebel against George III, he cautioned that "oppression will make even a wise man mad!"[11]

The crisis escalated in 1773–1774 when Bostonians destroyed the East India Company's shipment of tea and the British retaliated with the Intolerable Acts. Like other preachers, such as Israel Holly, Cleaveland feared that God was bringing judgment on Americans for their selfishness and immorality. If the colonists made themselves morally pure again, he believed, then God would hear their prayers for relief. Cleaveland combined spiritual and political tactics of opposition, calling on Americans both to repent of their sins and to resist the importation of British goods. If the colonists would seek God's protection, reform their sinful ways, and sacrifice personal gratification for the public good, then God would preserve their civil and religious rights. Holiness and virtue would lead to victory against their enemies, but sin and selfishness would lead to more judgments. Cleaveland's moral admonition to his fellow colonists was part of a long tradition of ascribing the public woes of Americans to their sinfulness, while summoning them to repentance that would lead God to establish justice on their behalf. For a century or more, colonial New Englanders had responded to times of political or military crisis with Cleaveland's sort of exhortation: a jeremiad, or cautionary lecture. Recalling the message of Jeremiah, the Old Testament prophet, ministers told the people that sin had brought them their trouble, but godliness would bring them deliverance.[12]

The battles of Lexington and Concord in April 1775 turned Cleaveland and many other Patriot leaders from resistance to revolution. The

British attack on the Patriots, and King George's apparent approval of it, shattered whatever remaining loyalty Cleaveland felt toward the British Crown. In a column in the *Essex Gazette*, he cried, "Great Britain adieu! no longer shall we honor you as our mother. . . . King George the third adieu! no more shall we cry to you for protection!" Colonists only reluctantly accused George III of precipitating the crisis, typically blaming devious officials surrounding the king instead. But now Cleaveland pointed to the king himself as the root of the problem and accused him of breaching his sacred covenant, which required him to protect the lives and liberty of his subjects. Cleaveland again warned the colonists to watch out for any immorality that might provoke God's judgment against them, yet he remained confident of God's favor on America and expected that God would defend their cause. In an open letter in the *Essex Gazette* in July 1775, Cleaveland called General Gage a "monster of falsehood and perfidy" and declared that "the God of glory is on our side and will fight for us." Even though colonists routinely agreed with preachers like Cleaveland and saw their own sins as the cause of their troubles, they never lost their trust that God would honor his promise to protect his people.[13]

The widespread belief that sin led to national punishment impelled the Continental Congress—the new, united legislature of the colonies—to proclaim days of prayer and fasting in 1774 and 1775, calling on all Americans to confess and repent of their sins. Thomas Jefferson later recalled that the Congress reviewed old Puritan proclamations for fast days, modernized the language, and called for the solemn occasion "to implore heaven to . . . inspire us with firmness in support of our rights." According to the Congress, the crisis's solution lay in nationwide spiritual quickening, as it called for prayer that "virtue and true religion may revive and flourish throughout our land." Robust faith and morality would lead God to intervene on the colonists' behalf, and to secure their civil and religious liberties. Even leaders like Jefferson, who did not share the evangelicals' faith, hoped that a resurgence of religion would help Americans win the war.[14]

In the South, evangelicals also helped fire the Patriots' resistance against Britain. William Tennent III, the evangelical pastor of the Independent

Presbyterian Church in Charleston, became a member of South Carolina's provincial legislature and one of the colony's chief agitators against British policies. Tennent had deep family roots in the evangelical movement; he was the nephew of renowned itinerant preacher Gilbert Tennent of New Jersey. In a 1774 sermon, William Tennent warned his congregation that their freedom itself was at stake in the controversy over Britain's taxing authority and the Intolerable Acts. If the imperial government could tax the colonists without their consent, shut down the Massachusetts government, and close the port of Boston, then what would prevent the colonists' descent into the "most abject slavery"? Tennent went on to note that active resistance against oppression was permitted by the Scriptures.[15]

So influential were Tennent and other evangelical pastors that southern legislators used them to raise support for an impending war of independence. In 1775 the South Carolina provincial assembly sent Tennent and Baptist pastor Oliver Hart on a mission into the South Carolina backcountry to convince reluctant residents to support the Patriot cause against Britain. Notwithstanding Tennent's and Hart's evangelical patriotism, a number of Baptists and Presbyterians in the rural Carolinas either remained committed to the British Empire or sought to stay neutral. Some trusted the British government more than they trusted the colonial authorities in Charleston, and some evangelicals believed that their religious faith precluded involvement in war. The colonial assembly sent Hart and Tennent as advocates for the American resistance, believing that the preachers' popularity would win over the largely religious audiences of the backcountry.

Tennent and Hart's mission met with considerable success. Tennent warned many large assemblies about the oppression threatened by the British government. At one meeting near the Little River in South Carolina, Tennent spoke for two and a half hours, exhorting the audience not to become complicit in their own enslavement. He believed that God moved in the room, he wrote in his journal, with results like those seen at revival meetings: People pressed around Tennent afterward, asking him to continue speaking, and the two preachers convinced many of them to sign a pledge of loyalty to the rebellious South Carolina government.[16]

Baptist minister Richard Furman also helped mobilize the Carolina backcountry in support of resistance against Britain. Furman became the pastor of the High Hills of Santee Baptist Church in 1774, and within a year he had begun to work with Hart and Tennent to rouse support for South Carolina Patriots. Furman often met with opposition, as he did in Camden, South Carolina, where the sheriff refused him access to the courthouse; nevertheless, the preacher spoke outside its door with such vehemence that even some of the town's leading Loyalists were convinced.

By late 1775, violence had erupted between Patriot and Loyalist forces in South Carolina. In the politically divided backcountry, the Revolution threatened to become a vicious civil war, with brother literally fighting brother. In November Loyalists carried out an assault on the trading post at Ninety Six, South Carolina; the following month Colonel Richard Richardson of High Hills led a Patriot counterattack, marching through a freak South Carolina snowstorm. In almost three feet of snow, the Loyalists surrendered to Richardson and signed a pledge not to take up arms for the empire again.[17]

As part of his campaign, Colonel Richardson distributed a letter from Pastor Furman appealing for the backcountry settlers to support the Patriot cause against Britain. Furman recognized that some of the most devout Christians balked at resistance because of Bible verses calling for obedience to the established authorities. Furman wrote that he did not mean for the colonists to oppose the legitimate actions of the king, but said that when the king acted contrary to the British constitution, he was not morally exercising power given to him by God. In such cases, the king ought not to be obeyed. Cooperating with such abusive actions would put the colonists under the "unlimited sway of arbitrary power," Furman said. He, Hart, and Tennent convinced many of the biblically minded residents of South Carolina's hinterlands to support the Patriot cause.[18]

Although he would later oppose the Revolution itself, Presbyterian pastor John Zubly of Savannah, Georgia, became one of the most articulate evangelical proponents of resistance before 1776. Zubly emigrated from his native Switzerland to Georgia in the mid-1740s and immediately came under the influence of George Whitefield. Zubly never believed that his pastoral ministry precluded commentary on politics, and he became heavily involved in the Stamp Act crisis in 1765. Even though Parliament repealed the Stamp Act in 1766, it attached a declaration to the repeal asserting that Parliament had the right to tax the colonists "in all cases whatsoever." Outraged by that claim of unbounded authority, Zubly posited that the colonial assemblies remained sovereign within their American spheres. Echoing his friend John Dickinson (the author of *Letters from a Farmer in Pennsylvania*), Zubly raised the assemblies to a coequal status with Parliament, granting Parliament sovereignty over the colonies only in matters of trade policy. Zubly deliberately repeated Dickinson's argument, telling him in a personal letter that he hoped to bring some of Dickinson's "fire with him to the South."[19] For Zubly, parliamentary sovereignty "in all cases whatsoever" meant slavery for the colonists. Even after the beginning of open conflict between Britain and the colonists in 1775, Zubly held that sovereignty remained the critical issue dividing Americans from the British government. He warned the British government that the "Americans are no idiots, and they appear determined not to be slaves."[20]

Yet Zubly argued against independence, believing that God had joined Americans and Britons as one people and that Christians should not take up arms against the established government. Even though he was chosen to serve as a representative from Georgia in the Second Continental Congress in 1775, he grew disturbed when the sentiments in that assembly slid toward independence, which he could not countenance. Zubly's case reminds us that resistance did not necessarily translate into support for revolution for all evangelicals, or for Americans generally. A strong minority of American evangelicals did not support the rebellion and became Loyalists or neutrals once war broke out. Zubly himself, after leaving the Continental Congress under a cloud of suspicion, refused to ally with Georgia's independence movement and hid in South Carolina's Black Swamp until the British captured Savannah in 1779. He returned home and became one of Georgia's leading Loyalist writers until his death in 1781.

Although Zubly's faith did not carry him all the way to rebellion, evangelical beliefs helped many others vault over the line from resistance to revolution. Christian rhetoric continued to frame the most fervent appeals for liberty once the crisis teetered at the edge of violence in the mid-1770s. As we have seen, some Patriot writers were evangelicals themselves; others simply employed the language of evangelicalism, even if they did not embrace the evangelical movement or traditional Christianity of any kind. Among the latter group, no writer was as influential as Thomas Paine.

When Paine left London for Philadelphia in 1774, he did not seem destined for fame. His second marriage had just collapsed, he had lost his job as a tax collector, and creditors were pursuing him for outstanding debts. Paine effectively threw up his hands and booked passage on a ship bound for the colonies and a fresh start. His one beacon of hope was Benjamin Franklin, who had met and taken a liking to Paine in England. In America, with Franklin's backing, Paine quickly found work as an editor, offering him an outlet for his uncanny writing talent.

Paine electrified the colonies with his January 1776 publication of *Common Sense*, the most influential political pamphlet in American history. Until the appearance of *Common Sense*, many Americans hesitated to reject the authority of the king, even though at that point the redcoats had been fighting Patriot soldiers, with the king's assent, for nine months. Paine had been associating with Philadelphia's most influential revolutionary leaders, including Franklin and the radical young physician Benjamin Rush, who helped him write *Common Sense*. Franklin and Samuel Adams also offered a few suggestions. In the pamphlet, Paine set aside political theory and spoke to the people in the language of the Bible and Protestant Christianity. The strategy worked. *Common Sense* became a national sensation and turned the tide in favor of independence, which the Second Continental Congress would formally declare six months later.

Paine was reared by an Anglican mother and a Quaker father, and apparently worked for a brief period as an evangelical Methodist preacher before coming to America. He knew the culture of Anglo-American Protestantism well. His use of religiously inspired language and arguments in *Common Sense* is ironic, because at the time he wrote the pamphlets he was already becoming skeptical about traditional faith. In the 1790s he would become well-known as one of the leading deist critics of

Christianity. But just as advocates for royal prerogative used the Bible to defend the divine right of kings, so Paine used the Bible to attack monarchy. He described monarchy as a kind of original political sin committed by the nation of Israel in I Samuel 8 and 9. In that biblical passage, God warns the Israelites that they should not desire a king because such an absolute ruler would abuse them; God alone should be their king. But out of fear and envy of the surrounding nations, the Israelites persist, choosing Saul to reign over them. Paine concluded that in this episode God had evidenced his displeasure with monarchical government. Abandoning monarchy would mean a return to God and his law. "But where," Paine asked, "is the King of America? I'll tell you friend, he reigns above, and doth not make havoc of mankind like the Royal Brute of Britain." Paine called for a symbolic American coronation day in which a crown would be placed on the word of God alone, "by which the world may know, that so far as we approve of monarchy, that in America THE LAW IS KING."[21]

Paine also used millennial language to anticipate the consequences of independence. The old world of Europe had given in to sin and corruption, but Americans had a chance to "begin the world over again." He likened America's opportunity to that in the book of Genesis when God flooded the earth, killing the world's population except for Noah and his family. Free from the debilitating influence of British rule, Americans would create a utopian society pleasing to God and noble for man. "The birthday of a new world is at hand," he proclaimed, if only the American Patriots would seize the moment.[22]

The rhetoric of evangelical dissent was everywhere in Paine's pamphlet. Anti-Catholicism, government limited by the law of God, and political millennialism all fueled his argument. The pamphlet became a sensation among biblically minded Americans, running through twenty-five editions and selling tens of thousands of copies. Hundreds of thousands of Americans either read the tract or heard its arguments recited publicly. Paine's personal religious skepticism did not keep him from appropriating biblical arguments and evangelical rhetoric to mobilize a population that understood that language very well.[23]

Paine was the most influential writer using biblical language to justify the Revolution, but he was hardly the only one. The Baptist pastor John

Allen, a recent immigrant from England to Boston and a man of dubious moral repute, penned *An Oration upon the Beauties of Liberty* (1773), another popular revolutionary pamphlet. Allen had worked as a pastor of a Baptist church in London in the 1760s, but like Thomas Paine, he fell into debt and legal trouble and lost his position in 1767. Two years later he was charged and tried for forging a promissory note, and even though he was acquitted, his reputation was fatally damaged. In the early 1770s Allen began publishing on liberty and the rights of Englishmen, and by 1772 he had decided, like Paine, to try his luck in America. In Boston he sought preaching work at Second Baptist Church; some members were skeptical of his qualifications, but a church committee noted that "a number of gentlemen were desirous to hear him (Sons of Liberty)." Some of those Sons of Liberty, Boston's leaders in the resistance against Britain, apparently liked Allen's oratorical blending of evangelical faith and republican liberty. But as more details of Allen's background became known, he lost his chance to work at Second Baptist Church. Instead, he found his calling as a writer.[24]

Like many in America, Allen was enraged by the British response to the burning of the British customs ship *Gaspee* in Rhode Island's Narragansett Bay in 1772. Although some colonists proposed that Indians had perpetrated the attack, it was clear that rebellious Rhode Island merchants were responsible. The British government set up a commission to investigate, with legal authority to bring any accused persons to England for trial. The commission could not produce any convincing suspects, but the mere prospect of the Americans' being deprived of the ancient right of trial by a jury of peers roused colonists like Allen to action. Allen vividly expressed popular resentment over the *Gaspee* affair in his *Oration*, which eventually went through five editions. Although he has largely been forgotten in the annals of the Revolution, his radical pamphlet anticipated the final rejection of King George's authority during a time when no American was yet calling publicly for independence. His verbal pyrotechnics also anticipated the excited, angry rhetoric of Paine's *Common Sense*. *An Oration* drew not on formal political sources but on a host of biblical stories and allusions to make its case. Allen especially commended the prophet Micah, a "SON of LIBERTY," who challenged the wicked king of Israel, Ahaz. No doubt Allen saw himself as operating in that same prophetic mode.

Allen maintained, like most colonists, that King George had been deceived by corrupt bureaucrats around him. But he still warned that if the king endorsed the tyrannical power represented by the *Gaspee* commission, he would forfeit his right to rule over the American colonists. Unlike John Zubly, Allen asserted that Parliament had no legislative authority over America at all. Americans had the right, by the "law of GOD, of nature, and of nations," to resist attempts to oppress and enslave them. To do so was not rebellion; it was a God-given right and duty.[25]

Many American evangelicals, including some primary leaders of the Great Awakening, also rallied their followers to resist Britain in the years before independence. Jonathan Parsons of Newburyport, Massachusetts, had become a leading Separate during the Great Awakening and had participated with his friend John Cleaveland in the new revivals of the 1760s. Like Cleaveland, Parsons called on his congregation (in whose crypt was buried George Whitefield) to defend their Christian liberty. In a 1774 sermon, he commemorated the "barbarous butchery" of the Boston Massacre of 1770, when British soldiers had fired into a menacing Boston crowd, killing five. Parsons opposed any taxes laid on people without their consent, whether the taxes were levied for church or state. Reflecting his continuing engagement with the Separate cause, he warned New Englanders that their very church establishments made their calls for civil liberty hypocritical. Nevertheless, he insisted that if the British government continued its efforts to enslave the colonists, they should take up arms in the "spirit of Christian benevolence" to defend their rights. In the face of arbitrary power, Christian benevolence mandated action, not passivity. Echoing Locke, Parsons described the colonists' rights as based on man's inherent nature and the English constitutional tradition, but he went on to say that ultimately their rights came from Christ himself, as the "purchase of his blood." Those rights were so precious that Christians should risk filling the "streets with blood," rather than submitting to slavery.[26]

Younger evangelicals roused their congregations to support Christian liberty also. Nathaniel Niles was one of the leading "New Divinity" theologians who defended the evangelical Calvinism propagated by Jonathan

Edwards. Although he was a pastor in Norwich, Connecticut, Niles traveled in the mid-1770s across New England to promote the colonists' resistance against British domination. Like earlier opponents of the Stamp Act, he did not endorse war with the mother country, but he did see religious and civil tyranny behind the encroaching power of the British government. In *Two Discourses on Liberty*, delivered at Newburyport, Massachusetts, in the summer of 1774, Niles envisioned a macabre future under a military government that would tyrannize American Christian Patriots who failed to resist its initial forays. He feared the imposition of a Catholic military state that would kill American men in battle and would lead American Protestants to see "their daughters ravished, their wives ript up, their children dashed against the wall, and their pious parents put to the rack for the religion of Jesus." Strongly linking the love of civil liberty with the freedom of the children of God, he proposed that "no man can be a Christian and not a friend to civil liberty." If a monarch began to harm the common good, Niles argued, then he should be removed "like other common nuisances." As the crisis began to peak, Niles, Parsons, Allen, and their evangelical colleagues helped fashion a godly sanction for violent resistance against the government and king.[27]

Many ministers escalated the fight with Britain by interpreting it through apocalyptic lenses. What might this terrible war portend? Many believed it could signal a critical epoch in the events leading to the return of Christ or the beginning of the millennium. Certain of the rationalist founding fathers, such as Jefferson, Washington, and Franklin, might have scoffed at any recourse to prophecy to bolster the Patriot cause, but mobilizing the people at large required a broader, religiously urgent appeal. Since the Great Awakening, evangelicals had anticipated that the Kingdom of God would arrive through a combination of spiritual, political, and military triumphs. Great numbers of sinners would convert to true Christianity as the last days approached, but the forces of tyranny and oppression would be defeated, too—and the brewing war with Britain seemed to evangelicals like the fulfillment of New Testament prophecy.

In this new formulation, the identity of Antichrist altered. Earlier American interpretations of Antichrist had typically associated the apocalyptic force as arising out of Catholicism and Islam, but as the crisis built in the 1760s and 1770s, some preachers and writers began to ascribe the spirit of Antichrist to the British. Most were not as blunt as an anonymous pamphleteer of 1777 who found that the Hebrew and Greek words for "Great Britain" and "Royal Supremacy" contained the hidden numbers 666, the number of the beast in Revelation 13. But several others anticipated that the war would fulfill biblical prophecy and hasten the coming of Christ's kingdom. Even the theologically liberal Congregationalist pastor Samuel West of Dartmouth, Massachusetts, called for resistance against the British government in 1776 using apocalyptic terms, exhorting his audience to "get the victory over the beast" of Revelation, which he interpreted as a symbol of political tyranny. For some of these spiritual-political visionaries, victory over Britain thus ensured the millennial triumph of God. Evangelical minister Ebenezer Baldwin of Danbury, Connecticut, boldly proclaimed that the war with Britain was intended by God to establish in America the headquarters of the millennial kingdom of God on earth. Baldwin asserted in November 1775 that the fighting would lead to American independence and the establishment of an "American empire" that would be the world's new utopia of Christian liberty.[28]

Some evangelicals experienced prophetic visions of the war. Evangelical layman Samuel Clarke (possibly a pseudonym) of Gloucester, Massachusetts, published accounts of his dreams about the divine significance of the conflict. Clarke originally produced a pamphlet, *A Short Relation Concerning a Dream*, in 1769 during the first wave of the crisis with Britain, but it went through many editions during the revolutionary period. In his dream (as recounted in 1776 in *The American Wonder*, the narrative's eighth edition), Clarke saw a great host of men coming from the east. A wizened old man by the roadside told him that the company of men was the "forerunner of great trouble that is coming on New England." Clarke believed that New England's sin provoked God's fury and that the suffering of the colonists under Britain represented the pouring out of the "first vials of God's wrath" referenced in the book of Revelation.[29]

In the 1776 edition of Clarke's dream, an editor calling himself "Publicola" glossed the account with reflections on the outbreak of the war. He assured readers of his confidence that Clarke's prophecy of New England's troubles was legitimate. It showed that God had begun the war as a chastisement of the colonists, he said, but revealed that God would also bring about victory for the colonists if they returned to him. Publicola noted that Clarke had been ridiculed in some circles as a deceiver or a "Newlight"—that is, a radical evangelical—but he insisted that God used the layman's dream to reveal the divine purposes behind the war. According to Publicola, if colonists put their confidence in God, then he would establish an American nation, granting the land of North America to the colonists "until time shall be no more."[30]

A similar dream account, *The Strange and Remarkable Swansey Vision*, also published at the outset of the war, recorded a man's dream, supposedly from 1734, foretelling the coming of the Revolution. The visionary recorded an encounter with a luminous person clothed in white—apparently either an angel or Jesus—who told the man that the North American colonists would face the wrath of God because of their sins and that God would raise up a nation against them "who were before your friends." Blood would run in America's streets until the colonists repented, the figure warned, but their repentance would help usher in the last days. Americans would become great missionaries, preaching the gospel even in Rome at the "seat of the Great Whore of Babylon." The true gospel would overwhelm the globe, the figure announced, and the millennium would commence, destroying all oppression and tyranny. Such visionary narratives as the *Swansey Vision* helped convince their readers that although God had brought on the troubles with Britain, God would redeem the Americans' suffering and give them a critical role in the coming millennial kingdom.[31]

No minister developed as elaborate a prophetic interpretation of the American Revolution as Reverend Samuel Sherwood of Fairfield, Connecticut. He warned the people of Connecticut in 1774 that an "infamous herd of vile miscreants" was plotting to oppress the colonists and subject them to everlasting "slavery and bondage." He argued that political power was exceedingly dangerous because of human sinfulness and that all citizens were obligated to keep watch over their governors to make sure they did not become tyrannical. Rulers were capable "of doing the greatest mischief and wrong, of any men in the world," Sherwood preached, when they lost their grip on justice and Christian morality. The principles of Christian liberty closely circumscribed the lawful power of any government.[32]

By early 1776, Sherwood had become convinced that a malign faction within the British government had actually seized control of the empire. Preaching on a passage from the book of Revelation, Sherwood asserted that the controversy between Britain and the colonists represented an apocalyptic confrontation between the people of God and the forces of Antichrist. Anyone promoting tyranny and slavery was affiliated with the devil, in Sherwood's view. The "tools and emissaries in general, of anti-Christian, tyrannical power, who are the spirits of devils," had gone out into the world looking to oppress the people of God. Tragically, the devil-spirits had snared the British government, which until recently had been the world's great defender of true Christianity. "Our own nation has been . . . infected" with the "wicked scheme of anti-Christian tyranny," Sherwood proclaimed. He insisted that the conflict between the Continental Army and the British redcoats was the human manifestation of a heavenly battle: "God Almighty, with all the powers of heaven, are on our side. Great numbers of angels, no doubt, are encamping round our coast, for our defence and protection. [The archangel] Michael stands ready; with all the artillery of heaven, to encounter the dragon, and to vanquish this black host." To Sherwood, the spiritual meaning of the war surpassed political theory or economic concerns.[33]

Secular political ideals and financial matters undoubtedly drove many of America's revolutionary leaders into supporting not just resistance but revolution, yet the evangelical tradition supplied spiritual propulsion to the Patriot cause that was unsurpassed by any other element of Patriot ideology. Millennial beliefs provided nearly unlimited resources for justifying the war to a biblically minded people while assuring them that God held the results in his hands. In the Protestant millennial vision, God would not ultimately give his people over to the forces of tyranny and slavery, and God's people had a right to revolt against those who stood on the wrong side of the millennial divide.

How much power did evangelical beliefs wield in the rise of political revolution? Some Loyalist leaders gave the evangelical clergy a great deal of credit. Writing in 1775, Massachusetts Loyalist Jonathan Sewall lamented the way the common people's "spiritual drivers" had whipped them into a frenzy with the "never failing topics of tyranny and popery." Sewall ultimately blamed the trouble on the dangerous spirit of religious frenzy—a mania he attributed to evangelicals—because "there is an enthusiasm in politics, like that which religious notions inspire." Enthusiasm deluded the people into thinking they could overthrow the established authorities because God was on their side, according to Sewall. Anti-revivalists of the 1740s had warned of the dire consequences that evangelical piety could have on the public order; now political enthusiasts, borrowing from evangelical rhetoric and ideology, stood ready to challenge the British Empire itself, driven by the conviction that a new world order was at hand.[34]

No wonder, then, that the greatest orators and writers of the Revolution, including Patrick Henry and Thomas Paine, employed biblical and evangelical rhetoric to make their case. Such rhetoric was the language of the people. Without evangelicalism's resources for criticizing political power and rousing popular sentiment, the Patriots would never have commanded the allegiance of so many Americans.

CHAPTER 5

"A Christian Sparta"

Virtue and the American Revolution

BY THE END OF 1780, as the Revolutionary War ravaged the South, Samuel Adams was worrying that the battle for public morality was being lost in the North, particularly in Boston. The Continental Army had fought the British to nothing better than a stalemate, yet politicians and merchants, among others, had begun to live indulgently, as if independence and freedom did not remain imperiled. When John Hancock was elected governor of Massachusetts in October, officials threw a lavish celebration at public expense, with "elegant entertainment" provided for the gentlemen thronging Faneuil Hall, complete with thirteen toasts.[1]

Adams and others decried such extravagance and waste when the Continental Army continued to be chronically undersupplied, its soldiers dying of combat wounds and disease. Only that May had Charleston, South Carolina, fallen to the British, after a six-week siege. Five thousand American troops surrendered, in the Continentals' biggest loss of the war. Then, in August, the British had badly defeated the Continentals at Camden, South Carolina, a clash that ruined the reputation of a hero of the Battle of Saratoga, General Horatio Gates. Gates's Patriot soldiers had been marching through grueling South Carolina heat, with nothing to eat but green corn, unripe peaches, boiled beef, and molasses. This explosive combination had given many men cramps and diarrhea, rendering them unfit for battle. Gates also bungled the troops' positioning on the field of battle, so that the inexperienced Carolina militia took the brunt of the redcoats' assault. The result was a rout of the Patriot army, with Gates himself galloping 170 miles north in three days, the very picture of a hasty retreat.[2]

After months of such gloomy news from the southern front, Adams was disgusted by Governor Hancock's insensitive celebration of his own inauguration with "pomp and parade." Writing to a friend, he keenly remembered the way revivalist George Whitefield had railed against the dances and balls of America's growing towns. Adams feared that the extravagance of the American people would steal their attention from their most precious jewel: liberty. Once he had hoped that Boston would become what he called the "Christian Sparta," but now he was losing faith that his young town would become a citadel of rigorous Christian rectitude. "Will men never be free!" he exclaimed. "They will be free no longer than while they remain virtuous."[3]

To Adams, the American Revolution was not exclusively either a secular or a religious endeavor. Instead, he integrated the legacies of the Reformation and the Enlightenment to propound a convergence of classical republicanism and Reformed Christianity that would provide America with a new moral vision. By likening Boston (and America) to a Christian Sparta, Adams expressed the hopes of those American Patriots who believed that the new American Republic could combine the best aspects of ancient political tradition and Protestant Christianity. Classical antiquity supplied the political ideals of the prospective Republic, including checks and balances, safeguards against tyranny, and the importance of civic virtue. Christianity supplied the Republic with its spirit and the power to preserve itself. In claiming the Spartan tradition but empowering it with the ideals of Christianity, Adams was articulating a new philosophy of the Patriot cause: Christian republicanism.

From where did Adams's fascination with Sparta arise? European political philosophers had for centuries returned to Greek and Roman antiquity for direction on the structure and ethics of republics. Sparta was not the most frequently referenced ancient republic (Rome and Athens were more common), but its memory did hold a particular resonance for Patriots like Adams. Revolutionary chaplain Hugh Henry Brackenridge, a classmate of James Madison at Princeton, also pointed to Sparta as the embodiment of public-mindedness, "general philanthropy, and benevolence of spirit." Sparta, to Adams, Brackenridge, and other Patriots, represented the republican model in which citizens had rigorously subjugated their individual rights to the common good.[4]

For Adams and many other Americans, private virtue was not enough to preserve and safeguard republics. Government power was so dangerous that only a public-minded, self-sacrificial citizenry could check a government's inexorable creep toward tyranny. Nor was republican government alone enough, because in the pre-Christian, pagan republics no divine assistance engendered holiness among the people. Adams, steeped in Calvinism, believed that men could not be good without the transforming power of God working in their lives. Not just a "Sparta," but a "Christian Sparta," was what Adams had in mind—a republic with both the ideals and the spiritual motivation to maintain the common good.

Adams's distress over the morality of Bostonians represented a broader American concern about maintaining public virtue during the Revolution. For many Patriots, public virtue emphasized honesty, self-sacrifice, and good will toward others, especially among political leaders. Although people disagreed about how best to promote morality, there was little doubt among the Revolution's leaders that only an ethical people could preserve good government and Christian liberty.

But there was a problem. For most Americans, the Christian (and often Calvinist) view of morality held that people were not naturally disposed toward virtue. Holiness and civic responsibility flourished primarily through the experience of salvation, they believed, even as virtue could also be fostered with the external restraints of law. Evangelical Christians emphasized the importance of God's power in creating virtue in sinful human hearts, whereas more rationalist students of political philosophy believed that education and good government could best foster public integrity.

Those who called America to virtue were not just indulging in self-righteousness. Many of them believed that America's lack of virtue had already born bitter fruit, with some blaming America's sins for having precipitated the crisis with Britain. God brought the trouble on Americans because of their neglect of moral law. As one 1776 pamphlet put it, "Sin alone is the moral and procuring cause of all those evils we either feel or fear" from the British.[5] Even the Continental Congress issued a proclamation for a day of prayer and fasting, to be held in May 1776, calling on Americans to "bewail our manifold sins and transgressions, and by a sincere repentance and amendment of life appease [God's] righteous displeasure, and through the merits and mediation of Jesus Christ, obtain his pardon and forgiveness."[6] The Patriots fought for liberty, but their liberty meant serving the country as a whole. This ideal of liberty as an opportunity to foster public virtue had diverse roots. The most obvious was the Christian tradition, in which Jesus had laid down his life to save others. But Greek and Roman antiquity also provided guidance, because the ancient republics by definition had sought the common good of the people.

Americans had contemplated the nature of public morality for decades prior to the Revolution. Leading writers of the Great Awakening, particularly Jonathan Edwards, had vigorously debated the question of virtue and the means by which people could become good. Because most of the main revivalists were Calvinists, they placed no confidence in man's innate ability to fulfill God's law. Edwards, as the preeminent evangelical theologian of the eighteenth century, argued that true virtue could come only from a converted Christian's love for God. In his treatise *The Nature of True Virtue* (posthumously published in 1765), Edwards admitted the value of law, which obligated all people to obey certain rules. But he believed that such public morality fell short of the best kind of virtue, which was found in a Christian's adoration of God. In promoting this God-centered idea of virtue, Edwards was fighting against the tide of most eighteenth-century philosophy associated with the Enlightenment, which asserted that people were naturally good, or at least could cultivate virtue without God's direct intervention.

Some moral philosophers in the eighteenth century tried to find a basis for universal standards of ethics separate from religious conversion or special revelation in the Bible. Many leading intellectuals in England, Scotland, and the colonies tried to place all ethical knowledge in a scientific framework. Accordingly, some thinkers worked to establish a natural grounding for the rules of morality, with most of them assuming that "natural" morality would complement the great principles of the Bible contained in the Ten Commandments and Jesus's teachings. But if morality and ethics were disentangled from quarrels over religion and the Bible, they believed, then public virtue could find a stronger common ground among people of all religious beliefs.

One of the most influential moral philosophers among Americans at the time of the Revolution was Scotland's Francis Hutcheson, a professor at the University of Glasgow in the 1730s and 1740s, who declared that all humans—whether Christian or not—possessed a God-given "moral sense" that, if cultivated, could guide them in making virtuous decisions. That faith in an innate moral sense gave Hutcheson and his followers hope that communities could find moral consensus outside the realm of the churches, where doctrinal divisions tended to divide rather than unify.[7]

Hutcheson's belief in an inborn moral sense was useful for revolutionaries who were trying to break with the British political tradition while not wanting to alienate Christian Americans by neglecting moral justifications for revolution. Patriots like Thomas Jefferson could appeal to universal moral principles established by God as "self-evident" truths while avoiding the thicket of theological specifics. American Patriots argued that God's moral law, or at least the moral law that God had revealed in man's nature, demanded a break with tyrannical Britain. They also believed that their own virtue must sustain the new Republic, or all would be lost. When Benjamin Franklin reportedly remarked that the Constitutional Convention of 1787 had created "a republic . . . if you can keep it," he meant that republican freedom required popular morality. A republic prone to moral license would inexorably descend into chaos and tyranny.[8]

From the outset of the crisis with Britain, Patriot leaders and pastors were consumed with the issue of virtue and morality. Pastor Joseph Emerson of Pepperell, Massachusetts, in a sermon celebrating the repeal of the Stamp Act in 1766, concluded with sharp warnings about the meaning of the crisis for colonists. Emerson was concerned that in their fear over losing their civil liberty, most colonists had missed the message God was sending them via the Stamp Act. God had orchestrated the Stamp Act, Emerson told his congregation, to warn Americans that if they did not repent of their rampant sinfulness, he would bring even greater judgments upon them. Such judgments would not be repealed like a bad human law. Emerson expected "an entire loss of our freedom" if Americans did not turn back to God; nations might be great and powerful, but if they persisted in sin, God would give them over to ruin and slavery. Emerson believed that only national revival, both in the colonies and in Britain, would avert future crises.[9]

Other colonial pastors and leaders believed it was Britain's pattern of sin and corruption that had produced the Stamp Act. Congregationalist minister Stephen Johnson of Lyme, Connecticut, attributed the act to "a most venal, covetous and arbitrary spirit of lawless ambition" among British bureaucrats. He particularly worried about a cabal of unelected officials working behind the scenes in London to deceive the king and Parliament and deliberately craft a scheme to destroy the colonists' liberties. Just as Rome had fallen due to state corruption, Johnson declared, so could the British Empire fall just as easily. Even as early in the revolutionary period as 1765, Johnson warned the British government that if faced with the choice of slavery to Britain or independence, the colonists would choose independence in an instant.[10]

American apprehension over British immorality had been growing for some time. During the Seven Years' War, the colonists had been impressed by the discipline and effectiveness of the British regular troops but were disgusted by their coarse behavior. Colonists complained that the British army failed to observe the Sabbath and cringed at the soldiers' vulgar talk and their using God's name in vain. Such violations were often prosecuted as misdemeanors in New England, but British army officers overlooked the behavior of their men. Even worse, many of the British regulars were lewd, promiscuous, and sexually aggressive.

Revulsion at the British troops' immorality made Bostonians even more wary when those same troops returned in 1768, this time to occupy their unruly town. Boston pastor Andrew Eliot remarked in 1769 that the British troops were delighted with the cheap cost of local liquor. Reports of military burglaries and rapes began to circulate, and by 1776 many Americans regarded the British regulars as mired in "shocking profanity"—all bad conduct that exacerbated the already prevalent fear that standing armies in peacetime precipitated the loss of civil liberty. In the Anglo-American political tradition, honest governments needed an army only in times of war; a standing army like the British regulars stationed in the colonies was surely up to no good.[11]

As the crisis with Britain escalated in the early 1770s, Americans became convinced both that God permitted the conflict because of Americans' immorality and that the trouble also sprang from deep-seated corruption in the British government. Preaching in the aftermath of the 1774 Intolerable Acts, minister William Tennent III of Charleston, South Carolina, warned that widespread degeneracy heralded a nation's imminent destruction. He pointed to a long list of common sins on both sides of the Atlantic as evidence that the British and the colonists deserved their impending doom. Infidelity, heterodox theology, lax child-rearing, failure to observe the Sabbath, swearing, drunkenness, and unmentionable sexual sins all made Britain and its colonies deserving of God's wrath. If the ancient cities of Sodom and Gomorrah "had showers of burning sulphur rained down upon them, it is surely of the Lord's mercy that our cities, our nests of iniquity, are not consumed!" Tennent proclaimed. Yet that day of reckoning might still be at hand, he warned—and only public prayer, repentance, and reformation could save the British nation.[12]

Looking to the history of previous civilizations, a number of colonists came to believe that like that of Rome, the British Empire's glory had dimmed because of moral corruption. This decline was perceived as part of the natural life cycle of republics and empires. Pastors and political leaders frequently quoted the French political philosopher Montesquieu on the subject: "As all human things have an end, the state we are speaking of (England) will lose its liberty, will perish. Have not Rome, Sparta, and Carthage perished?" Colonists found in the ancient world not only models for proper republics but also warnings of how such republics declined and fell. All ascribed the decline of the great ancient empires to moral decay. John Adams perceived the English people as irredeemably depraved, their government thoroughly corrupt, having descended to the same point as Rome just before the rise of the Caesars. Quoting a famous line from the ancient historian Sallust, Adams declared that Britain had become like Rome, "a venal city, ripe for destruction, if it can only find a purchaser."[13]

Like John Adams and many other American observers, South Carolina Patriot leader William Henry Drayton, a close friend of William

Tennent, directly associated the histories of Rome and Britain. Writing in 1776, he explained that both empires had become overextended and indulgent because of the wealth they created. Britain, he concluded, "experienced the invariable fate of empire" when its American colonies declared their independence. God ultimately wrecked empires that had lost their virtue, according to Drayton, and God "made the choice of the present generation to erect the American empire." That empire, he went on to say, also would only last as long as its people remained moral.[14]

Samuel Adams went further, accusing both the British and the Americans of immorality and ascribing to the British a conscious plot to undermine American virtue in order to make the colonists vulnerable to oppression. True religion and godly education made a people free, but tyrants sought to make people immoral and ignorant, Adams wrote. Rome had fallen because its morals had declined, thus allowing it to be conquered by the Goths: "The diminution of public virtue is usually attended with that of public happiness, and the public liberty will not long survive the total extinction of morals." He believed that God rewarded or punished peoples according to their ethical character. Adams confessed that he could not be entirely confident of the Americans' virtue. If he trusted his new nation's moral stature, he would have no doubts about the colonists' ability to defeat the British. But as the war continued, brazen episodes like Hancock's inauguration made him wonder and worry.[15]

No one better articulated the need for American virtue than the Presbyterian pastor John Witherspoon. The Scottish-born Witherspoon had studied at the University of Edinburgh, where he had been influenced by the writings of Francis Hutcheson. Witherspoon became one of the chief American advocates of Hutcheson's moral sense philosophy when in 1768 he became president of the College of New Jersey in Princeton. Trustees there saw him as the key to shoring up the college's intellectual and Christian bona fides, and his friends, including evangelist George Whitefield and Philadelphia physician Benjamin Rush, encouraged him to make the move across the Atlantic for the good of the college and the colonies.

In America, Witherspoon hardly limited his activities to school and church. The roiling controversy with Britain soon drew in the pastor, and in 1774 he joined the resistance movement against the British government, going on to lead New Jersey's Patriots into independence in 1776 as a member of the Continental Congress. When conservative members of the Congress argued that Americans were not ready for independence, Witherspoon declared that the colonies were so ripe for liberty from Britain that they were "in danger of becoming rotten for the want of it." The Congress agreed, and that July he became the only clergyman to sign the Declaration of Independence.[16]

As a pastor, educator, and congressman, Witherspoon promulgated a persuasive vision for the moral American Republic. Shortly before leaving for Philadelphia in 1776, on a day mandated for fasting and prayer, he delivered a sermon in Princeton, *The Dominion of Providence over the Passions of Men,* that would become his most influential address. In appointing this fast day, the Continental Congress called on Americans to repent of their sins, acknowledge God's sovereignty in the war, and pray for God's favor in the Patriots' "cause of freedom, virtue, and posterity." As a Presbyterian pastor and expert on the science of virtue, no American was better prepared to respond to this summons than Witherspoon. In his sermon, he called for a vigorous, public-oriented religion that would sustain Americans' virtue and lead to victory. He assured the Patriots that their troubles with Britain would lead to God's glory and their benefit, with all Americans soon recognizing the folly of remaining under British rule. Selfish men should never be given as much power as the British government sought to exert over the colonists, Witherspoon warned: "I do not refuse submission to their unjust claims, because they are corrupt or profligate, although many of them are so, but because they are men, and therefore liable to all the selfish bias inseparable from human nature." Witherspoon, speaking out of a tradition of Christianity that held that original sin corrupted all people, likewise believed that any ruler would abuse the rights of others when given too much authority.[17]

But if Americans maintained a sincere devotion to Christianity and virtue, Witherspoon went on to say, they could avoid the fate of the corrupt British Empire. God would preserve the liberty only of the morally pure. Conversely, "nothing is more certain than that a general profligacy and corruption of manners make a people ripe for destruction. A good form of government may hold the rotten materials together for some time, but beyond a certain pitch, even the best constitution will be inef-fectual, and slavery must ensue." Other founders, such as John Adams and James Madison (one of Witherspoon's students), placed more confi-dence in the beneficial effects of good government, but Witherspoon avowed that no republic could survive without robust morality. Such morality could only arise out of authentic Christian faith; that is, com-mitment to Christ that was active, heartfelt, and not hypocritical. Every person, in Witherspoon's ideal republic, would take responsibility for what he called the "public interest of religion."[18]

Witherspoon recommended certain moral duties that would bolster America's communal health, such as industry, hard work, and frugality. Even within their families, Patriots would limit their consumption of food, dress modestly, and furnish their homes simply. Such virtuous prac-tices would free them from the love of money and the snares of bribery and empower them to serve the poor. In wartime, modest living by citi-zens would augment the military's resources. The Christian Patriot, Witherspoon declared, would make whatever sacrifices were necessary to preserve the liberty of the whole—and only such unselfish devotion to the good of the Republic would save Americans from the British threat.[19]

Loyalists mocked Witherspoon's vision of American virtue. Anglican priest Jonathan Odell of Burlington, New Jersey, a prominent Loyalist writer, deplored Witherspoon's promotion of the Patriot cause. Like many Anglican clergymen in America, Odell was critical of British trade and tax policy but did not believe that Americans had the moral right to over-throw their government. Odell penned Loyalist poetry during the war, painting Witherspoon and other revolutionary leaders as treasonous monsters:

Unhappy Jersey mourns her thrall,
Ordained by vilest of the vile to fall;
To fall by Witherspoon!—O name, the curse
Of sound religion, and disgrace of verse.
. . .
I've known him seek the dungeon dark as night,
Imprisoned Tories to convert, or fright;

Whilst to myself I've hummed, in dismal tune,
I'd rather be a dog than Witherspoon.[20]

Witherspoon presented the war as a compelling opportunity for Americans to seize their moral destiny apart from Britain, but in a land divided fiercely by rebellion against Britain and support for the mother country, these sentiments met angry opposition from other Christians such as Odell.

The religious zeal that fueled the war's early years inevitably faded as the conflict bogged down in the late 1770s. Americans won a major victory at Saratoga, New York, in 1777, which was followed by the heartening alliance with the French. But in 1778 the battle of Monmouth, New Jersey, ended in a draw, signaling the end of most major combat operations in the North. The British put most of their focus on the South, capturing Savannah in 1778 and Charleston in 1780. Then came the Americans' galling defeat at Camden, South Carolina, concluding with Horatio Gates's cowardly dash.

As the war seemed to turn against the Patriots, many—Samuel Adams chief among them—worried that Americans lacked the moral fortitude to win. By 1778, America faced fiscal, social, and moral crises on every front. Recruitment for the army became increasingly difficult, desertion rates grew, and Americans found all kinds of ways to evade conscription. Financial problems also dogged the Congress, which came up with few solutions other than printing more money, which drove up inflation, making prices exorbitant and leading some merchants to overcharge in order to compensate for anticipated future losses. Other businessmen carried on a very profitable illegal trade with the British during the war.[21]

Some of the war's most zealous advocates began to worry about the effects of greed and extortion on the war effort. Were these signs that Americans had lost their virtue, just like the British? Long Island Presbyterian minister Abraham Keteltas supported the war passionately, yet he also recoiled at what he saw as evidence of American immorality. Like Witherspoon, Keteltas had become involved in the American resistance

movement fairly early, chairing in 1774 the Committee of Correspondence of Jamaica, New York. Keteltas had to flee Long Island when the
British invaded in 1776 and stripped his home of all valuables. No wonder,
then, that Keteltas would describe the Revolution as "the cause of heaven
against hell." But Keteltas also keenly felt Americans' moral responsibility,
and in 1778 he preached a scathing sermon against the epidemic of extortion he saw sweeping his new country. He warned that not only did
greed and price-gouging hurt the most vulnerable Americans, but it also
caused General George Washington—a friend of Keteltas—to struggle to
supply his army. Short-term gain would turn into long-term slavery for
the extortionists, he preached, because their personal profit undercut the
Patriot cause. By exploiting inflation, the extortionist "is making a sword
to pierce his own bowels, and he is pulling down the pillars that support
the goodly fabric of liberty and property." Selfishness was self-defeating,
because it would strangle the fragile American Republic.[22]

Confronting extortionate business practices, Keteltas put Christianity's reputation itself at stake, comparing ancient Roman virtue and
Protestant righteousness to shame Christian Americans. If they could see
the conditions prevailing in America, the morally upright citizens of ancient Rome would deplore the Americans' selfishness and wonder
whether Christianity itself led to immorality. Keteltas believed that Christianity was indeed the root of true virtue, but in light of Americans' ugly
greed, he wondered, "Shall Pagan zeal and patriotism excel Christian?"
and urged, "O my brethren, suffer it not to be said, to the disgrace of our
most holy religion." Three years into the war, Christian Patriots like
Keteltas and Samuel Adams had begun to wonder if enough Americans
really manifested Christian virtue. Extortion would provoke God and
cause him to turn his wrath against Americans instead of against the
British oppressors.[23]

The Revolution presented an opportunity not only for repentance but
also for framing new national and state governments that would foster public virtue. For leading Patriot politicians, this was the most excit-
ing political prospect of 1776: Independence offered a chance to start

governments from scratch. As Virginia started working on its state constitution in 1776, George Washington cautioned that forming "a new government requires infinite care and unbounded attention, for if the foundation is badly laid, the superstructure must be bad."[24]

Patriots believed that although religion might provide inner motivation for virtue, good governments could also foster benevolent behavior. In *Common Sense*, Thomas Paine argued that the power of the king poisoned the republican element of the English constitution, an element that was to be found in the House of Commons. "When republican virtue fails, slavery ensues," Paine concluded. He saw monarchy as inherently corrupt because of the power it vested, through heredity, in a single man or woman. Republics distributed power among representatives chosen by the people.[25]

John Adams agreed that a republic had the best chance of preserving virtue. In his influential *Thoughts on Government* (1776), Adams recommended that the states adopt a mixed republican government of a bicameral legislature, a governor, and a judiciary, a proposal that many of the states adopted in framing their new governments. Adams fervently believed in the separation of powers among branches of government. To him, the happiness of society was the chief end of government, and human happiness and dignity lay in possessing and demonstrating virtue. Therefore, the best kind of government promoted public virtue. Republican governments, by representing the interests and dividing the power of all segments of society, best ensured moral liberty. Indeed, to Adams the "principle and foundation" of a republic was virtue.[26]

Patriots like Adams got their ideas about virtue as the essential quality of republican citizens from the many eighteenth-century political philosophers who developed this connection, most explicitly the Baron de Montesquieu. Montesquieu's writings, especially *The Spirit of the Laws* (1748), became the most frequently cited political source in revolutionary America. Because it was the people who ruled in republics, Montesquieu wrote, virtue was more necessary for them than for authoritarian governments that ruled by force and fear. But he also downplayed the Christian origins of virtue, defining political virtue as a naturally available love of humanity and as a belief in equality among all men. Even though these humanistic ideas might undermine exclusively Christian beliefs, conservative American Christians seemed to embrace the republican ideal of virtue as eagerly as their more liberal colleagues did.[27]

Many American Christians called for the new state governments to separate the powers of government and promote morality and religion. Pastor Peter Whitney of Northborough, Massachusetts, cautioned in 1776 that the new state government should not only reject monarchy and fully represent the people but should also separate its powers; too much power in any one person's hands could become intoxicating. He also believed that America should promote the public interests of Protestantism. "God has ever been the friend and patron of the American Israel," he said, "and he will continue so, if we act up to our character and obligation." By establishing good government and preserving moral behavior, Americans would maintain their covenant with God. Whitney anticipated that God would establish America as a republic of righteousness from ocean to ocean, "'till time shall be no more."[28]

Some Patriots posited an almost unbreakable link between Christianity and republican government—a bond best articulated by leading Patriot and physician Benjamin Rush of Philadelphia. Rush grew up in a revivalist Presbyterian church and was well connected with leading Presbyterians on both sides of the Atlantic, including John Witherspoon. But Rush grew more liberal in his theological views and eventually became a universalist, believing that all people would be saved whether Christian or not. By the 1780s Rush had come to believe that Christianity and republicanism served essentially an identical aim: to bring about the happiness and liberty of people. In a treatise on public education, he advocated the transformation of children into "republican machines," which could be best effected by training them in religion. "The only foundation for a useful education in a republic is to be laid in RELIGION," he wrote. "Without this, there can be no virtue, and without virtue there can be no liberty, and liberty is the object and life of all republican governments."[29]

Rush believed that any religion that taught about God's attributes and the rewards and punishments of the afterlife would help people become better republican citizens. He even claimed that he would prefer that America's youth learn the principles of Islam or Confucianism than learn no religion at all. But to him, Christianity was the best religion for republican government, because a "Christian cannot fail of being a republican." The account in the book of Genesis of a single human origin, and the fact that we are all descended from Adam and Eve, was the best proof of equality and the best refutation of the divine right of kings, Rush asserted. The life of Jesus, moreover, inculcated the principles of humility and self-sacrificing kindness. Because Christianity's values perfectly suited the civic-minded imperative required of a healthy republic, Rush believed that all children should be taught those principles by state schools. Rush's Christianity served primarily earthly, social purposes: producing virtuous citizens who could preserve the Republic from corruption.[30]

As Rush pointed out, the most obvious instrument of government for inculcating virtue was public education. The new states set up systems of public education to instill moral principles (often through explicitly Christian instruction) in children. The Massachusetts Constitution of 1780 stated that because wisdom, knowledge, and virtue were necessary for the preservation of people's liberties, public schools should spread these gifts among all the people, regardless of class. When New York's constitution was adopted, Patriot leader John Jay proclaimed that if "virtue, honor, the love of liberty and of science" were to remain at the heart of the Republic, then rising generations had to be taught to be free. Jay, Rush, and other Americans already worried about the negative effects that corrupt schools and teachers could have on children. Abigail Adams wrote to her husband John in 1783 wondering what would happen to their boys when they entered college. Would they be led astray by infidel philosophers? A Christian education before college would teach the boys values such as "moderation, humility, and patience." She hoped that John would be able to return soon from his political duties to train the children in morality, so that when they entered college they could "keep the path of virtue."[31]

The Patriots' discussion of public virtue was fraught with tension. In retrospect, it was rarely clear whether Christian faith was essential to true virtue, or whether republican morals could be practiced by all people, regardless of their spiritual state. On one end of the debate were evangelical Calvinists such as the heirs of Jonathan Edwards, who insisted that

Christian conversion alone produced true virtue in people's lives. On the other end were those such as Rush who abandoned evangelical faith in favor of a utilitarian religion of public morality. But these perspectives rarely clashed because of America's widespread acceptance of Christian republicanism. Whether evangelical or rationalist, most Patriots assumed that Christianity would, in some sense, be the cornerstone for the preservation of the new American Republic.

No one would better express the integration of religion and republican virtue than George Washington in his 1796 Farewell Address. These were his final words to his beloved country upon his retirement from the presidency, a retirement that was not required by the Constitution but that set the standard of two terms for the president and a willing relinquishment of power that was perceived as an act of public virtue in itself. Alexander Hamilton, James Madison, and John Jay—the authors of *The Federalist*—all helped Washington pen this address, making it an almost uniquely representative expression of the political philosophy of the founders. In the speech, Washington powerfully articulated his confidence in religious republicanism:

> Of all the dispositions and habits which lead to political prosperity, religion and morality are indispensable supports. In vain would that man claim the tribute of patriotism, who should labor to subvert these great pillars of human happiness—these firmest props of the duties of men and citizens. The mere politician, equally with the pious man, ought to respect and to cherish them. A volume could not trace all their connections with private and public felicity . . . and let us with caution indulge the supposition, that morality can be maintained without religion. Whatever may be conceded to the influence of refined education on minds of peculiar structure; reason and experience both forbid us to expect that national morality can prevail in exclusion of religious principle.

Washington and Hamilton were alarmed by the anticlericalism and violence of the French Revolution, which by the mid-1790s had turned into an ugly anti-Christian crusade. Priests were decapitated by the guillotine, and churches—including Notre Dame Cathedral—were vandalized and turned into "temples of reason." The cautious Washington insisted that the practice and prevalence of religion would help the American Republic survive. He was merely stating in 1796 what most of the major founders believed. Like others, Washington derived his view on virtue and republics from Montesquieu, whose language in *The Spirit of the Laws* Washington employed almost verbatim. "Virtue or morality is a necessary spring of popular government," he said, echoing Montesquieu's conviction that only a selfless people could govern themselves.[32]

To Washington, religion ensured the health and happiness of a republic. He said that Providence had "connected the permanent felicity of a nation with its virtue." Washington had less interest in the eternal benefits of religion or in a doctrinaire kind of Protestantism. He cherished the disestablishment of the churches won during the revolutionary era, which had been capped by the First Amendment to the U.S. Constitution. Washington also repeatedly assured patriotic American Jews and Catholics that under his leadership the government of the United States would give "bigotry no sanction, [and] persecution no assistance." Still, Washington believed that the government should support the interests of general, nonsectarian religion.[33]

Well before Washington bade farewell to Americans, however, many revolutionary-era leaders were beginning to doubt whether Americans were sufficiently virtuous to sustain the Republic they had won. In the fractious, unabashedly selfish political atmosphere of the 1780s, the ideal of political virtue—the denial of self-interest for the good of the whole—seemed a foolish dream. Some even began to wonder whether virtue was actually a vital element of a republic. The great Montesquieu's views on virtue actually came under fire in some quarters during the 1780s, with the young Federalist writer William Vans Murray going so far as to say that "Montesquieu had never studied a free democracy" and that in America the great philosopher would have seen that, in practice, a republic could survive on the principles of self-interest and capitalist freedom. An article in the *Providence Gazette* contended that an equal distribution of property was the key to preserving equal power in a republic; its author argued that Montesquieu's republican philosophy could only be sustained by substituting property for virtue, because "virtue, patriotism, or love of country, never was nor never will be, till men's natures are changed, a fixed, permanent principle and support of government."[34]

Few American political leaders went as far as these anti-Montesquieu writers, but many champions of Christian republicanism worried in the 1780s and 1790s that Americans did not have the fortitude to keep their Republic. Such concern helps explain why Samuel Adams wondered whether Boston ever could become a Christian Sparta. Alexander Hamilton concluded in 1782 that America's leaders could preach about selfless virtue until they were exhausted, but they would probably not win a single convert. John Adams similarly wrote to his cousin Samuel in 1790 confessing that "all projects of government, founded in the supposition or expectation of extraordinary degrees of virtue, are evidently chimerical."[35]

Yet even though many Americans after the Revolution grew pessimistic about political virtue's potential to sustain the Republic, they still believed that good government could help restrain man's natural selfishness. James Madison, who rarely seemed sanguine about Americans' potential for public benevolence, asserted that government should account for human failings, writing, in one of *The Federalist*'s most famous phrases, that "if men were angels, no government would be necessary." If a republic could not regenerate people's moral nature, then the best political way to handle people's natural selfishness was to accept the tenuousness of human virtue. Madison wanted America to build a government that would channel its citizens' self-interest into the good of the Republic. But in spite of the serious reservations about the viability of virtue as sustenance for the republican experiment, through the era of the Civil War most Americans would continue to believe that the Christian religion should assist government in lifting people's moral dispositions, so that they might contribute positively to the freedom of the Republic. Even the skeptical Thomas Jefferson believed that Christianity, in its original purity, "is a religion of all others most friendly to liberty."[36]

CHAPTER 6

"A Time of War"

Chaplains, Virtue, and Providence

PASTOR PETER MUHLENBERG of Woodstock, Virginia, a German Lutheran turned Anglican, became intimately involved with the Patriot cause in 1774 when he was elected to Virginia's legislature. In January 1776 he ascended the pulpit of his church and preached on Ecclesiastes 3, "To every thing there is a season . . . a time of war, and a time of peace." Finishing the sermon, Muhlenberg shed his clerical gown—and revealed a uniform underneath. The twenty-nine-year-old pastor had accepted an appointment as a colonel of a Virginia regiment. He and Patrick Henry were the only nonmilitary appointees for such offices in Virginia. The overflowing congregation, moved by Muhlenberg's example, produced three hundred recruits for the army that day. Muhlenberg was appointed to the rank of brigadier general by Congress the next year and would continue to serve in the army for most of the rest of his life, along with a brief stint in the U.S. Senate in the early nineteenth century.[1]

American pastors like Muhlenberg, and especially the chaplains who ministered to soldiers on the battlefield, helped infuse the Revolutionary War with sacred meaning—sometimes regardless of what the war required the troops to do. On Sunday, July 4, 1779, the third anniversary of the Declaration of Independence, Baptist pastor and military chaplain William Rogers addressed Continental troops on their way to subdue

Iroquois Indians who had sided with the British in the Revolutionary War. He reminded the men of the sanctity of their cause:

> Politically as a nation we are exhorted to trust in the Lord. God hath hitherto blessed our arms and smiled on our infant rising states . . . provided we fear God and are publicly as well as individually honest; what have we now to alarm us? American exertions have hitherto been crowned with success; let us still under the banners of liberty, and with a Washington for our head, go on from conquering to conquer. . . . "Our fathers trusted and the Lord did deliver them; they cried unto Him and were delivered; they trusted in Him and were not confounded." Even so may it be with us, for the sake of Christ Jesus, who came to give freedom to the world.

Thus roused by their chaplain, the troops attacked and burned forty Iroquois towns, razing their fields and orchards, during their campaign.[2]

Many pastors supported the revolutionary cause not only through their words at home but also by their service as chaplains. The chaplains focused on two primary tasks: explaining the godly meaning of the war and fostering moral, obedient behavior among the troops. To Patriot generals like George Washington, the chaplains' work was absolutely essential for sustaining the enormous sacrifices required of the soldiers and for assuring the army that God was on their side.

For revolutionary military and civilian leaders, the primary moral and strategic mandate of army chaplains was to inculcate virtue among the soldiers. About 117 men served as chaplains in the Continental Army. Although New Englanders represented only about a quarter of the American population, a disproportionate number of the chaplains—about half—were Congregationalists from that region, with many of them conservatives or evangelicals. Many Americans believed that success in the war depended on their individual moral character and that of their new nation. But nowhere was virtue more emphasized—and nowhere did it prove a source of more anxiety—than in Washington's army. Soldiers were expected not only to fight but also to shoulder the moral burden of winning the war.[3]

Wars in America had long included the clergy. In the 1750s and 1760s, chaplains in the Seven Years' War provided moral exhortation, spiritual counsel, and a redemptive framework for the British-American cause. Nathaniel Taylor, chaplain to a Connecticut regiment and pastor at New Milford, thanked God in a 1762 sermon for delivering Americans from the threat of French and Spanish Catholics. God, instead of giving the British colonists over to civil and spiritual tyranny, had fought on behalf of Protestant liberty. "Glory to God for maintaining the Protestant cause," he declared. Taylor also warned the men about the dangers they courted by indulging in immorality.[4]

The chaplains of the Seven Years' War encouraged spiritual revival among the troops as well. This was no surprise, as the chaplains were disproportionately evangelical. John Cleaveland, the Separate minister from Ipswich, Massachusetts, one of the most influential evangelical pastors from the Great Awakening to the American Revolution, served as a chaplain during both the Seven Years' War and the Revolutionary War and sought to convert as many soldiers as he could. In 1758, as the Seven Years' War was turning in favor of the British and the colonists, Cleaveland prayed that God would "follow the wars with his blessing, and make me an instrument of convincing and converting sinners and edifying and comforting the small number of saints that appear amongst us here." Thus, the themes of conversion, morality, and providence were well established among American troops in the signal conflict before the Revolution.[5]

During the Revolution, George Washington became the Patriots' most important advocate for army chaplains. Even though Washington seems personally to have held a rather distant view of the deity, he still believed that God was providentially active in human affairs. The general was convinced that chaplains could help preserve virtue and proper deference to authority among his troops. Moreover, he believed that God, through acts of providence, would judge wicked nations, so he remained especially vigilant about maintaining morality and religious devotion in the Continental Army. His chaplains were on the front line of that internal contest in the war.[6]

Washington and the evangelical chaplains may not have seen eye-to-eye on personal theology: The spiritually reticent Washington was an active Anglican, yet he seems not to have experienced the new birth, the signature moment of evangelical faith. But the general was more than willing to accept evangelical chaplains if they promoted the morale and morality of the soldiers. The Loyalist critic Peter Oliver scoffed at one of Washington's favorite chaplains, Abiel Leonard of Connecticut, who "with a stentorian voice and an enthusiastic mania, could incite his army to greater ardor than all the drums of his regiments," but Washington specifically commended Leonard as an effective advocate for the American cause. The evangelical chaplain was particularly good at explaining to the soldiers the sacred value of their political rights and liberties. Washington was also pleased that after an outbreak of desertions, Leonard chastised the troops about their duty to obey their superiors.[7]

When the Continental Congress appointed chaplains to each Continental Army regiment, Washington ordered the soldiers to attend Sunday services under the chaplains' supervision. He insisted that the regimental colonels hire only chaplains of exemplary character and mandated that the chaplains be shown proper respect, lest a soldier invite the wrath of God, for the "blessing and protection of heaven are at all times necessary but especially so in times of public distress and danger—the General hopes and trusts, that every officer and man, will endeavor so to live, and act, as becomes a Christian soldier defending the dearest rights and liberties of his country." Widespread immorality or contempt for authority, in the general's view, might cause God to withdraw his protective covering from the army.[8]

Washington consistently fought to maintain the chaplains' positions and pay, even when budget constraints might have made them expendable. In 1777 Congress tried to switch to brigade chaplains instead of regimental chaplains (increasing the chaplains' responsibilities about fivefold), but Washington insisted that Congress retain regimental chaplains and preserve the pastors' effectiveness. Washington also argued that a multiplicity of regimental chaplains would avoid religious disputes by giving regiments the choice of the kind of Christian chaplain and services they preferred. Washington bothered little with the particulars of the

chaplains' theology, but he deeply cared about the chaplains' ability to address the soldiers' spiritual needs and maintain discipline.[9]

What roles did these clergymen play in the war itself? Americans have
long been fascinated with the image of the "fighting parson" in the American Revolution. Some pastors, such as Peter Muhlenberg, did take up
arms in moments of urgency; a few actually enlisted as common soldiers
in the army or militia. Most clergymen who served in the Revolution did
not take on combat or strategic roles, however. Instead, they worked to
maintain courage, piety, wholesome behavior, and good order. From the
outset of the conflict, pastors, chaplains, and commanders worried about
the morality of the Continental troops, knowing through experience that
soldiers faced many temptations to sin, including profanity, drunkenness,
sexual immorality, and religious apathy. Baptist pastor and chaplain
Hezekiah Smith wrote to his wife in 1776, "Vice prevails greatly in the
army, which is a matter of lamentation and very discouraging in this dark
and gloomy day. Religion alas how rare! True godliness where is it?" Many
chaplains believed they faced a daunting challenge in reforming the soldiers' behavior.[10]

John Witherspoon, president of the College of New Jersey, offered
special words of caution to the men of the Continental Army in 1776.
God judged the moral character of nations, he said, and the behavior of a
nation's military was a particularly critical matter. "The cause is sacred,
and the champions for it ought to be holy," he insisted. He especially
warned the soldiers about the dangers of profanity and of using God's
name in vain. Americans regarded the British army as shockingly lewd,
but Witherspoon hoped that the Continental Army would, by contrast,
maintain their personal rectitude and discipline and so secure the blessings of God on their battles.[11]

Chaplains embraced Witherspoon's call to preserve the moral integrity of America's military men. Abiel Leonard, the Connecticut
chaplain and favorite of Washington, poured everything he had into
maintaining the godly fervor of the Continental Army. His *Prayer Composed for the Benefit of the Soldiery, in the American Army* (1775) exemplified the attitude chaplains were trying to produce in the Continentals.
The pamphlet offered a sample prayer that presented the American

cause as righteous and committed the soldier to personal holiness and courage. In the prayer, the soldier declared that God had called Americans to armed resistance and asked that the Lord "be the God of the American army." He implored God for skill and purity in the service of Christ and the new nation:

> Teach, I pray thee, my hands to war, and my fingers to fight in the defense of America, and the rights and liberties of it! Impress on my mind a true sense of my duty, and the obligation I am under to my country! And enable me to pay a due and ready respect and obedience to all my officers. Grant unto me a courage, zeal and resolution in the day of battle, that I may play the man for my people, and the cities of my God; choosing rather to lay down my life, than either through cowardice or desertion betray the glorious cause I am engaged in. And, O Lord, if it seem good in thy sight, shield and protect me; cover my head in the day of battle; and suffer not the arrows of death that may fly around me, to wound or destroy me. . . . Enable me to flee all those vices of gaming, rioting, chambering and wantonness which have a destructive and fatal tendency: but as a stranger and pilgrim may I abstain from fleshly lusts which war against the soul! . . . And may I prove myself a faithful follower of Jesus Christ, whom all the armies of heaven follow; fight the good fight of faith; and have my present conflicts against the world, the flesh and the devil crowned with victory and triumph!

And, the soldier asked, just as God had once delivered the Israelites of the Old Testament from Egyptian slavery, so should God also spare Americans from British slavery.[12]

General Washington valued Leonard's service so much that he wrote letters to the pastor's congregation in 1776 requesting that Leonard be allowed to remain on an extended tour. By 1777 he had become the most trusted chaplain in the Continental Army. But military service took its toll on him. He felt that many of the chaplains were enduring disrespectful treatment from soldiers and poor pay from Congress. The inoculation he received to protect him from the smallpox that was ravaging the Continental Army left him weak and troubled. Leonard had a history of mental illness, which resurfaced in the summer of 1777, leading him to attempt suicide by cutting his throat. He died eighteen days later.[13]

Even for successful chaplains of great equanimity, the work could involve a great deal of stress and danger, but many relished the opportunity to provide spiritual direction in what they believed was the glorious cause of American liberty. In a March 1776 sermon before the soldiers he ministered to in Carlisle, Pennsylvania, Dutch Reformed minister William Linn insisted that God held the course of the war in his hands but that if victory were to be preserved, the army must maintain its moral standards. Linn reminded the men of the reasons Britain had caused them to rebel: "breaking charters, blocking up harbors, establishing popery, and sending an armed force to dragoon us to submission." He assured them that Providence controlled the outcome of battles and that God favored the relatively untrained American forces. Nonetheless, Linn maintained that although Britain's cause was unjust, America's own sins had caused God to bring down war on the colonists. He recommended that all soldiers "enlist under the banner of Jesus" and avoid the common sins of drunkenness, dishonesty, and debauchery. A holy army would have no reason to fear death and would not provoke God's judgment in their battles. Anticipating Christ's millennial kingdom on earth, Linn concluded his sermon by praying, "May the peaceful reign of King Jesus soon commence, when the earth shall be filled with the knowledge of the Lord, and the inhabitants thereof learn war no more." By spiritualizing the meaning of the war, Linn assured soldiers that they were fighting to establish peace, and perhaps even to inaugurate the kingdom of God.[14]

Although northern pastors dominated the ranks of the chaplains, some southerners also served to bolster the Patriots' cause. John Hurt, an Anglican parson who labored as a chaplain with Virginia troops for ten years during the era, addressed soldiers in New Jersey in early 1777 in a sermon that offered his listeners an exemplar of Christian republicanism. Unlike the more traditional evangelical exhorters, Hurt based his sermon not so much on biblical principles as on the responsibilities of the virtuous Patriot. Sounding very much like his fellow Virginian Thomas Jefferson, Hurt proclaimed that Americans would never accept British tyranny "while the cause of religion, the cause of nature and of nature's God cry aloud." He warned the soldiers that the most grievous threat among Americans was "luxury," which turned Patriots into self-serving weaklings. Civic-minded virtue would win the war for Americans. Although the British regular army might not "dread our strength, [they] will certainly stand in awe of our virtue," he trumpeted.[15]

Hurt told the troops that "the love of your country" should be "the governing principle of your soul." It might seem strange for a Christian minister to have made such a statement (shouldn't the love of God be a Christian's governing principle?), but Hurt insisted that no other loyalty should compete with love of nation. The colonists' mother land, Britain, had betrayed them. Now Hurt and the revolutionary pastors pledged filial devotion to a new country, America. To Hurt, the colonists' allegiance was clear: "We are all children of one common mother, *America*, our country; she gives us all our birth, nurses our tender years, and supports our manhood." Only a few years earlier the colonists had spoken of Britain in this same adoring way.[16]

As the war ground on, the soldiers in the Continental Army badly needed reminders of their devotion to God and country. In addition to frequent humiliating losses and retreats, the army constantly struggled to maintain supplies of food and clothing. Its nadir came at Valley Forge, Pennsylvania, Washington's winter quarters in 1777–1778. With disease and near-starvation conditions ravaging his men, an anguished Washington wrote to Congress just before Christmas and told the congressmen that "unless some great and capital change suddenly takes place in that line this army must inevitably be reduced to one or other of these three things. Starve—dissolve—or disperse, in order to obtain subsistence in the best manner they can." Help was slow in coming, and about 2,500 of the 12,000 soldiers died pointlessly at Valley Forge.[17]

That spring, as the Continental Army emerged from the scourging winter, John Hurt kept beating the drum of civic virtue and American nationalism. Speaking to Virginia troops as they celebrated the French alliance (secured by the American victory at Saratoga months earlier),

Hurt called for redoubled efforts at maintaining devotion to the public good, declaring, "The more we do for ourselves the more reason have we to expect the smiles of Providence." He ended his address with a poem:

America *shall blast her fiercest foes!*
Out-brave the dismal shocks of bloody war!
And in unrivaled pomp resplendent rise,
And shine sole empress of the western world!

Hurt envisioned a virtuous American Republic becoming the dominant power of the Western Hemisphere. Despite the torturous winter the soldiers had just endured, he promised that a few more months of fighting would probably win the war and open a new era of American ascendancy.[18]

David Avery, the chaplain who had opened the war by praying over Massachusetts troops fighting at Bunker Hill, also agonized about the immorality he saw in the army. He confessed, "[My] heart trembles on account of the sin, vanity, and almost every vice, which are rampant through the camp. *Jehovah's* name is daily, hourly, and almost continually profaned by most all characters among us." Even sick and dying soldiers had to struggle to focus on their need for forgiveness and holiness, Avery saw. Some died with no interest at all in Christ. He praised the generals, especially Washington, but he feared they could do nothing to secure God's blessing on a sinful army. If Americans could just purge themselves of unrighteousness, Avery anticipated that the "Lord's spiritual empire and love, joy, and peace will flourish gloriously in this Western World!"[19]

The fears chaplains expressed about immorality and lack of rectitude in the army help explain why Patriots saw General Benedict Arnold's treachery as such a disaster. America needed its military heroes to be unswervingly virtuous; Arnold had presented himself as such a figure, only to prove himself a fraud. After establishing himself in the top rank of Continental Army leadership by his heroism in the Saratoga campaign—in which he successfully blocked the retreat of the British from the battlefield and nearly lost a leg in the fight—Arnold was beset by financial troubles and squabbles with American authorities, which led him to become a British spy. In 1780 he obtained command of West Point, the key American fort on the Hudson River, and began plotting to turn it over to the British. When his scheme was exposed, Americans portrayed him as a dupe of Satan. Crowds in American towns paraded and burned effigies of Arnold and the devil. Disgusted former admirers wrote that Arnold had only mimicked the virtuous qualities of other American heroes, that his heart was really controlled by greed and vanity. Some compared him to Judas, Jesus's betrayer, and to Cain, the Bible's original murderer. One poem portrayed Arnold as an embodied demon:

> *Curse on thy malice! what a fiend thou art!*
> *A fiend incarnate, of the worst degree,*
> *To spit the infernal venom of thy heart*
> *At honest men, who never injured thee.*

For religiously fervent Americans, a betrayal like Arnold's could only have malevolent spiritual origins. His treachery also became a perfect foil for the virtue Americans saw—or hoped for—in the Patriot cause. The incessant deploring of Arnold's deceit may have helped Americans avoid noticing their own failings, especially the lack of provision for the army. To the devotees of the Patriot cause, Arnold was everything the true Patriots were not.[20]

No chaplain played a more critical role in sanctifying the American Revolution than Israel Evans. Evans studied at the College of New Jersey under John Witherspoon and graduated in the same class as the Pennsylvania chaplain William Linn. Evans had just graduated with his M.A. degree when the war broke out, and instead of pursuing a church position he accepted a chaplaincy. He served through the entire war and became one of Washington's trusted subordinates, despite their divergent religious beliefs. In early 1778 Washington told Evans, "It will ever be the first wish of my heart to aid your pious endeavors to inculcate a due sense of the dependence we ought to place in that all-wise and powerful being on whom alone our success depends." Washington continued to believe that God's favor was essential to military victory and that divine assistance was best cultivated by good chaplains like Evans.[21]

Accepting Washington's confidence, Evans exalted Washington's character. Evans's encomiums to Washington began with his first published sermon of the war, a thanksgiving meditation offered following the dramatic American victory at Saratoga in 1777, on a day the Continental Congress had set for Americans to express their gratitude to God and pray for forgiveness of sins, military success, and the "promotion and enlargement" of God's kingdom. Evans, preaching before his New Hampshire brigade, reminded the troops of their just war against British tyranny. He also thanked God for backing them in their surprising military successes, particularly at Saratoga. But it was for his Christian hero Washington that Evans reserved his most exceptional praise. The general had a totemic quality, and Evans told the soldiers to "look on [Washington], and catch the genuine patriot fire of liberty and independence. . . . Like him love virtue, and like him, reverence the name of the great Jehovah." According to the chaplain, merely gazing upon Washington was enough to bolster one's courage and holiness. Evans even set aside the normal evangelical standard of spiritual salvation achieved through faith alone when he envisioned Washington's eternal destiny, praying that legions of angels would guard the general and, at the end of his life, "safely convoy him to the regions of eternal liberty and happiness, and seat him high, as the most renowned heroes of liberty and religion." Evans's Washington achieved greatness as a moral exemplar and a standard-bearer for virtue. The general's stewardship of liberty and public morality seemed by themselves sufficient to qualify him for heaven.[22]

Evans closely conflated the divine and the worldly in another sermon delivered upon his brigade's return from fighting the Iroquois in 1779, the same campaign that chaplain William Rogers had heralded that July. In this sermon, Evans's references to Washington could be mistaken for references to Christ. He promised the weary troops that "once more see[ing] the illustrious CHIEF of the armies of the United States, and obtain[ing] his approbation, for he knows your worth, will make you forget all your past dangers and toils, and make you pant for an opportunity to distinguish yourselves in his presence." For Evans, just being in Washington's presence would lift the soldiers' burdens.[23]

Despite the brutality of the campaign against the Native Americans of New York, Evans assured the troops that in burning Iroquois towns of the Finger Lakes region and razing their orchards and crops, they had paved the way for the expansion of the Christian gospel into the western lands. Ever since the founding of New England, British American colonists had often spoken of their desire to evangelize Native Americans, even as they fought vicious wars with them. Evans continued this tradition, promising the victorious men that they represented the vanguard of the Christian faith spreading inexorably into Indian lands. They were "the instruments in the hand of GOD, for accomplishing so great a revolution, and extending the kingdom of his Son so far. Liberty and religion shall have their wide dominion from the Atlantic through the great continent to the western ocean." Subduing the Iroquois heightened the prospects not only for an independent America but also for the westward flow of the gospel; in Evans's vision of providence, God blessed these goals simultaneously.[24]

Evans was present at the war's denouement at Yorktown, Virginia, where the British general Charles Cornwallis surrendered his forces to Washington. Frustrated by his inability to defeat the Patriots decisively in the Carolina backcountry, Cornwallis had moved into eastern Virginia and entrenched at Yorktown, on a peninsula between the James and York rivers. Washington moved his combined army of American and French troops out of the North and rendezvoused with a French fleet outside Yorktown, giving the Patriot forces an overwhelming advantage. For days, the Americans and French mercilessly bombarded the British forces, sending Cornwallis and his men into earthen hovels and overhangs at the York River's edge. On October 14, 1781, Alexander Hamilton finally led the Americans in a charge against one of the British redoubts, which they secured by fierce hand-to-hand combat. Three days later the battle was over, and surrender negotiations began.[25]

Israel Evans remained with Washington during the fighting at Yorktown. According to one anecdote, the two men were standing together during part of the siege and narrowly avoided being struck by a British

cannonball. Washington naturally appointed Evans to deliver a thanksgiving sermon to available troops immediately following Cornwallis's surrender on October 19, 1781. On that occasion Evans may have addressed
the largest assembly gathered in America since George Whitefield's gar-
gantuan evangelistic meetings of the early 1740s. In his sermon, and in a
poem appended to the published version, Evans still reminded the troops
that, out of gratitude for their providential deliverance, they needed to
uphold moral purity and worship God:

> To him who led in ancient days
> The Hebrew tribes, your anthems raise;
> The God who spoke from Sinai's hill
> Protects his chosen people still.
>
> Not to ourselves success we owe
> By help divine we crushed the foe,
> In sword or shield who vainly trust
> Shall soon be humbled to the dust.
> . . .
> Praise him who gives us to repel
> The powers of Britain and of hell,
> With thankful hearts his goodness own,
> And bow before Jehovah's throne.[26]

Yorktown ended the war's active combat, and John Adams, Benjamin
Franklin, and John Jay negotiated the terms of peace at Paris in 1783.
Britain granted the colonies their independence and conceded the borders
of the new United States, roughly bounded by Canada, the Mississippi
River, and Spanish-controlled Florida. It was an excellent resolution for
the new nation, and arguably the greatest diplomatic achievement in the
history of the United States, because it put America on remarkably strong
footing with plenty of room to grow. With the signing of the treaty, Israel
Evans saw unlimited, even millennial potential in the outcome of the war.
One-quarter of the globe would now be devoted to true religion and

liberty. "Hail auspicious morning of the rising empire of this western world!" he exulted. Such sentiments were apparently common among the chaplains. George Duffield of Philadelphia, a Presbyterian pastor who worked as a chaplain both to Congress and to the army, predicted in late 1783 (quoting Isaiah 35) that "justice and truth shall here yet meet together, and righteousness and peace embrace each other: And the wilderness blossom as the rose, and the desert rejoice and sing. And here shall the various ancient prophecies of rich and glorious grace begin their complete divine fulfillment; and the light of divine revelation diffuse its beneficent rays, till the gospel of Jesus have accomplished its day, from east to west, around our world."[27]

Chaplains were hardly the only Patriots to predict the millennial significance of the war. Even John Adams, writing to his wife Abigail shortly after Yorktown, asserted that "the great designs of Providence must be accomplished;—great indeed! The progress of society will be accelerated by centuries by this Revolution. . . . Light spreads from the day-spring in the west; and may it shine more and more until the perfect day."[28]

Chaplains had a unique opportunity to focus the soldiers' attention on the broader moral challenges and religious possibilities the war and its outcome offered. They not only comforted the sick and injured but also heralded the good spiritual principles embodied in the war. As seen through the chaplains' eyes, the war was not simply about political control or Americans' disinclination to pay new taxes; it was also about godly freedom, that gift that, as chaplain William Rogers told the Iroquois-fighting troops on the Fourth of July, 1779, Jesus had come into the world to give. Such motivations could sustain the American army when battles turned against them or when the American people failed to support them, and certainly when victory was at long last won.

More problematically, however, the framing of the war as the action of Providence could make it difficult for American leaders to maintain a critical perspective on the war or its tactics. Rogers, for instance, seemed not to wonder whether the spirit of Christian freedom licensed the destruction of Iroquois towns and fields.

Indeed, the war seemed only to bring bad consequences for Native Americans. Some evangelical Native Americans tried to encourage neutrality, but the war constantly encroached on their territory, livelihood, and lives. The Mohegan pastor Samson Occom—the most influential Native American evangelical of the eighteenth century—wrote in a letter circulated to his fellow Indians that they should not "meddle with the family contentions of the English, but will be at peace and quietness, peace never does any hurt. Peace is from the God of peace and love. . . . Jesus Christ is the Prince of Peace." Although Occom sympathized with the plight of the American colonists, he thought that the devil had stirred up the conflict, so Native Americans should stay out of it. The war would ultimately hurt Native Americans caught between the two sides, he believed, and damage the reputation of white Christians trying to evangelize the Indians.[29]

By the war's end, Occom's dire predictions had come true. He believed that the American Revolution had damaged Native Americans' communities more than any other force in his lifetime. Occom bitterly wrote that his former friend, the Presbyterian missionary Samuel Kirkland, "went with an army against the poor Indians, and he has prejudiced the minds of Indians against all missionaries, especially against white missionaries, seven times more than anything, that ever was done by the white people." Kirkland had become one of the Continental Congress's chief diplomats to the Iroquois League and had helped persuade the Oneidas and Tuscaroras to support the Patriot side, a move that created serious divisions among the Six Nations of the league. Kirkland went on to serve as a chaplain and provided intelligence for John Sullivan's devastating 1779 campaign against the Iroquois in New York. He later became wealthy from land speculations in Iroquois territory appropriated by Americans as a result of the war.[30]

It was not only Native Americans who challenged the problematic wartime actions committed in the names of God and Providence. Loyalist writer Peter Oliver sneered that the Christian Patriots of the Revolution invoked God's name "to sanctify any villainy that was committed for the good old cause." The chaplains, proponents of Providence, did admirable work in bringing solace to the suffering while pointing to the great American ideals of liberty and virtue, but their insistence— encouraged by supportive generals and politicians—that the war was divinely sanctioned tended to limit their perspective. If the cause was godly, then everything done in the name of the cause seemed godly too. From the Revolution to the conflicts their nation engages in more than two centuries later, Americans want to believe that their wars reflect the will of the Almighty. But as we hear in the echoes of Samson Occom's lament and in the ringing tones of William Rogers's endorsement of the destruction of Iroquoian towns, using God's might and right to justify one's cause can easily obscure the complexity or injustice of war. Providentialism was the most morally problematic religious principle of the Revolution.[31]

CHAPTER 7

"God Has Made of One Blood All Nations of Men"

Equality by Creation

THOMAS JEFFERSON would not seem a promising candidate to have produced the greatest statement of human equality in world history, "All men are created equal." His views on equality were complicated, at best. Jefferson was the foremost proponent of the American Enlightenment, which held as one of its key convictions that slavery was wrong because of the equal creation of all people by God. Yet in his livelihood, finances, and means of living, Jefferson was utterly dependent on slavery. Moreover, as Americans would learn close to two centuries after his death, Jefferson carried on a sexual relationship with one of his slaves, Sally Hemings, following the passing of his wife Martha in 1782. Sex between masters and slaves was not unusual in the eighteenth century; indeed, Sally Hemings herself was Martha Jefferson's half sister. Jefferson freed only a few of his slaves near the end of his life, some of them almost certainly his own children.

The gap between Jefferson's beliefs and his behavior is indicative of the struggle of revolutionary Americans to grasp new implications of what they saw as an ancient truth: the common creation of mankind by God. The assertion of this truth became the heart of the case for American independence and for human equality in the newly established nation.

But the application of the principle of equality by creation faced tremendous obstacles erected by traditional belief in inequality, monarchy, and slavery. It would take decades—even centuries—for the nation to live up to "the proposition that all men are created equal," as Abraham Lincoln put it in the Gettysburg Address. America's Civil War president was speaking at a battlefield cemetery that memorialized how bloody the struggle over equality had become. How could it have been easy for the revolutionary generation, or its descendents, to sort out the meaning of equality by creation, when a slaveholder proposed it?

The elites of seventeenth-century Europe and America believed that God had created people unequal, possessing different capabilities and serving different roles in society. John Winthrop, the governor of the Massachusetts Bay Colony, made this conviction clear in his *Model of Christian Charity* sermon (1630), delivered on board the ship carrying Puritan settlers to Massachusetts. Winthrop opened his sermon with the claim that "God Almighty in his most holy and wise providence has so disposed of the condition of mankind, as in all times some must be rich some poor, some high and eminent in power and dignity; others [lowly] and in subjection."[1] Although Winthrop believed that all men were created by God and stood equally in need of God's grace, he believed that God made people in various situations and stations so that everyone would provide for the communal needs of each other. In his ideal godly society, inequality meant that the strong would protect the weak and the rich would bless the poor. And as the New Testament instructed, slaves would work diligently, and masters would treat their bound laborers with kindness, generosity, and fairness.

In the decades after Jefferson wrote "all men are created equal," the doctrine of created inequality would come under increasing assault by critics of slavery. In 1813 James Forten, a prominent African American sailmaker of Philadelphia, wrote, "We hold this truth to be self-evident, that God created all men equal, and [this idea] is one of the most prominent features in the Declaration of Independence and in that glorious fabric of collected wisdom, our noble constitution. This idea embraces the Indian and the European, the savage and the saint, the Peruvian and the Laplander, the white man and the African." Although many American defenders of slavery would continue to believe in inherent human inequality, the American Revolution had severely undermined slavery's ideological foundation. Essential to the attack on slavery was the basic principle of the equality of all humans by creation, and nowhere was that doctrine stated more simply and powerfully than in the Declaration of Independence.[2]

The Christian faith has for two millennia had a complex influence on the idea of human equality. On one hand, the belief in a common creation by God puts all humans on the same spiritual footing, their lives originating from the same divine source. Although the Bible also depicts all people as sinners in need of God's grace, it seems to accept vast differences in power and authority among humans, even to the point of tacitly accepting slavery. The same Apostle Paul who told slaves to obey their masters also wrote, "There is neither Jew nor Greek, there is neither [slave] nor free, there is neither male nor female: for you are all one in Christ Jesus" (Galatians 3:28). The biblical characterization of equality therefore seems not to require parity of condition, or even of opportunity. Nevertheless, the Bible endorses a fundamental equality of humans in their standing before God, which can have profound social implications. Americans of the revolutionary era put a dramatic new emphasis on human equality by creation and began haltingly to consider what changes that doctrine might require in social relations between the wealthy and poor, men and women, and masters and slaves.

Some Christians before the Revolution had already begun to act on the implications of equality by creation by attacking slavery. In seventeenth-century England and America, the Quakers spoke out especially early against slavery, basing their argument on their belief in the equality of the races before God. Their advocacy was not surprising; the early Quakers were the most radical of all Protestants and believed that the "Inner Light" of God's presence was available to all people. In their daily lives, Quakers refused to acknowledge their social superiors with honorific terms or by doffing their hats, which often earned them public beatings for insubordination. They were pacifists and saw all war as evil, allowed women to speak openly in their meetings, and believed that Europeans, Africans, and Native Americans would have equal places in the Kingdom of God. English Quaker leader George Fox, having visited the English colony of Barbados, made an appeal to the Quakers of the Caribbean to consider freeing their slaves, not only because all people were equal by creation but also because Christ had died for all races: "He died for the tawnies [Native Americans] and the blacks, as well as for you that are called whites." Fox encouraged Quakers to teach their slaves Christianity and also to free them after a limited term of service.[3]

Non-Quakers, such as Puritan judge Samuel Sewall in his antislavery tract *The Selling of Joseph* (1700), made an argument similar to Fox's. Because all people are descended from Adam and Eve, they all have an equal right to liberty and freedom from slavery, he wrote. Like Fox, Sewall cited Acts 17:26, in which the Apostle Paul proclaimed that God "has made of one blood all nations of men." This verse became the most commonly cited text used to demonstrate human equality by creation, and it was often employed by Christians making a biblical case against slavery.[4]

Early New Englanders' high view of local church authority also supplied resources for new notions of equality. The Puritans and many of their eighteenth-century heirs rejected church hierarchies above the congregational level and believed that Christians should have the right to govern themselves without the interference of bishops or denominational councils—a disavowal of hierarchy that encouraged a broader commitment to human equality. John Wise, the pastor of Chebacco parish in Ipswich, Massachusetts, was the most outspoken advocate of congregational rule, basing his arguments on the equality of people before God. In his tract *A Vindication of the Government of New-England Churches*, a 1717 book that was republished shortly before the Revolution, Wise wrote that in civil and religious government, "the natural equality of men amongst men must be duly favored." God never meant for governments to abuse the rights of men, he said; instead, all persons should expect the government to defend their happiness, life, liberty, and honor equally. Yet despite early efforts to translate equality by creation into a program for social or religious reform, most Christians before the American Revolution remained comfortable with all kinds of social inequalities, including slavery, and saw them as ordained by God.[5]

The radicals of the Great Awakening certainly introduced new possibilities of equality into the American landscape by giving prominent roles to African Americans, Native Americans, the poor and uneducated, and women. But the chief leaders of the Awakening, including Jonathan Edwards and George Whitefield, held a complicated view of human equality. Whitefield believed that all people, including Native Americans and African Americans, needed to find salvation in Christ. He chastised those in the American South who balked at preaching the gospel to the slaves; some southerners believed that if the slaves converted to Christianity it would give them newfangled ideas about equality and freedom. Whitefield assured slaveholders that a Christian slave would only become more obedient to his or her master. In 1740 the evangelist penned a sample prayer for a servant that exemplified the sort of attitude he imagined a pious Christian slave might exhibit. Even though this prayer cites Acts 17:26, the slave's belief in equality by creation would serve as an aid to enduring his bondage—in the hope that God would treat him fairly at the day of judgment. Whitefield's model servant prays for the grace to obey his master in all circumstances, and not just when the master is watching. Whitefield would go on to own slaves himself and to promote the legalization of slavery in the newly founded colony of Georgia.[6]

Jonathan Edwards also distinguished between spiritual equality and social equality, and he too owned household slaves. In his treatise *The Nature of True Virtue*, Edwards praised orderly, hierarchical communities, where "different members of society have all their appointed office, place and station, according to their several capacities and talents, and every one keeps his place, and continues in his proper business." More than a century had passed since John Winthrop had sermonized aboard his immigrant ship, but the words sounded the same. Edwards encountered his own problems in obtaining the social obedience he propounded. He expected the people of his congregation to defer to him as their pastor, but he found Northamptonites dangerously unruly. In 1744 Edwards tried to confront several young men who were wielding a midwifery manual and using its details to harass young women about their genitalia. When

Edwards tried to crack down on this behavior, one of the men told Edwards he wouldn't cooperate and that he wouldn't "worship a wig." When Edwards tried to institute major changes in the church's membership standards soon afterward, he lost the support of the church's elite members; the evangelical luminary was dismissed from his pastorate in 1750.[7]

In Northampton Edwards had become a victim of his own hierarchical views, but his Calvinist theology contained surprising reservoirs of egalitarian thought. Although Edwards believed that some people were chosen by God for salvation and others were not, he did not believe that any person merited salvation on his or her own. All individuals stood the same before God, corrupted by original sin and in need of salvation. Through conversion, the lowliest saint vaulted above the loftiest lost sinner. Many people honored by the world "are wicked men and reprobates," Edwards told his congregation, "and they are not of so great value in God's sight as one true Christian, however humble his birth and low his standing; however poor, or ignorant, or unknown." To Edwards and his fellow evangelicals, the essence of real religion—the converted heart—leveled the social distinctions that men made according to wealth, education, and family background.[8]

Edwards developed these views most fully during his time at the Indian mission town of Stockbridge, Massachusetts, where he lived after his expulsion from Northampton. Whereas many European colonists saw Native Americans as degraded and hopeless, Edwards viewed them as having both the same debility and the same promise as whites. "All are sinners, and exposed to condemnation," he wrote in *Original Sin*, penned during his Stockbridge pastorate. "This is true of persons of all constitutions, capacities, conditions, manners, opinions and educations; in all countries, climates, nations and ages." Especially after his bitter experience in Northampton, Edwards did not believe that Native Americans were inherently more sinful than Europeans. He expected that in the millennial kingdom, Africans, Turks, and Native Americans would be among the greatest saints. Although Edwards hardly held a positive view of human nature, he did see all humans as equally in need of God's grace.[9]

During the Great Awakening, the revivalists relentlessly preached that everyone needed to be born again, an emphasis that led to novel views on spiritual equality. Reverend William Cooper of Old South Church in Boston, speaking in 1740 at the outset of the revivals, declared that salvation made all social distinctions irrelevant. God would redeem people from every class and rank; some of the poor and humble would rejoice eternally in heaven while some of the mighty and wealthy would languish in hell. Most provocatively, Cooper reminded his congregation that some of all races would be saved. Noting that some slaves had been converted already, he declared that those new believers had become "the Lord's free-men, brought into the glorious liberty of the children of God." Citing Acts 17:26, Cooper warned that all needed salvation, suggesting that some slaves might experience it while some masters remained under God's judgment.[10]

Evangelical Christianity was only one of several sources that helped forge the revolutionary concept of human equality. Another factor was the relatively egalitarian social conditions in colonial America as compared to those in Europe. Make no mistake: colonial America was hardly a land of equality, and it was becoming more unequal as the Revolution drew near. Hundreds of thousands of African Americans were owned by white masters, Native Americans' rights were largely ignored, and small groups of elite whites exercised social, economic, and political authority over the common whites of the colonies. But there were also many ways in which American society did not feature the stark social divisions that immigrants had known in Europe. America had no titled nobility, and although Americans revered the king, the British court's presence hardly extended to the colonies (at least until they began raising new taxes in 1765). Profound distinctions of wealth existed among whites, but such divisions were nothing like those in England. Wealthy Americans' estates and incomes seldom rivaled those of their English counterparts. England—especially London—teemed with landless poor, whereas in America most farmers owned their own land, and cities remained small. The distribution of property reached unparalleled levels. Two-thirds of the white colonial population owned land.[11]

The relatively egalitarian nature of white American colonial society gave a less deferential, more democratic cast to prerevolutionary life.

Average Americans would bristle at suggestions that they were anyone's inferior. One visitor to New Jersey remarked that the people there "held their heads higher than the rest of mankind and imagined few or none were their equals." Similarly, an Anglican minister observed that the "poorest laborer on the shore of the Delaware thinks himself entitled to deliver his opinions in matters of religion and politics with as much freedom as the gentleman and the scholar." Many evangelicals also rejected the notion that they should defer to a minister because of his education, instead making the indwelling of the Holy Spirit the ultimate qualification for a preacher.[12]

Over the course of the eighteenth century, republican and Enlightenment writers began to make the doctrine of inherent human equality more acceptable in America. Although these philosophers were often unfriendly to traditional Protestantism, they still assumed that people's fundamental rights came from their creation by God. Chief among the philosophers of equality in the English Enlightenment was John Locke. Locke took a medical science degree from Oxford and in the 1660s began working as a personal physician for Lord Anthony Ashley Cooper, who went on to found the colony of South Carolina. Locke also involved himself in English politics, becoming one of the leading opponents of absolute monarchy under Charles II and James II, which forced him into exile in Holland during the 1680s. Upon his return during the Glorious Revolution, Locke became one of the foremost advocates of republican government, exercising significant influence both on American evangelicals of the Great Awakening and on the leaders of the American Revolution.

Locke held that such ancient republics as Rome and Sparta had been formed voluntarily by men "amongst whom there was no natural superiority or subjection." Each person had chosen to enter the republican compact, and each deserved equal treatment under that government. The philosopher also saw people in their prepolitical "state of nature" as equal to each other primarily because of their common creation by God: "For men being all the workmanship of one omnipotent, and infinitely wise maker: all the servants of one sovereign master, sent into the world by his order, and about his business; they are his property, whose workmanship they are." Although animals were made by God for human use, no human could claim God-ordained dominion over another. All were naturally subject to only one master, their creator. Locke also believed that God had given the world to men to use in common. Differences between men could be attributed largely to varying levels of education and experience, he believed, because all came into the world with their minds a "tabula rasa," or an equally blank sheet. Thomas Jefferson, by his own testimony, appropriated Locke's ideas as part of the ideological blend behind the Declaration of Independence.[13]

In the decades before the American Revolution, evangelicals also appropriated Locke's brand of equality by creation and used it to appeal for the individual right of religious conscience. The evangelicals' case for fair treatment sounded a great deal like the Patriots' arguments against Britain several decades later. Reverend Elisha Williams, the evangelical opponent of Connecticut's anti-itinerancy law, wrote in his pathbreaking *Essential Rights and Liberties of Protestants* (1744) that humans are born free and rational and are "born thus naturally equal, i.e. with an equal right to their persons; so also with an equal right to their preservation." Following Locke, Williams argued that the main purpose of government was to protect citizens' life, liberty, and property. People retained their God-given right of free conscience; they did not surrender it to the state.[14]

Equality by creation began to take more revolutionary form as conflict between Britain and the colonies developed. As early as 1762, Massachusetts lawyer James Otis was appealing to equality by creation in a dispute with the royal governor of the province. Asserting the power of the colonial legislature over monarchical authority, Otis declared that "God made all men naturally equal" and that kings and royal governors should serve the interests of the people, not vice versa. Soon colonists appealed to their equality with their fellow Britons in order to protest British tax laws, making the claim based on their rights under the British constitution, but also on people's fundamental equality before God.[15]

After the passage of the Stamp Act, Americans like John Adams still defended the British constitution as an ideal political system because they thought it was based upon man's God-given equality. The documents that made up the British constitution did not endorse domination by the king or the aristocracy, Adams wrote, and they opposed the notion that the people, "the multitude, the million, the populace, the vulgar, the mob, the herd, and the rabble, as the great always delight to call them, have no rights at all." Instead, the British constitution stood on the principle that "by the unalterable, indefeasible laws of God and nature . . . all men are born equal." Adams and his elite American colleagues hardly represented the common "herd," but he and other Patriots set forth the concept of universal human equality as they clamored for relief from the taxes imposed by the British government.[16]

In early 1776, the idea of equality by creation finally evolved into an assault on George III and monarchy itself. Thomas Paine's *Common Sense* condemned the institution of monarchy because it violated human equality. Americans had been devoted to the British monarchy for so long that rejecting the king's authority proved to be their most difficult step prior to declaring independence, and to encourage their urge to dissolve ties with the mother country, Paine argued that the office of monarch, set above the rest of mankind, represented an unnatural assertion of the superiority of one man or woman over others. "Mankind being originally equals in the order of creation, the equality could only be destroyed by some subsequent circumstance," Paine wrote. The "subsequent circumstance" that destroyed God-given equality was monarchy. Nature, reason, and the Bible testified against the exaltation of rulers above their fellow men, according to Paine.[17]

As the movement for independence grew in momentum in the summer of 1776, the belief in equality by creation became a rallying cry for those fighting the British. In a speech delivered by a "Farmer of Philadelphia County" in May, the orator echoed Locke in reminding his audience that it was "God Almighty who gave me my life, and my property . . . and it is he only that hath an absolute and unlimited right and power to take either or both away. . . . Of all earthly benefits my Creator hath bestowed on me, I do most esteem my liberty." Then, echoing Patrick Henry, he declared to his listeners that he would resist attempts to take his God-given right to liberty, even to the point of death.[18]

By 1776 the avowal of equality by creation had spawned extraordinarily militant ideas, notions much more radical than those the leading revolutionaries would endorse. The anonymous author of the New England pamphlet *The People the Best Governors* reasoned that if everyone was equal before God, then the people should rule directly. "God gave mankind freedom by nature, made every man equal to his neighbor, and has virtually enjoined them to govern themselves by their own laws." In this writer's ideal republic, the people would directly elect every officeholder. The legislature of ancient Athens had been composed of common workers, or so the writer said, and therefore America should have a congress of laborers as well. However, this radical populist had no patience for deists and skeptics in public office and would have required that all elected officials believe in the one true God and the Bible as God's word.[19]

It took Jefferson's felicitous phrase "all men are created equal" to establish equality by creation as the essential principle of the American creed. Fighting had begun at Lexington and Concord in April 1775, more than a year before the Continental Congress had even considered a declaration of American independence from Britain; the incipient nation lacked a document defining its autonomy or justifying its own existence. On June 7, 1776, Virginia's Richard Henry Lee moved that the Continental Congress sever the united colonies' ties with Britain. Congress appointed a committee to write a preamble to the resolution for independence, and Jefferson was selected by the committee to draft the Declaration of Independence.

Every phrase of the Declaration's opening paragraphs has been dissected by scholars—yet the claim that all men are *created* equal, and that they are *endowed by their Creator* with rights, has received less attention than other parts of the famous first passages of the document. It is likely that this historical neglect reflects the awareness by scholars of Jefferson's skepticism about traditional Christianity; some interpreters might believe that Jefferson was casually employing a widely recognized yet theologically neutral description of the deity and of the divine act of creation. But the motivation behind Jefferson's use of the phrase is at once simpler and more significant: When Jefferson needed a firm foundation for his plea for American rights, he turned to the broadly accepted notion of equality by creation.

For the rendering of this section of the Declaration, Jefferson borrowed from his fellow Virginian George Mason and the recently drafted Virginia Declaration of Rights. In that document, Mason spoke of men as "by nature equally free and independent." Jefferson rewrote this phrase to show more clearly the action of God in creation. Jefferson originally wrote that all men are "created equal and independent," but then cut out "and independent" to leave the simple phrase "all men are created equal."[20]

Jefferson's next phrase "and are endowed by their Creator" was also more theologically explicit than Mason's wording, which had simply asserted that all men "have certain inherent rights." In a rough draft of the Declaration, Jefferson had been even more forthright, writing that "from [men's] equal creation they derive rights inherent and inalienable." Mason's Declaration of Rights did speak of God as creator, but only later in the document and with specific reference to religious liberty. Overall Mason's phrasing was less theologically direct than what Jefferson employed. The use by Jefferson, and the endorsement by Congress, of equality and rights by creation—twice—in this essential sentence was no mistake or afterthought. Jefferson recognized that the wording of the Declaration of Independence would root his case for equality in the widely assumed common creation of mankind by God—and thus provide a more transcendent basis for equality than merely referring to the rights of Englishmen or to simple reason.[21]

Propounding national independence because God had created humans as equal beings was a profoundly significant example of the willingness of Jefferson and the other founders to use religious concepts to mobilize Americans for the Patriot cause. Congress even added two references to God ("the supreme judge of the world" and "divine providence") at the end of the Declaration. As Jefferson famously explained later, he meant the Declaration's language to reflect "the harmonizing sentiments of the day," using language that would resonate with the American public and rise above sectarian differences in theology. By 1776, the discourse around the concept of equality by God's creation possessed that broadness of appeal. Although Jefferson, a Virginia aristocrat and slave owner, only tentatively envisioned the Declaration as a catalyst of social change, Americans quickly began to realize that his words could be used to stimulate a much deeper egalitarian transformation.[22]

Jefferson's language of equality immediately provoked suspicion among his fellow members of the southern elite. Virginia's Edmund Randolph recalled that Robert Carter Nicholas, who had served as the last royal treasurer of Virginia before independence, opposed the claim in the Virginia Declaration of Rights that all men were equally free and independent because it could become a "forerunner or pretext of civil convulsion," or slave insurrection. Nicholas was apparently told that because Virginians were fighting the British, they should not be too cautious in their appeals to equal human rights.[23]

Decades later, as the nation increasingly fractured over slavery, leading southerners would come to regret Jefferson's appeal to equality by creation. South Carolina's John C. Calhoun, the champion of southern slavery and states' rights, railed against the Declaration of Independence in an 1848 speech, ridiculing the notion that all men are born or created equal. "They are not so in any sense . . . ; and thus, as I have asserted, there is not a word of truth in the whole proposition," Calhoun proclaimed. Everyone was born into a social world of various inequalities, and not every person deserved liberty; only those of the highest virtue and intelligence could manage the responsibility that freedom required, according to Calhoun.[24]

Slavery's defenders could and did protest those opening sentences of the Declaration, but it would be the embrace of these words by other Americans that would make Jefferson's invocation of equality by creation the most powerful and productive ideological force to come out of the Revolution. The social implications of the notion that "all men are created equal" would prove very difficult to contain. If God had made people equal, then how could anyone justify the vast inequalities in American society? Starting not long after the war for independence itself, the new American nation became a republican forum where people attempted to reconcile with social and political realities the belief that men were created equal. South Carolina Patriot leader and physician David Ramsay told a Fourth of July (1778) audience in Charleston that the chief difference between monarchies and republics was the doctrine of equality. Monarchies were suffused with hypocrisy, vanity, entitlement, and nepotism, he said, but with a republic's principle of "equality, the life and soul of commonwealth," people could be assessed according to their true merit and worth, Ramsay concluded.[25]

Following the adoption of the Declaration, hosts of Americans came to believe that the common creation of mankind was the firmest basis on which to fight for equal treatment. Many pastors and Christian politicians also asserted that American republicanism and Christianity combined to promote what Bishop James Madison (cousin of the future president) called "the gospel of equality and fraternity." Madison, a militant Episcopal Patriot and the president of the College of William and Mary, believed that the American Revolution had been fought to restore man to his original, God-given state of equality. "How were those sentiments of equality, benevolence and fraternity, which reason, and religion, and nature enjoin, to reassume their sovereignty over the human soul?" he asked. For Bishop Madison, God had chosen America as his favored place to reestablish the equality with which he endowed humans at birth.[26]

American Christians across the theological spectrum agreed with Madison's sentiments. Baptist pastor Samuel Stillman of Boston, for instance, regretted that in times past Christian ministers had defended the divine right of kings to rule over subjects. The Revolution had inaugurated a new era in the Christian view of man, in which equality by creation became the guiding principle, he said. Quoting Locke, Stillman concluded that whatever government America or the states instituted within its borders (he was speaking in 1779, as Massachusetts was still struggling to frame its state government), the authority in that government should, under God, be derived from the people. As a Baptist, Stillman particularly wanted the American and state governments to encourage the interests of religion by protecting the people's right to practice their faith as their consciences dictated. He envisioned a republic in which all believers would be equally "protected, but none established!"[27]

As Jefferson's words were disseminated around the new nation, evangelicals, liberal Christians, and deists took them to heart, crystallizing their own agreement that nature and reason indeed confirmed the Bible's view of the essential equality of all men. Samuel Cooper, an irenic, liberal pastor at Boston's Brattle Street Church, declared that no one needed biblical revelation in order to understand equality and its implications for fair government: "These are the plain dictates of that reason and common sense with which the common parent of men has informed the human bosom." Not only had God created men the same, but he had given them the common moral sense to understand their equality, Cooper said, citing Acts 17:26 to argue that the Bible also defended equality. Reason and revelation both affirmed God-given human parity.[28]

By 1793, when Samuel Adams became the governor of Massachusetts, wise American politicians knew they should defend equality by creation, because their constituents expected it. At this point in the new nation's existence, equality was not only a justification for national independence but a common cause: In the quest to establish equality, Americans would find their God-ordained mission in the world. Assuring Massachusetts legislators that he understood the limits of his power, Adams reminded them that God had imprinted divine laws on the hearts of all men. Through the Declaration of Independence, the Massachusetts Declaration of Rights, and other documents enshrining the principle, equality had become a foundational "article in the political creed of the United States," he said. Adams noted that France had recently adopted the same principle as an animating tenet of its revolution, which suggested that equality was spreading across the globe. If that trend continued, Adams postulated, "the whole family and brotherhood of man will then nearly approach to, if not fully enjoy that state of peace and prosperity, which ancient prophets and sages have foretold." Employing in another context the millennial language with which Americans by now were so familiar, Adams averred that the implementation of equality by creation might herald the coming of the Kingdom of God on earth. Although Adams had been deeply influenced by his family's Puritan heritage, in the matter of human equality he had largely jettisoned the Puritan legacy of Winthrop's *Model of Christian Charity* and embraced instead the notion that no man was created to rule over others; governors were responsible to those who elected them, for all were created equal.[29]

The Revolution and Declaration of Independence made equality by creation part of the American creed. Once it had done its work against

Britain, however, the belief in human equality could not simply be set aside, as Samuel Adams, Jefferson, and others well recognized. People like the sailmaker and activist James Forten urged Americans to accept the implications of equality by creation and thus, by the logic of equality, to end slavery. But Thomas Jefferson and other leading Patriots long resisted those connotations of the Declaration. By the mid-1780s, Jefferson had begun to scale back the broad implications of the Declaration, arguing that the physical differences between whites and blacks demonstrated that the two were fundamentally different races, one fit for liberty, the other not.[30]

Three quarters of a century after the Declaration, the tension between the professed American creed of equality and the practiced reality of slavery would become untenable. Abolitionists like Frederick Douglass denounced the hypocrisy of American Christianity and American republicanism because they forged the ideological principles behind abolitionism while maintaining slavery as an institution. In July 1852 Douglass, an escaped slave, vented his wrath, telling his fellow Americans that the "existence of slavery in this country brands your republicanism as a sham, your humanity as a base pretence, and your Christianity as a lie." For many African Americans, the creed of human equality only made more bitter the disappointment and suffering of the revolutionary era. America would sweep onward toward the bloody Civil War that would wreck Jefferson's self-contradictory republic of white equality and black bondage. The underlying impetus toward this grievous end was the inexorable logic of equality by creation.[31]

CHAPTER 8

"The Bands of Wickedness"

Slavery and the American Revolution

I N A REMARKABLE letter from 1773, Patrick Henry lamented the existence of slavery in a Christian land. The lawyer and orator was writing to Robert Pleasants, a Quaker in Virginia who had freed his slaves, thanking him for sending a tract by the Quaker antislavery activist Anthony Benezet. "Is it not amazing," Henry asked, "that at a time, when the rights of humanity are defined and understood with precision, in a country, above all others fond of liberty, that in such an age and in such a country, we find men professing a religion the most humane, mild, gentle and generous, adopting a principle [slavery] as repugnant to humanity, as it is inconsistent with the Bible, and destructive to liberty?" Noting the contrast between Pleasants and himself, Henry declared, "Would anyone believe I am the master of slaves of my own purchase! I am drawn along by the general inconvenience of living here without them." Some white slaveholding Americans like Henry agonized over the tension between American slavery and American liberty, yet Henry himself was willing to live with this profound inconsistency. In spite of his misgivings, he never freed his slaves.[1]

Massachusetts minuteman Lemuel Haynes had no such ambivalence about slavery. He knew it was wrong, and it was the emerging American movement of Christian republicanism that gave him the words to oppose it. Haynes was born in 1753 to a white mother and African American father and worked for a family in Granville, Massachusetts, as a servant. When the revolutionary crisis erupted, he joined the minutemen and then the Continental Army. His biracial presence apparently drew little notice from his fellow soldiers, as small numbers of African American recruits were fairly common in the New England regiments. Haynes also experienced an evangelical conversion around the same time and came under the influence of the disciples of Jonathan Edwards. Inspired by the revolutionary cause and the principles of evangelical faith, Haynes became one of the most trenchant critics of slavery in revolutionary America. In 1776 Haynes wrote "Liberty Further Extended: Or Free Thoughts on the Illegality of Slave-Keeping," an unpublished document that was privately circulated among New England Calvinists, especially those in the growing antislavery movement. This brilliant text took the Declaration of Independence's recent promulgation of the idea of equality by creation and turned it into an argument against American slavery. Haynes included the key sentence from the Declaration, "We hold these truths to be self-evident, that all men are created equal," as the opening quotation of his essay. Citing Acts 17:26 ("God has made of one blood all nations of men"), he insisted that "liberty is equally as precious to a black man, as it is to a white one, and bondage equally as intolerable to the one as it is to the other." Haynes warned that Americans invited the wrath of God if they did not give up slavery.[2]

The consequences of the Revolution for African Americans reveal the era's greatest moral failing. The moral struggle for independence implied a promise to end American slavery—a promise the Revolution did not fulfill. For Haynes and many other American Christians, the ideal of equality by creation inescapably pointed to the immorality of slavery. The Revolution unleashed an unprecedented flood of antislavery thought, much of which came from evangelical Christian sources. Enlightenment ideals also boosted some Americans' antislavery convictions, but most of the early activists against slavery in America came out of denominations such as Haynes's Congregationalists, the Quakers, or the new evangelical Methodists and Baptists. Although the war did help ensure the gradual end of slavery in most of the North, it did not in the South. The glorious cause of liberty left human bondage intact in the areas where freedom for all was the most urgent issue—in the South of such defenders of Anglo-American freedom as Patrick Henry and Thomas Jefferson. The experiences of African Americans in the war and afterward compromised the aura of moral virtue bestowed on the Revolution by white American Christians.

Slavery was widespread in America in 1776. It was legal in every single colony. Most religious leaders expressed few qualms about slaveholding, although many acknowledged that its practice in America was morally questionable. Many of its critics decided it was more effective first to attack not slavery itself but the international slave trade, because few advocates of slavery could justify the brutal transatlantic traffic in humans. With about 500,000 slaves already living in America, banning the slave trade would not threaten the institution. In fact, a ban could actually make slaveholders wealthier because the supply of slaves would become smaller. The southern economy was deeply dependent on slavery, but many northern merchants and shippers had a great deal invested in it as well. Ultimately, abandoning slavery in America would be a wrenching experience, driven by the revolutionary ideal of equality by creation. Yet ideas alone could not conquer slavery, and its persistence would lead to the great scourge of civil war.

Evangelical faith held great potential as a source of radical antislavery thought. In the most extraordinary case during the Great Awakening, the South Carolina planter Hugh Bryan, a convert of George Whitefield's, came temporarily to believe that he was a prophet of God destined to deliver South Carolina's slaves from their bondage. In 1742 Bryan sent a book of prophecies to the South Carolina legislature that predicted that the slaves would destroy Charleston. The colony's authorities, worried that Bryan was communicating his prophecies to the slaves themselves, went to arrest the planter but found him repentant. He had tested his calling by trying, like a latter-day Moses, to part the waters of a local river. One account reported that the Holy Spirit "directed him to go and take him a rod, of such a certain shape and dimensions, from such a tree, in such a place as he told him of; and therewith to go and smite the waters of a river, which should thereby be divided, so as he might go over, on dry ground." He did as he was told, and after cutting the rod he drove "full tilt with it into the river, and falls a smiting, splashing and spluttering the water about with it, till he was quite up to the chin; and his brother, who had pursued him as fast as he could had enough to do to save him from being drowned." Bryan, humiliated, followed the example of his mentor Whitefield and soon reconciled himself to the notion that faithful Christians could also own slaves.[3]

Evangelicals, white or black, did not typically entertain notions about slavery as subversive as those of the prophet Hugh Bryan. Nevertheless, as the Revolution approached, some slaves began to speculate that the time of their deliverance was near, thanks to their conviction that the Bible's prophecies of liberty for the captives applied to them. In 1775, as the struggle between the Americans and the British broke out into armed conflict, reports of slave insurrections in the South were rampant, with many slaves apparently believing that the British forces would rescue them from their American oppressors. One slave preacher named David reportedly told an audience in Charleston that "God would send deliverance to the negroes, from the power of their masters, as he freed the children of Israel from Egyptian bondage." At almost exactly the same time, a slave preacher named George was sentenced and hanged for fomenting rebellion southwest of Charleston. He reportedly told followers that King George III had received a divine mandate to "alter the world and set the negroes free."[4]

African Americans widely viewed the arrival of British forces in America as an opportunity for freedom, and droves of them fled to British lines when they had the chance. The British made halting efforts to encourage slaves to run away from their masters and thus disrupt American business and agriculture. Most notably, Lord Dunmore, the royal governor of Virginia, offered in late 1775 to free slaves who joined his army and fought against the Patriots. At least eight hundred slaves responded to the offer, and Dunmore composed an "Ethiopian Regiment" whose members wore on their uniforms badges declaring, "Liberty to Slaves." Such actions seemed to the Patriots one more example of British oppression of Anglo-Americans and elicited Thomas Jefferson's complaint in the Declaration of Independence that the British had "excited domestic insurrections amongst us."[5]

Other slaves left their masters when the turmoil of the war presented an opening for escape. One such slave was the Baptist pastor David George, who had been converted to evangelical faith while on a plantation near Silver Bluff, South Carolina. Around 1773 he became the pastor of the Silver Bluff Church, which is generally regarded as the oldest continually operating black church in America. When George's master fled from invading British forces, George led his family and much of his congregation to British-controlled Savannah, Georgia, where he operated a butcher's stall and his wife washed clothes for the redcoats. George soon left for Nova Scotia, where large numbers of African American Loyalists, including many evangelicals, found refuge during the war. The British, who had once detained George as a suspected Patriot spy, now gave George and his family free passage to Nova Scotia. He eventually relocated to Sierra Leone in west Africa, hoping to bring the gospel to his African brethren.[6]

As the revolutionary struggle escalated and Christian liberty increasingly became the Patriot rallying cry, many African American Christians used the tenets of their faith to denounce American slavery. The evangelical Christian poet and former slave Phillis Wheatley rarely spoke against slavery directly, but she said enough to make her sentiments clear. As a young girl in west Africa in 1761, Wheatley had been kidnapped and sold into slavery. When she arrived in Boston, she was purchased by the Wheatley family, evangelical Christians who gave her a last name and an education and introduced her to Christianity. The Wheatleys freed Phillis in 1773. In 1774, the poet corresponded with Mohegan minister Samson Occom about the rights of Africans. In a letter intended for a wide readership—it was published in several New England newspapers— she referred to the concept of human equality by creation and threw into sharp relief the moral hypocrisy of slavery. "In every human breast, God has implanted a principle, which we call love of freedom; it is impatient of oppression, and pants for deliverance; and by the leave of our modern Egyptians I will assert, that the same principle lives in us," Wheatley wrote. For her, the white Americans' calls for liberty and their enslavement of Africans were diametrically opposed.[7]

The 1770s produced a rush of antislavery polemics, coming primarily from Christian writers, both white and black. There was a great deal of cross-fertilization between British and American antislavery thought, despite the growing tensions between the colonists and the British government. The leading British abolitionist Granville Sharp and American Quaker abolitionist Anthony Benezet, for example, distributed one another's writings and were influenced by them. Sharp, a devout Anglican, won the 1772 *Somerset* case in England, in which the runaway slave James Somerset was legally freed in a decision by the Court of King's Bench. Although the actual decision did not clarify the status of other slaves, it was widely believed in Britain and America that the decision had abolished slavery in England. This victory inspired greater agitation against slavery in America.[8]

Although the Quakers were not unanimously opposed to slavery, their denomination did produce some of the most forward-thinking antislavery critics in England and America, including Benezet. Thomas Paine regularly attended Quaker meetings as a child, and he wrote a scathing 1774 essay against slavery before his more famous pamphlet *Common Sense*. Paine argued that God had brought the crisis with Britain against the colonists because they engaged in slavery. "How just, how suitable to our crime is the punishment with which providence threatens us? We have enslaved multitudes, and shed much innocent blood in doing it; and now we are threatened with the same," Paine lamented. Slavery, he believed, would drive African slaves away from the Christian gospel. In late 1775 Paine expressed the hope that when Americans became independent—and "dependent only upon [God]"—their first act of gratitude would be to pass a law abolishing the slave trade and providing for gradual emancipation.[9]

The Quakers were not, however, the primary religious source of antislavery thought in the revolutionary era. Unlike Paine, the Quakers in America were disproportionately Loyalist, due to their pacifism and their deep financial and political connections with Britain. The Quakers did not embrace the Christian republican synthesis that produced the most challenging antislavery writing of the time. Instead, that challenge arose out of northern evangelical Calvinism, the Christian tradition that transformed Lemuel Haynes and many others into antislavery polemicists.

Antislavery sentiment had become widespread among New England Calvinists in the generation after Jonathan Edwards's death, even though Edwards's own views on slaveholding were ambiguous at best. Edwards's successors championed the moral code of "disinterested benevolence," or acting graciously on behalf of the wretched and weak. No one in America needed benevolence more than the slaves, so the New England Calvinists became particularly concerned with their plight. Edwards's son, Jonathan Jr., became an outspoken critic of slavery in the 1770s, noting that although the colonists had been "so jealous of our own liberties, and so cautious to guard against every encroachment upon them from our mother country; we have been so inattentive to our own conduct in enslaving the negroes." Northern-based Congregationalist writers from Edwards Jr. to Wheatley saw the hypocrisy in white Americans' fear of enslavement by the British, even as the Americans enslaved hundreds of thousands of Africans. To them, this contradiction was the height of selfishness.[10]

The Reverend Samuel Hopkins, one of Jonathan Edwards's chief disciples, was the most influential Calvinist writer on the question of slavery. Hopkins came face-to-face with the grim realities of American slavery when he became pastor of a church in Newport, Rhode Island, a city that was one of the hubs of the transatlantic slave trade. Although his words won him the disapproval of many in Newport, by 1776 Hopkins had begun vociferously condemning slavery as an affront to Christian republicanism.

Like Paine and Edwards Jr., Hopkins indicted American slaveholders as hypocrites and argued that slavery was a "sin which God is now testifying against in the calamities he has brought upon us." If Americans refused to reform that sin, then Hopkins did not believe they could reasonably expect God to deliver them from the British threat. Later in 1776, following America's declaration of independence, in an incendiary sermon delivered in Newport, Hopkins depicted slavery as a vicious violation of God's will. "This whole country have their hands full of blood this day," Hopkins proclaimed. "Enslaving of fellow creatures as these American states do, is a most abominable wickedness; and equally against the law of nature and the law of Christ. 'Tis self-evident, as the honorable

Continental Congress observed: 'that all men are created equal, and alike endowed by their creator with certain unalienable rights.'" Hopkins warned his audience that God would not only deny America its freedom but would destroy the new nation if it did not repent and rid itself of slavery.[11]

In 1776 and afterward, Hopkins's kind of admonition—that God would not let the Patriots win the war if they did not forsake slavery—became common. The anonymous writer of the tract *A Discourse on the Times* asserted that if Americans "would have the Lord on our side, we must set at liberty those vast numbers of Africans, which have so long time been enslaved by us, who have as good a right to liberty as we have." More positively, David Avery—the chaplain who prayed over the minutemen at Bunker Hill—argued that if the states would begin the process of emancipation, it would be a "pleasing omen of the happy issue of our present struggle for liberty." New Jersey Presbyterian minister Jacob Green forecast in 1778 that even if God allowed Americans to win the war without emancipation, guilt would dog them and perpetuate national calamities until slavery was abolished.[12]

The evangelical sentiments about the hypocrisy of slavery influenced a number of prominent founders. Benjamin Rush, a Philadelphia physician and key agitator for independence, became an exemplar of those promoting the Christian republican critique of slavery, even though he had shed the evangelical Presbyterian piety of his youth. In 1773 Rush called slavery a "hydra sin" that violated every biblical precept, warning Americans that they courted the judgment of God if they did not begin the process of emancipation. Similarly, John Jay of New York, a devout Episcopalian and future chief justice of the United States, wrote in 1780 that all the states should adopt plans for gradual emancipation. Until they did, he believed, all Americans' prayers for liberty would remain "impious" and hypocritical.[13]

Somewhat more surprising were the comments that leading southern founders—many of them slaveholders—made regarding the hypocrisy of Christian slaveholding. Probably the most memorable was Jefferson's statement in *Notes on the State of Virginia* that human liberty was a gift from God and that men provoked God's wrath when enslaving others. "I tremble for my country when I reflect that God is just," Jefferson wrote, and "that his justice cannot sleep forever." Jefferson never freed most of his own slaves, of course. He justified Virginia's lack of progress toward emancipation by claiming that ending slavery would unleash a race war between blacks and whites. Slavery might be morally repugnant to Jefferson, but for him, perpetuating it meant postponing a genocidal clash between the oppressors and the oppressed.[14]

At the Constitutional Convention of 1787, the Virginian George Mason aggravated the contradiction of southerners who lamented the existence of American slavery while at the same time owning slaves. In a debate over how much power a new national Congress would wield over slavery, Mason warned that slavery would cause Providence to curse America: "Every master of slaves is born a petty tyrant. They bring the judgment of heaven on a country. As nations cannot be rewarded or punished in the next world they must be in this. By an inevitable chain of causes and effects providence punishes national sins, by national calamities." Like the evangelical Christians who were critics of slavery, Mason saw a direct relationship between a nation's moral characteristics and its future welfare. Yet like Jefferson, Mason believed that freeing his own slaves would have been impractical and dangerous, and he never liberated any of them.[15]

George Washington stands out among the well-known southern founders in taking decisive, if late, action to free his slaves. In his will, he mandated the emancipation of his slaves following his wife's death. As early as 1794, when he was president, Washington had begun to express an interest in freeing, as he put it, "a certain species of property which I possess, very repugnantly to my own feelings." We can only speculate what drove the taciturn Washington actually to emancipate his slaves, whereas others like Jefferson, Henry, Mason, and James Madison shirked such an action.[16]

It is illuminating, however, to note that among the many factors influencing his beliefs and actions around slavery was Washington's correspondence with Phillis Wheatley, who in late 1775 had penned a poem extolling him. Wheatley was already well-known for her fervent antislavery letter written to Samson Occom, but even in the face of potential controversy, Washington invited her to visit him at his wartime residence in Cambridge, Massachusetts. Washington wrote personally to her and praised her "great poetical talents." Jefferson, by contrast, mocked Wheatley's poetry, writing that religion "has produced a Phillis Wheatley; but it could not produce a poet. The compositions published under her name are below the dignity of criticism." Jefferson's racism could not concede the talent of the African American poet, whereas Washington's encounter with Wheatley helped convince him of blacks' potential for education and refinement.[17]

Although the founders' aversion to taking action against slavery demonstrates the moral limitations of Christian republicanism, the new antislavery movement did produce some practical reforms, especially regionally. It won many quick and impressive legislative victories once the new nation had declared its freedom, putting slavery on the road to extinction in all northern states by the early nineteenth century. Vermont's constitutional ban on slavery in 1777 was followed by a series of gradual emancipation laws in the other northern states, concluding with New Jersey's in 1804. These laws usually declared that slaves born after the act's passage were free, and that young blacks should serve their mother's owner only until they reached adulthood, often age twenty-one.[18]

These considerable successes fade in light of the reality that emancipation efforts failed in the South, the states with the greatest numbers of slaves. Although antislavery movements made very little progress in the lower South, in the upper South in the 1770s and 1780s proposals for gradual emancipation were seriously discussed by state legislatures. A number of southern states passed laws that made private manumission easier. Thus, before the start of the nineteenth century, these small signs of progress offered hope to the southern antislavery movement.[19]

Also a factor in changing southern attitudes were the Separate Baptists, who, after their emergence from the Great Awakening, began to infiltrate the South during the 1750s, bringing with them radical notions about race. They established a Baptist stronghold at Sandy Creek, North Carolina, where they targeted blacks as well as whites for conversion—a practice they continued in their other mission areas across the South. Numbers of African Americans joined their churches in the revolutionary period. Separate Baptists often gave African Americans, Native

Americans, and women higher-ranking leadership positions than other churches, with nonwhites serving as exhorters, deacons, and even elders in the new Baptist congregations.

Some Baptists in the South viewed slaveholding as a sin, denouncing it with the moral clarity lacking in Jefferson's and Henry's equivocations. The Baptist pastor John Leland—Jefferson's ally, who would later bring him the "mammoth cheese"—labored in Virginia for fifteen years. He saw some of his greatest evangelistic successes during the war itself: In an eight-month stretch in 1779–1780, he baptized 130 converts. Leland did not restrict his work to the conversion of souls, however; he became one of the greatest advocates of the emancipation of slaves. Leland successfully promoted a resolution at the General Committee of Virginia Baptists in 1790 characterizing slavery as "a violent deprivation of the rights of nature, and inconsistent with a republican government; and therefore recommend it to our brethren to make use of every legal measure, to extirpate the horrid evil from the land."[20]

Although many of the local churches dismissed Leland's resolution, saying that slaveholding was a matter between a person and God, some Baptists in Virginia were convinced. Reverend John Poindexter wrote that he had once supported slavery, "but thanks be to God, my eyes have been opened to see the impropriety of it, and I long for the happy time to come, when the church of Christ shall loose the bands of wickedness, undo the heavy burdens, and let the oppressed go free." As for Pastor Leland, after leaving Virginia to return to Massachusetts in 1791, he continued to exhort his fellow Baptists to pray for the slaves' liberation, anticipating the millennial era when Christians would rejoice to witness "the great jubilee usher in, when the poor slaves, with a Moses at their head, should hoist up the standard, and march out of bondage!"[21]

Reverend David Barrow, Leland's Baptist colleague in Virginia, exemplified the evangelical antislavery impulse in the South. Like many other Baptist preachers in Virginia, in the 1770s Barrow came under sharp persecution by antievangelical Anglicans for his Christian radicalism. In 1778 a group of his tormentors nearly drowned Barrow in a mock baptism. Undeterred, the evangelist kept preaching, declaring his conviction that slaveholding was a sin that contradicted the best principles of the Revolution; he freed his own two slaves in 1784. Barrow stated in the deed of manumission that he was "sensible and fully persuaded that freedom is the natural and unalienable right of all mankind; and also having a single eye to that Golden Rule prescribed in sacred writ, 'do to all men as you would they should do to you.'" On the basis of natural rights and of the Bible, he felt compelled to liberate his slaves.[22]

The decision took its toll financially on Barrow. He relocated to Kentucky in 1798, worried that he could not support his family in Virginia without the use of slave labor. Nevertheless, Barrow continued to hope for the time when the slaves would be freed from the "iron talons of their task-masters." Barrow promoted emancipation in Kentucky and even corresponded with Thomas Jefferson, who told him in 1815 that although slavery would only disappear slowly in the South, the former president prayed that it would happen eventually. Like Leland, Barrow believed that one of the distinctive features of Christ's millennial reign would be the abolition of slavery. But because of slavery's economic value among white Baptists and many of their southern neighbors, and the conviction that slavery was an issue best left to one's private conscience, antislavery advocates like Leland and Barrow rarely saw their views translate into action in the Baptist churches of the South.[23]

Methodists in the South advocated even harder than the Baptists for emancipation of the slaves, going to incredible—although ultimately futile—lengths to remove the sin of slavery from their churches and country. The Methodists were a very small denomination in America at the outset of the Revolution, but they would grow explosively in the years following. Their great leader, the Englishman John Wesley, declared in 1774 that blacks were created equal to whites and that Christ had died for all. American Methodist leaders took up the cause of antislavery, too. In 1780 American Methodist preachers as a group denounced slavery, saying they were freeing their own slaves. Then, in 1784, the denomination made the most aggressive move against southern slaveholding of any group in the entire revolutionary era. Meeting in Baltimore, Methodist leaders denounced slavery, blending biblical authority with republican principles in declaring that slavery was "contrary to the golden law of

God . . . , and the unalienable rights of mankind, as well as every principle of the Revolution." These kinds of statements had been made before
by Americans, but the conference went on to add that in order to "extirpate this abomination from among us," they would require all members of
Methodist churches in America to begin emancipating their slaves. Those
who refused to comply would be expelled from the church, as would anyone who trafficked in the slave trade.[24]

Many Methodists found these decrees too extreme, and within six
months the antislavery policy was suspended. When Methodist leaders
petitioned the Virginia legislature in support of emancipation in 1785,
opponents reminded Virginians that most of the Methodists had not supported the American Revolution and suggested that British agents might
be behind the antislavery movement. The Methodists slowly backed away
from most penalties related to members' slaveholding and eventually even
published two different sets of church regulations, one for the lower
South with no comment on slavery, and one for the North and upper
South expressing opposition to slavery but containing few expectations
beyond obedience to state laws. After 1785 all the major Protestant denominations in the South removed the topic of slavery from official
church discussions, believing that the issue would only cause dissension
among their white members.[25]

In spite of diluting or rescinding their church policies on emancipation, the Methodists made considerable progress in encouraging individual members to free their slaves. One Methodist planter named Daniel
Grant decided in the early 1790s that despite the economic hardship, he
must begin freeing his slaves, who were "human creatures endued with
immortal souls capable of everlasting happiness or liable to everlasting
misery as well as our selves," he wrote privately. Other Methodist farmers followed this example. Hundreds, if not thousands, of manumissions
in the upper South in the 1780s and 1790s can be traced to the spread of
Methodist principles.[26]

Maryland evangelist Freeborn Garrettson freed his slaves after receiving a message from God telling him, "It is not right for you to keep
your fellow creatures in bondage; you must let the oppressed go free."
Garrettson recalled that he had never thought slaveholding was wrong

until that moment, but he immediately told his slaves that "they did not belong to me, and that I did not desire their services without making them a compensation." Garrettson became a traveling preacher, ministering to slaves and free blacks and agitating for their freedom. He recalled that one slaveholder, angered by Garrettson's emancipationist views, "came to the house to beat me: soon after he entered he began to swear, affirming I would spoil all his negroes." The man punched him in the face, but Garrettson refused to retaliate and continued imploring the man to stop his profane behavior. The assailant eventually gave up and left Garrettson alone. Garrettson took his message into North Carolina, where he preached regularly to slaves and privately sought to "inculcate the doctrine of freedom" in them, which caused more whites to turn against him. In addition to preaching to whites, Garrettson sometimes spoke in separate services for blacks, recording that "many of their sable faces were bedewed with tears, their withered hands of faith were stretched out, and their precious souls made white in the blood of the Lamb."[27]

Irish-born Methodist itinerant James O'Kelly also faced physical attacks because of his antislavery views. Even after most Methodist churches lost interest in the cause, he continued promoting emancipation, painting slaveholding as a debilitating, demonic kind of sin, "a work of the flesh, assisted by the devil; a mystery of iniquity, that works like witchcraft, to darken your understanding, and harden your hearts against conviction." As many white Methodists came to accept or even defend slavery, preachers like O'Kelly and Garrettson found themselves more isolated in the South. Black Methodists, who had converted by the thousands in the 1780s, understood the direction that the white Methodists were headed. When O'Kelly seceded from the Methodists in 1792 to form the Republican Methodist Church, many African American converts in the Southside region of Virginia followed him instead of remaining with the neutral or proslavery white Methodists. A few Methodists continued to promote emancipation and encountered vicious opposition. In 1800, when South Carolina Methodists tried to circulate petitions supporting gradual emancipation, Charleston residents burned the handouts. A mob dragged one of the Methodist preachers through the streets and nearly drowned him in a well.[28]

Southern Presbyterians, typically more socially moderate than their Baptist and Methodist brethren, showed less inclination toward emancipationist views. But a few exceptions did occur. One was the declaration by the Darien, Georgia, Committee of Correspondence in 1775, which would be the clearest antislavery statement produced in the lower South during the Revolution. Darien was populated largely by Scottish Presbyterians and had a decades-old record of antislavery opinion. In their resolutions against the British government, the Darien committee called slavery "a practice founded in injustice and cruelty, and highly dangerous to our liberties, (as well as lives,) debasing part of our fellow-creatures below men, and corrupting the virtue and morals of the rest" and stated that it was "laying the basis of that liberty we contend for (and which we pray the Almighty to continue to the latest posterity) upon a very wrong foundation." Only a tiny minority of white Georgians would agree with these sentiments, but the Darien committee argued that slavery contradicted the principles of American liberty and implied that it would provoke God's disfavor on the Patriot cause.[29]

Few Presbyterians would take as aggressive a stance against slavery as the Reverend David Rice, a pastor in Virginia and Kentucky. When Kentucky drew up its constitution in 1792, Rice made an eloquent plea for keeping slavery out of the state. Like many other antislavery activists, Rice used America's own egalitarian ideology to attack the institution, portraying African Americans as equal to whites before God. Slavery to him was America's great national sin. "The slavery of the negroes began in iniquity; a curse has attended it, and a curse will follow it. National vices will be punished with national calamities. . . . We now have it in our power to adopt [slavery] as our national crime; or to bear a national testimony against it." Despite Rice's powerful Christian republican arguments, he failed to convince the Kentucky convention, which adopted a measure legalizing slavery.[30]

The southern evangelical antislavery movement, a serious but limited force in the revolutionary era, was provocative enough to generate a proslavery Christian backlash, with writers arguing that the Bible countenanced or even promoted slavery. Although this backlash did not fully develop until the 1840s and 1850s, it began to appear before 1800. In

1798, John Lawrence of South Quay, Virginia, penned *Negro-Slavery Defended by the Word of God*, which asserted the popular belief that Africans were the descendants of Canaan. Canaan was the man mentioned in Genesis 9 as the son of Ham, cursed by his grandfather Noah to live in perpetual servitude. The Africans' blackness was, to Lawrence and his ilk, ostensibly a mark of that curse. Moreover, because the New Testament never forbade slavery, Lawrence reasoned, it must therefore be lawful to own slaves.[31]

The curse of Canaan theory had been in circulation among Christians long before the Revolution, but in the early national period it became the central tenet of biblical defenses of slavery. No traditional Christian would argue that Africans, as humans, were not descended from Adam and Eve, although some heterodox thinkers like Thomas Jefferson had speculated that the black and white races might actually have different origins, implying either that Africans were not fully human or that the Genesis creation account was simply not true. The curse of Canaan offered proslavery advocates the prospect of a time after creation when God condemned the putative forefathers of modern Africans to enduring servitude. But others challenged this interpretation. The Baptist preacher David Barrow mocked the notion of the curse of Canaan, noting that out of a relatively obscure Bible reference proslavery partisans had fashioned "a saddle for every horse" that answered every challenge to the morality of slavery. He thought no passage of the Scriptures had been more abused than Genesis 9, the chapter in which Noah curses Ham's son to be "a servant of servants."[32]

Whatever momentum the southern antislavery movement still possessed was blocked in 1800 by the rebellion led by a Virginia slave named Gabriel. Gabriel, a blacksmith, planned to raise an army of his fellow slaves and march against Richmond. But his plan was exposed, and Governor James Monroe called out the militia to quash the revolt. In the months after the rebellion was put down, hysterical fear of slave insurrection spread across the South; hundreds of slaves were executed, mutilated, or deported for their suspected roles in plots against slaveholders. Gabriel was rumored to have been inspired by the story of the Israelites' liberation from Egyptian slavery, which led southerners increasingly to fear the effect of evangelical faith on the slaves. Virginia and South Carolina subsequently passed laws forbidding slaves from attending religious meetings after dark, even in the presence of whites.[33]

Two decades later, in 1822, rumors of another revolt, this one instigated by a slave named Denmark Vesey, shot through Charleston, South Carolina. Vesey and many of his supposed conspirators had been involved with the African Methodist Episcopal Church in Charleston. (The African Methodist Episcopal denomination traced its origins to a separate black Methodist church founded in the 1790s by Richard Allen in Philadelphia.) At Vesey's trial, Benjamin Ford, a white teenager, claimed that Vesey applied his religious beliefs to slavery and politics. Vesey, he testified, "would speak of the creation of the world in which he would say all men had equal rights, blacks as well as whites [and] all his religious remarks were mingled with slavery." Richard Furman, the evangelical pastor of First Baptist Church of Charleston, rejoiced in the suppression of Vesey's rebellion and insisted that true Christianity was not to blame for the plot. Instead, he argued that truly Christian slaves obeyed their masters and that a correct interpretation of the Scriptures "tends directly and powerfully, by promoting the fear and love of God, together with just and peaceful sentiments toward men, to produce one of the best securities to the public, for the internal and domestic peace of the state." In Furman's ideal society, slaveholders would treat their slaves fairly, and slaves would revere and obey their masters. According to Furman's teaching, God not only tolerated but endorsed that kind of slave society.[34]

Some southerners still blamed evangelical faith for agitating slaves and encouraging restiveness in them. Frederick Dalcho, an Episcopal minister in Charleston, pointed to Vesey and his conspirators' association with Methodism, and to Methodism's tolerance of African American religious expression, and ascribed to that the origins of their plot. He asked rhetorically why his own Episcopal Church produced no conspirators among the slaves owned by its parishioners. Was it not because among Episcopalians, "there is nothing to inflame the passions of the ignorant enthusiast; nothing left to the crude, undigested ideas of illiterate black class-leaders [Methodist leadership positions]? Is it because the colored leaders in that Church, were not permitted to expound the Scriptures, or to exhort, in words of their own; to use extemporary prayer, and to utter at such times, whatever nonsense and profanity might happen to come into their minds?" Episcopal rationality and sobriety kept the slaves in check, Dalcho believed; the independence of mind and spirit offered by Methodists to blacks, particularly in the African Methodist Episcopal Church, led to insurrection.[35]

Dalcho also suggested that slaves should be kept away from Fourth of July celebrations, where they would hear invocations of human equality by creation. The combination of Christianity and republican ideals was just too dangerous, Dalcho believed; for him, the Fourth of July "belongs exclusively to the white population of the United States. The American Revolution was a family quarrel among equals. In this, the negroes had no concern; their condition remained, and must remain, unchanged. . . . In our speeches and orations, much, and sometimes more than is politically necessary, is said about personal liberty, which negro auditors know not how to apply, except by running the parallel with their own condition." To white southerners like Dalcho, the best way to prevent more insurrections was to keep slaves ignorant of evangelical faith and of America's egalitarian ideals. Then they would remain in their place.[36]

Once evangelicalism entered African American culture, its radical implications proved hard to contain. Once again in 1831, white southerners faced the terrifying prospect of a faith-driven insurrection among African Americans. This time the revolt was led by the visionary Nat Turner in Virginia. In the 1820s Turner began to receive a series of revelations from the Holy Spirit convincing him that he was a prophet (like Hugh Bryan eighty years earlier) chosen to liberate his people from slavery. The Spirit told him, he said, that the "Serpent was loosened, and Christ had laid down the yoke he had borne for the sins of men, and that I should take it on and fight against the Serpent, for the time was fast approaching when the first should be last and the last should be first." The insurrection began on August 22, 1831, when Turner and some seventy slaves killed about sixty white men, women, and children. The uprising was swiftly suppressed, and Nat Turner executed, but the revolt unleashed a paroxysm of violence by whites against suspected black conspirators, many of whom were dismembered and decapitated, their heads placed on poles as a warning to local slaves. Many white southern critics blamed evangelical itinerants for the revolt, because they incautiously filled their sermons to slaves "with a ranting cant about equality."[37]

The virulent reaction of white southerners to the antislavery movement would provide an unhappy end to the great promise of equality offered by the Christian republicanism of the American Revolution. Led by courageous activists like the minuteman and evangelical pastor Lemuel Haynes, antislavery advocates put northern slavery on a path to extinction by appropriating the ideal of equality by creation. Where slavery was most prevalent, in the agricultural South, antislavery sentiment flowered with early religious revivalism. Then, under the cultural pressures of southern society, it wilted. Leading slaveholders like Patrick Henry and Thomas Jefferson expressed ambivalence about slavery, but ultimately the weight of economics and racial prejudice made the antislavery movement anathema to white southerners. Evangelical and republican ideals combined to make the antislavery movement possible—an alliance of beliefs that triumphed in the North. In slavery's citadel, Christianity and republicanism instead came to bless the perpetuation of bound servitude. To dislodge slavery in the South would require not just faith or ideas but a terrible war.

CHAPTER 9

"One God, Three Gods, No God, or Twenty Gods"

Disestablishing America's State Churches

URING THE REVOLUTION, many of America's state-supported churches suffered, and none more so than the Anglican Church in Virginia. It effectively lost its state funding and struggled to pay its priests and maintain its churches. The Anglican Church also carried the burden of a close association with England and Loyalism. After the war, American Anglicans began calling themselves "Episcopalians" instead, to distance themselves from England, and reconstituted themselves as the Episcopal Church, but their problems persisted—and the church became the arena for a nationwide conflict over the official position of religious denominations in public life.[1]

Some Virginians sought to disestablish the Anglican Church and get the state out of the business of subsidizing any denomination. But Patrick Henry, for one, was not among their number; he and many of his allies wanted to resume public financial support for religion, because they saw well-funded churches as an essential component of a virtuous republic. At the same time, Henry knew that Virginia's non-Anglican churches were too strong to allow the state to return to an exclusive establishment of the Episcopal Church. Instead, he proposed what he called a "general assessment" for religion, which would require people to support, through taxes, the denomination of their choice. Henry's bill explained that "the general diffusion of Christian knowledge hath a natural tendency to correct the morals of men, restrain their vices, and preserve the peace of society; which cannot be effected without a competent provision for learned teachers [pastors], who may be thereby enabled to devote their time and attention to the duty of instructing such citizens." For Henry, strong religion required an established and thriving structure of churches of various denominations.[2]

Henry faced an uphill battle in promoting the general assessment, for dissenting evangelicals of Virginia and elsewhere hated established churches of any kind, whether Anglican or Congregationalist. Some loathed state-supported churches so much that they associated establishment with the diabolical beast of Revelation. Elisha Rich, a Baptist minister from Chelmsford, Massachusetts, wrote that the devil had imposed civil authority on the churches of England and America. State-sponsored churches replaced Christ with politicians who tried to govern the Kingdom of God by "worldly compulsion; which is open anti-Christianism."[3]

For many evangelicals in America, the Revolution presented an opportunity to end all forms of religious discrimination and let the gospel run free. They hardly sought a strict "separation of church and state" because they still expected the government to protect public morality and defend the general interests of religion. They believed, however, that official government preferences for particular denominations had to end. They further believed that as the establishments crumbled, Americans might set the stage for the downfall of Antichrist, the coming of the millennial kingdom, and the return of Christ.

Enlightenment rationalists like Thomas Jefferson and James Madison had little use for this talk of Antichrist and the millennium. Their desire for disestablishment came from their commitment to liberty of conscience, their belief that people should believe what they wanted, or not, with no interference by the government. But the rationalists and evangelicals arrived at the same conclusion: The government should stop policing religious beliefs, and no denomination should get favored treatment. This agreement on the public role of religion would become the American way of church-state relations.

For religion in America, disestablishment would prove to be the most significant political outcome of the Revolution. It meant that, outside of New England, the states would stop public funding for any particular denomination. Likewise, as stipulated by the First Amendment in 1791, the national government would be prohibited from creating a national established church. Increasingly, disestablishment also meant less restrictive theological tests for officeholders, or no such tests at all. Disestablishment did not mean that religion became a private matter, however. Almost no one in the revolutionary era expected that ending direct government support for religion would also remove faith from the public sphere.

O ver the course of the revolutionary period, every American state altered its church-state relationship. In states like Pennsylvania and Rhode Island that had had no established church prior to the Revolution, these changes were as modest as an official clarification of the religious qualifications for office holding, or a reassertion of the state's commitment to the free practice of religion. Pennsylvania's constitution of 1776 stated that all men had the natural right to worship God according to their own consciences and that no one should be forced to support any church financially. Benjamin Franklin, who chaired Pennsylvania's Constitutional Convention, tried to prevent the adoption of any religious test. The irenic Franklin was one of the only leading founders who announced himself publicly to be a deist. As he wrote in his *Autobiography*, however, Franklin's deism did not equate to atheism: He did not doubt "the existence of a deity, that he made the world, and governed it by his providence; that the most acceptable service of God was the doing good to man; that our souls are immortal; and that all crimes will be punished, and virtue rewarded either here or hereafter; these I esteemed the essentials of every religion." He did question the divinity of Jesus, and he believed that morality was the essence of true religion, not correct doctrine. As with Jefferson, Franklin's relative skepticism fed into a strong belief in liberty of conscience. Franklin wrote, "When a religion is good, I conceive that it will support itself;

and, when it cannot support itself, and God does not take care to support, so that its professors are obliged to call for the help of the civil power, it is a sign, I apprehend, of its being a bad one." The Pennsylvania convention did not agree with him on this point, and Franklin failed in his effort to abolish the religious test. Pennsylvania would require officeholders to declare their faith in God and the Christian Bible by swearing, "I do believe in one God, the creator and governor of the universe, the rewarder of the good and punisher of the wicked. And I do acknowledge the Scriptures of the Old and New Testament to be given by divine inspiration."[4]

Despite the efforts of Franklin and others opposed to religious tests, most of the revolutionary state constitutions included basic theological standards that public officials had to embrace. Delaware, for example, required officials to profess a belief in the Father, Son, and Holy Ghost, as well as the Old and New Testaments. As the century drew to a close and the newly formed states rewrote their constitutions and passed new laws, there arose a trend toward less theological specificity in tests. In 1790, a new Pennsylvania constitution expanded the qualifications for people in public office to include those who simply believed in God and in a system of future rewards and punishments—a standard that would include Jews.[5]

In New York, the move for disestablishment was fueled by widespread hostility toward elite Anglicans. The legislature had established the Church of England in four counties in colonial New York, but at the beginning of the Revolution anti-Anglican mob violence temporarily shut down most of its churches in and around New York City. Influential Anglican lay leaders like John Jay wisely cooperated in the move for disestablishment, helping institute in the state a new Episcopal Church aligned with the Patriots. The state constitution of 1777 allowed for the free exercise of religion with no discrimination against any denomination. Jay and others tried to insert a test designed to exclude Roman Catholics from serving in office, but the provision was voted down. A naturalization provision in the New York constitution, however, required citizens to renounce all foreign authorities "ecclesiastical as well as civil," a clear reference to the pope.[6]

In the northern states, Massachusetts saw the hottest contest over dis-establishment, but, over the protests of Baptists, the new state constitution of 1780 ultimately maintained a Congregationalist establishment. Baptist leader Isaac Backus of Middleborough emerged as the most articulate opponent of the Massachusetts establishment; he and the Separate Baptists had long suffered under a variety of fines and bureaucratic pressures for their resistance to supporting the Congregationalist churches. As New England entered the revolutionary crisis, the weight of establishment began to lighten, but a 1771 episode in Ashfield, Massachusetts, high-lighted the continuing conflict. When Massachusetts passed a law re-quiring them to support the local Congregationalist pastor financially, Ashfield's majority Baptists successfully appealed to London to overturn the statute—which led some Baptists to believe that the king was more committed to religious liberty than their home colony was. But most New England Baptists did support the Revolution, even as they used the Pa-triots' ideology of freedom to argue for relief from the Massachusetts es-tablishment. In his influential 1773 text on disestablishment, *An Appeal to the Public for Religious Liberty*, Backus contended that God would not hear the Americans' pleas for liberty from unfair taxes if they imposed such taxes on their own people.[7]

In 1774 Backus took his case for disestablishment to the members of the Continental Congress, where he got a cool reception from Massa-chusetts delegates John Adams and Samuel Adams; they told him that the Massachusetts establishment placed negligible burdens on dissenters and that (in Backus's words) they "might as well expect a change in the solar system, as to expect they would give up their establishment." The Baptists continued to agitate against the Congregationalist establishment during the Revolution, and in doing so they developed a largely unde-served reputation for disloyalty to the Patriot cause.[8]

Massachusetts attempted to adopt a new state constitution in 1778 that would endorse free exercise of religion but at the same time tacitly provide state support to Congregationalist churches. In response, Bap-tists garnered over seven hundred signatures on a petition insisting that the state constitution should adopt the basic principle that "religious ministers shall be supported only by Christ's authority, and not at all by assessments and secular force." The people of Massachusetts rejected the new constitution partly because it lacked a bill of rights, but the Baptists still worried about what form the state's governing document would eventually take.[9]

In these constitutional debates, Baptists became the objects of furious scorn and disdain, with their opponents accusing them of undermining the public virtue of the commonwealth. Reverend Phillips Payson, the Congregationalist minister of Chelsea, delivered a sermon before the Massachusetts assembly in May 1778, railing against attempts to disestablish his denomination. Because the fear of God represented the most powerful restraint on the sinful behavior of men, Payson avowed, only a state-supported church could properly inculcate dread of divine wrath. He disdained the lower-class, fanatical evangelicals who dared to challenge the established order—these ignorant ruffians only thought of their own freedom, not the good of the state. "Persons of a gloomy, ghostly and mystic cast, absorbed in visionary scenes, deserve but little notice in matters, either of religion or government," Payson told the state's lawmakers.[10]

Loathing of Baptists sometimes took more violent forms. In June 1778 a mob in Pepperell, Massachusetts, carrying clubs and poles and led by some town officials, confronted a group of Baptists gathered for a riverside baptismal service. The crowd demanded that the Baptists leave Pepperell and accused them of hatching "a Tory plan, the work of the devil, and such like." Some in the crowd dragged a dog into the river and baptized him in mockery of the Baptists. Others baptized men in a bowl of liquor. The Baptists quietly dispersed but were soon caught again by a crowd brandishing whips and demanding they get out of town. The Pepperell government passed resolves threatening violence against any Baptist preachers who included the town in their itinerations. Although this conflict was more extreme than most, it reflected the growing hostility toward Baptists among the backers of the Congregationalist establishment in Massachusetts.[11]

Baptists continued to push for an end to tax support for religion, but to little avail. The 1780 Massachusetts constitution (which, unlike the rejected 1778 version, was approved by voters in town meetings) included a provision for tax support of "public Protestant teachers of piety, religion, and morality." This system functioned as a general assessment for pastors, with taxpayers able to designate which pastor should receive their contribution. Previously, dissenters could apply for an exemption from paying the established pastor; now all had to pay but could choose the recipient. Baptists would still have to file certificates to redirect taxes to their own churches. The constitution also permitted the state legislature to require citizens to attend church services at certain times, but it made an allowance for those who would not attend a local church for reasons of conscience. Baptists found these regulations unacceptable because, in the words of John Leland, when a pastor receives his salary by legal force, "he ceases to be a gospel ambassador, and becomes a minister of state."[12]

A number of dissenting evangelicals objected vehemently to the religious terms of the new constitution. Dissenters in the town of Granville dryly noted that Jesus needed no help from the Massachusetts legislature to support his church. The town of Ashby recalled that most martyrs of the Christian faith had fallen victim to political authority over church affairs; Ashby's residents inferred that, by placing temporal authority over Christ's church, the people of Massachusetts were saying, "We will not have Christ to reign over us, . . . the laws of his Kingdom are not sufficient to govern us, [and] the prosperity of his Kingdom is not equally important with the kingdoms of this world." A popular writer using the name "Philanthropos" penned a series of articles against the constitution arguing that the document failed to distinguish between the Kingdom of Christ and the kingdoms of this world, while reminding readers that citizens of other states, such as New Jersey, Pennsylvania, and New York, supported religious institutions voluntarily without governmental coercion. Philanthropos also noted that the ancient Greek and Roman republics had supported excellent civil governments without the support of orthodox religion. Philanthropos's opponents accused the writer of representing Loyalist elements within Massachusetts. A writer named "Irenaeus" asserted that Philanthropos represented a pro-British force within the state, "a certain junto composed of disguised Tories, British emissaries, profane and licentious deists, avaricious worldlings, disaffected sectaries, and furious, blind bigots." The dissenters sought to factionalize Massachusetts, making it ready for British invasion, Irenaeus claimed; the opponents of establishment were the real enemies of religious liberty, because disestablishing the church would lead to rampant immorality and irreligion, destroying the freedom of all.[13]

Despite these kinds of attacks against them, Baptists in Massachusetts continued to push against establishment. They tested the legitimacy of the religious provisions of the 1780 constitution in the 1781 *Balkcom* case, a legal decision that seemed temporarily to end discrimination against evangelical dissenters. A Baptist layman in Attleborough, Elijah Balkcom, had been threatened in 1781 with imprisonment if he did not pay taxes to support the local Congregationalist church (he and others refused to file certificates to pay only the Baptist church). Balkcom decided to pay rather than go to jail, but he sued to recoup his money. A county court found in his favor, agreeing that the system of certificates legally preferred the Congregationalists and that this violated the principle of religious fairness endorsed by the Massachusetts constitution. Understandably, Isaac Backus and others saw the case as an enormous breakthrough, thinking it heralded the end of religious discrimination in Massachusetts. Backus equated the verdict's significance with the end of the American Revolution itself (which also came in 1781): In both events he divined the approach of Jesus's millennial kingdom, where the power to enslave men politically or religiously would be destroyed. The Baptists' joy was short-lived, however; in 1784 the Massachusetts Supreme Court held in a similar case that a Baptist was required to file the certificate.[14]

Despite their protests, the dissenting evangelicals could not convince the Congregationalists of New England that the principles of the Revolution logically required disestablishment. The evangelicals who sought equal treatment would have to wait until the Congregationalists ceased to be the majority in a significant number of Massachusetts towns. This development occurred in the 1820s when Unitarians (who believed in the moral authority but not the divinity of Jesus) formally broke off from the Congregationalists and formed their own denomination. Now religious pluralism—and competition among Unitarians, Congregationalists, Baptists, Methodists, and others—marked Massachusetts religious life. Ironically, a number of traditional Congregationalists, fearing that they themselves were becoming minorities in some areas, joined with the Baptists in 1833 to amend the state constitution and disestablish their church. No one was forced to pay religious taxes or file certificates redirecting their contributions any more.[15]

Connecticut also retained its church establishment during the revolutionary era, but with less controversy than in Massachusetts—thanks to the fact it did not adopt a new state constitution but simply revised its colonial charter to remove references to the king of England. Connecticut maintained public support of Congregationalist ministers through the efforts of pastors like Judah Champion of Litchfield, Connecticut, who was not only one of the most ardent supporters of the Patriot cause but a great defender of the established church. One weekend early in the war, a Continental Army cavalry regiment stopped in Litchfield for Sunday service. Everyone was worried about reports of the imminent British invasion of New York and Connecticut. Looking over the assembled regiment, Champion thundered that the British meant to destroy American liberty and religion, and he prayed from the pulpit, "O Lord, we view with terror and dismay the enemies of our holy religion; wilt thou send storm and tempest to toss them upon the sea, to overwhelm them in the mighty deep, or scatter them to the utmost parts of the earth." He prayed for the soldiers, as well: "Gird up the loins of these thy servants, who are going forth to fight thy battles. . . . Give them swift feet, that they may pursue their enemies, and swords terrible as that of thy destroying angel, that they may cleave them down."[16]

Champion defended not only the Patriot army but the established church, lauding it as a key safeguard of American liberty. He believed that people's civil and religious liberties were inextricably linked and should both be supported by state mandates. Although believers were individually free to read their Bible, pray to God, and join the church of their choice, for Champion the state had a responsibility to promote public morality and the health of religion. "In favor of virtue, to suppress immorality, and support religion, we have a system of excellent laws enacted, while different persuasions enjoy the most generous liberty and freedom," Champion declared. Like the Litchfield pastor, defenders of establishment in New England saw their constitutions as balancing the need for communal morality and individual religious liberty. Without virtue, the vengeance of God might turn against America, too.[17]

Radical evangelicals in Connecticut saw the establishment much differently than did Champion. The Separate evangelical movement there had been calling for relief from religious taxes since the 1740s, when Solomon Paine of Canterbury had called freedom of conscience an "unalienable right." With the outbreak of the Revolution, Separates led by Israel Holly of Suffield again petitioned the Connecticut legislature for complete religious freedom. Holly declared the time auspicious for such a move, because across America people were clamoring for equal rights and privileges in their fight against Britain. Echoing the language of the Declaration of Independence, the Connecticut Separates began their petition with the assertion that they had "an unalienable right, by the two grand charters, of nature, and scripture, to choose our religion." They denied that they had any ill will toward the Revolution and portrayed themselves as the truest Patriots. Many of the Separates fought for the American cause, but they found it disheartening to suffer religious oppression from the state on whose behalf they took up arms. In response to this compelling argument, the Connecticut assembly did offer some relief in 1777, exempting Separates who produced certificates from paying taxes to support the Congregationalist churches.[18]

Although this move nullified the most obnoxious feature of the establishment, Separates and Baptists continued to clamor for full religious freedom in Connecticut. In 1791 a law that tightened certification requirements for dissenters precipitated a memorable response from John Leland. Leland had recently returned to New England from Virginia and confronted the Connecticut establishment with the delightfully titled *The Rights of Conscience Inalienable, and Therefore Religious Opinions Not Cognizable by Law; or, The High-Flying Church-Man, Stripped of His Legal Robe, Appears a Yaho.* In words reiterating Jefferson's, Leland wrote that "government has no more to do with the religious opinions of men, than it has with the principles of mathematicks. Let every man speak freely without fear—maintain the principles he believes—worship according to his own faith, either one God, three Gods, no God, or twenty Gods; and let government protect him in so doing." The preacher had no doubt that the gospel of Christ would triumph in open competition with other religious beliefs.[19]

Even after the ratification of the U.S. Constitution, evangelical dissenters continued to struggle to win full disestablishment in Connecticut, and Leland and others found reason to rejoice when Thomas Jefferson was elected president in 1800. Although the personal religious sentiments of the Baptists and Jefferson could hardly have been more different, their views of religious establishments were very similar, which led the Danbury Baptist Association to write to Jefferson in 1801 hoping he might pressure Connecticut to drop its establishment. The new president replied kindly to the Baptists' letter and assured them that he did indeed share their convictions. He knew he could not change the minds of the Federalists who controlled the Connecticut legislature and who remained committed to the establishment of the Congregationalist denomination, but he hoped that they would take comfort in the fact that the national government, under the U.S. Constitution, could never institute an official religion. In words that have rung loudly through the constitutional debates over religion and the First Amendment, he wrote,

> Believing with you that religion is a matter which lies solely between man and his God, that he owes account to none other for his faith or his worship, that the legitimate powers of government reach actions only, and not opinions, I contemplate with sovereign reverence that act of the whole American people which declared that their legislature should "make no law respecting an establishment of religion, or prohibiting the free exercise thereof," thus building a wall of separation between church and state.

Jefferson surely wished that the states too would build such walls, but he and the Baptists would have to wait for the people of Connecticut to make that decision for themselves.[20]

The change finally came in 1818, when a new Connecticut constitution ended the establishment of the Congregationalist Church. Many Congregationalist ministers were devastated, blaming the debacle on a conspiracy of scoundrels and dissenting evangelicals. Prominent Congregationalist pastor Lyman Beecher believed that the opposition to establishment included "nearly all the minor sects, besides the Sabbath-breakers, rum-selling tippling folks, infidels, and ruff-scuff generally." Thomas Jefferson, on the other hand, celebrated "the resurrection of Connecticut to light and liberty."[21]

New Hampshire and Vermont also had Congregationalist establishments but supported them inconsistently, which, along with increasing religious diversity, wore down the state churches' strength. New Hampshire's 1783 constitution committed the state to freedom of conscience in religion. It also asserted, however, that "morality and piety, rightly grounded on evangelical [biblical] principles, will give the best and greatest security to government," and accordingly permitted state support for churches.[22]

The most explosive church-state issue in New Hampshire would occur well after the revolutionary era and focus on the control of Dartmouth College. Dartmouth was an evangelical Congregationalist school at its founding, but as the only college in New Hampshire it also received state support. When in 1815 the college president—an evangelical himself—tried to liberalize teaching and hiring policies in order to serve the public more fully, conservative Congregationalist trustees removed him from office. Critics of the trustees saw a malevolent design behind their action. "Junius" wrote in the *New-Hampshire Patriot*, "Lift the curtain, and you will behold a monster, horrid to the sight, grasping in his right hand the crown and mitre—his left hand pointing to the inquisition— trampling under foot religious freedom—and on his forehead labeled— UNION OF CHURCH AND STATE." A legal battle between the state government and the Dartmouth trustees landed in the U.S. Supreme Court, resulting in the landmark case *Trustees of Dartmouth College v. Woodward* (1819). Although the Court's decision affirmed Dartmouth's protected status as a private corporation, it also helped establish a much clearer distinction between private religious organizations and public nonsectarian ones. Private sectarian organizations like Dartmouth could no longer expect to receive state support. The Dartmouth controversy led to disestablishment in New Hampshire, which came in 1819 when the legislature enabled residents personally to exempt themselves from religious taxes.[23]

Vermont, like several other states, embraced religious freedom in its 1777 constitution, but it also insisted that all people must observe the Sabbath day and support some form of religious worship. Officeholders had to be Protestants and profess belief in the authority of the Old and New Testaments. Towns were allowed to determine their own systems for supporting the churches. Even under this light and local form of establishment, evangelical Baptists protested. Caleb Blood, a Baptist minister of Shaftsbury, Vermont, succinctly stated the Baptists' view of the establishment: "I am far from wishing to have America involved in the great error of blending the government of church and state together. But I heartily wish that all her rulers may be truly virtuous, and such as shall rule in the fear of God." Officeholders should not try to promote or support specific churches, Blood believed, but he certainly wanted faithful Christians in office to promote public virtue. In 1807 Vermont went on to make individual support for churches voluntary.[24]

With government subsidies for the Congregationalist churches persisting into the nineteenth century, the New England states maintained their official establishments of religion longer than anywhere else in the new nation. This arrangement was legally acceptable even under the First Amendment to the U.S. Constitution, which banned only a national establishment of religion. But the hypocrisy of maintaining unjust religious taxes, the tireless efforts of evangelical dissenters, and the growth of religious diversity would ultimately doom state support for New England's most long-standing religious denomination.

In the South, all states began the revolutionary era with Anglican establishments—and all substantially modified their relationship with the established church during that period. In most cases, the Anglican Church had a limited infrastructure in the South and held less popular sway than the Congregationalist Church in New England. Moreover, growing evangelical influence in the South weakened the Anglicans' hold. The Revolution's ideals of liberty helped end state financial support for southern religion as well.

In South Carolina, the state's 1776 constitution retained the primacy of the Anglican Church. Evangelical dissenters, led by William Tennent III of the Independent Presbyterian Church in Charleston, petitioned the assembly for relief in 1777. Tennent had developed impeccable patriotic credentials on the basis of his earlier tour of the backcountry promoting the rebels' cause—which he now employed on behalf of his religious cause. Tennent called for a repudiation of the Anglicans' favored status, declaring that the state constitution should give all Protestants equal religious and civil privileges. In his impassioned speech in support of the petition, Tennent used the logic of Christian liberty to expose what he saw as the hypocrisy of establishment. A love of liberty and equality inspired the Revolution, he said, and the evangelical dissenters should not be blamed for wanting rights equal to those possessed by citizens belonging to other churches; instead, the state should favor the general interest of Christianity without discriminating against any Protestant denomination. Dissenting congregations far outnumbered those of the Anglicans in South Carolina, yet dissenters still had to fund Anglican parishes. "EQUALITY OR NOTHING! ought to be our motto," Tennent declaimed. "In short, every plan of establishment must operate as a plan of injustice and oppression."[25]

The South Carolina constitution of 1778 disestablished the Anglican Church, but replaced it with a more general Protestant establishment: Officeholders had to be Protestants, and only Protestant churches could legally incorporate, which gave them favorable privileges under state law. Dissenters like Tennent were pleased with this general establishment system, for under it their churches were equal to those of the Episcopalians, with no church of any denomination receiving public funding. Even the Charleston Baptist Association was delighted, proclaiming that under the state constitution "our civil and religious privileges are established on the broadest bottom, and most permanent foundation." Moreover, inspired by the federal Constitution of 1787 and a recognition of contributions to the Revolution by Catholics and Jews, the 1790 South Carolina constitution removed even the provision incorporating Protestant churches alone, as well as theological tests for office holding.[26]

Georgia went through a process roughly similar to South Carolina's. Its 1777 constitution approved a general tax for Protestant churches, but in 1798 Georgia decreed that all financial support of churches should be voluntary.

North Carolina, however, was a more religiously complex place than its southern neighbors, which meant its path to disestablishment would be relatively brief. By the time of the Revolution, it had developed a reputation as a wild and irreligious place. Anglican itinerant Charles Woodmason lamented the conditions in the colony, saying that it was a "stage of debauchery, dissoluteness, and corruption." Evangelical Baptists and Presbyterians had begun to make serious inroads in the North Carolina backcountry, where dissenters now resented the privileged status of the Anglican churches. The 1776 state constitution abandoned the establishment, but required all officeholders to be Protestants and to affirm the inspiration of the Old and New Testaments. In 1809 the theological test for officeholders was challenged by the election of Jacob Henry, a Jew, to the North Carolina legislature. Although some protested that Henry could not assent to the truth of Protestantism or the New Testament, he responded that the unalienable right of conscience affirmed by the state constitution superseded the religious tests. Henry was able to assume his office.[27]

Of all the southern states, Maryland took the most circuitous path to disestablishment. The 1776 constitution there left the Anglican Church in place as the preferred state denomination and gave the legislature the right to lay a tax for support of Christianity. But its wording also seemed to prevent counties from collecting the revenues that had previously supported the Anglican parishes. The state legislature made periodic attempts to institute a general assessment to support all Protestant churches, but non-Anglicans saw these efforts as a plot to resume tax support primarily for Anglicans. Patrick Allison, a Presbyterian minister in Baltimore, warned that plots to coerce support for the Anglican Church would "ever raise a powerful alarm, unless the people are enslaved or asleep—an attempt of this sort has raised a powerful alarm, and a prosecution of it shall, with the countenance of heaven, be resolutely and successfully opposed." Non-Anglicans successfully opposed repeated schemes to resume state financing of the churches, and in 1810 Maryland repealed the constitutional provision that allowed the legislature to levy taxes for religion.[28]

The most fascinating and broadly significant effort toward disestablishment in the South—and in fact, in all the United States—transpired in Virginia. It would be there that the synthesis of evangelical and Enlightenment opposition to religious establishments would win its most important victory. Rationalist leaders, including especially James Madison and Thomas Jefferson, lent the evangelicals the weight of political influence that they lacked in the North, with evangelicals providing ballast as rank-and-file opponents of a state-supported church. The resulting combination would produce a stunning repudiation of Virginia's powerful Anglican Church.

By 1776 Virginia had halted its active persecution of dissenters and had promised religious freedom in the Virginia Declaration of Rights. But non-Anglicans in Virginia would hardly let the matter rest there, and in late 1776 they bombarded the Virginia House of Delegates with petitions calling for an end to the establishment of the Anglican Church. Baptists circulated a "ten-thousand name" petition praying that the legislature would follow the logic of freedom, and the Hanover Presbytery, where evangelical piety in Virginia had originated in the 1740s, made an articulate case for full religious liberty by appealing to the principles of the Enlightenment and Christian republicanism. "In this enlightened age, and in a land where all are united in the most strenuous efforts to be free, [we] hope and expect that their representatives will cheerfully concur in removing every species of religious as well as civil bondage," they declared. The logic of establishment, they wrote, was used to cruelly establish Islam in Muslim lands, and Catholicism in Catholic lands—did Protestant Virginia want to follow the example of Muslims and Catholics?[29]

Led by Jefferson and Madison, the Virginia legislature in 1776 did exempt dissenters from financially supporting the Anglican Church. This raised the thorny problem of how to distinguish genuine dissenters from tax evaders. Instead of confronting that issue, Virginia simply suspended the religious taxes altogether. From that point forward, the debate over church-state relations in Virginia centered around two primary options: complete disestablishment, or Patrick Henry's general assessment system in which every Virginian would be taxed for religion but would be allowed to designate the recipient of the funds. The general assessment had some powerful friends in Virginia, including George Washington. Washington deplored the controversy over assessment, but he wrote, "I am not amongst the number of those who are so much alarmed at the thoughts of making people pay towards the support of that which they profess, if of the denominations of Christians; or declare themselves Jews, Mahometans or otherwise, and thereby obtain proper relief." Even the Hanover Presbytery registered tentative support for the general assessment in 1784, arguing that the government had the right to support Christianity in a pluralistic fashion in order to maintain public virtue.[30]

Despite the formidable support for the general assessment plan, the partisans of disestablishment won the day. The alliance of Enlightenment rationalists and evangelicals defeated the plan through a combination of shrewd politicking and ideological appeals. Madison battled in the legislature against Henry and the supporters of the assessment and wrote the most famous document opposing the assessment, his *Memorial and Remonstrance* (1785). Madison argued that Christianity did not need state support to flourish and that state support actually enervated religion. More strikingly, Madison challenged the premise that the government needed a religious establishment to maintain public morality. Instead, the best government would protect the interests of religion "by neither invading the equal rights of any sect, nor suffering any sect to invade those of another." In Madison's view, disestablishment would protect anyone from having to financially support churches whose beliefs they did not share, and it would energize the expansion of Christianity in America.[31]

When Henry left the legislature to become Virginia's governor in 1784, Madison and the opponents of assessment got the assessment bill referred to the voters of the state. This move elicited an avalanche of popular protests against the assessment. A Baptist petition struck much the same tone as Madison's *Memorial and Remonstrance*, arguing that the bill contradicted the spirit of the gospel, for the "holy author of our religion needs no such compulsive measures for the promotion of his cause." About ninety petitions, mostly coming from evangelical churches, opposed the general assessment. Only about ten petitions supported the plan, leading the legislature to set it aside.[32]

The assessment's defeat led Madison to reopen debate on Jefferson's Bill for Establishing Religious Freedom, which had originally been proposed in 1779. Although Jefferson at that time was serving as American ambassador to Paris and was not present to advocate for it, Madison won the statute's passage in early 1786. Just as the Declaration of Independence based its argument for rights on equality by creation, Jefferson based the Virginia Bill for Establishing Religious Freedom on the principle of freedom of conscience by creation, asserting that "Almighty God hath created the mind free." Jefferson based religious voluntarism on the example of Jesus, who possessed the power to coerce people to follow him yet chose not to do so. Jefferson also marshaled the ideals of Christian republicanism, arguing that forcing people to support churches was both "sinful and tyrannical." He uncoupled theology and civil rights, however, asserting that "our civil rights have no dependence on our religious opinions, any more than our opinions in physics or geometry." He did not deny that public morality was essential to the health of a republic, but he did not believe that any particular doctrinal opinions promoted ethics better than others.[33]

At the end of the bill, Jefferson's language turned more purely toward Enlightenment principles. He confidently proclaimed that "truth is great and will prevail if left to herself, that she is the proper and sufficient antagonist to error, and has nothing to fear from the conflict, unless by human interposition disarmed of her natural weapons, free argument and debate." Although Jefferson personally believed that the unfettered progress of truth would reveal many errors in traditional Christianity, he still lived in a world where no one could conceive of a basis for public morality outside the realm of Christian ethics. This practical necessity explains his recourse to theistic, and even specifically Christian, claims for the rights of conscience. The bill concluded by mandating that no one should be compelled to support any church or denomination and that no one should suffer any civil penalties or disadvantages for their religious beliefs.[34]

The 1786 Statute for Establishing Religious Freedom did not end the controversy over church-state relations in Virginia. Baptists and others continued to push for Episcopalians to lose the benefits of their previously established status, especially their glebes (lands provided by the state for the support of the Anglican ministers). In an effort led once again by Madison, the state authorized the seizure and sale of the Episcopal glebes in 1802.[35]

From the early years of the Revolution to the start of the nineteenth century, Madison, Jefferson, and the evangelical dissenters had won a remarkable success in their repudiation of the religious establishment. They ensured that "free exercise" meant no privileged status for any denomination. Despite their considerable religious differences, the evangelicals and Enlightenment liberals of Virginia made common cause around their views of conscience and the public good. Nor was the alliance of Madison, Jefferson, and the evangelicals an arrangement of convenience alone. They shared significantly similar views on the public role of religion. They saw religious opinion and participation as a voluntary matter under the authority of God, not the state, and they did not want the state to discriminate against any group or individual for their religious beliefs, whether skeptical or evangelical. As of 1786, when the Bill for Establishing Religious Freedom was adopted, no one seems to have seriously contemplated that separation of church and state meant that the state should stop promoting public virtue or that the state should be hostile to the interests of religion. The need for public virtue remained a largely unquestioned belief of Americans steeped in Christian republicanism.

The essential question of church-state relations in the era of the Revolution was whether public virtue required the funding of a state church. If morality was so critical to the health of the Republic, then how could the state not fund churches? Dissenting evangelicals and Enlightenment skeptics like Jefferson and Madison ultimately won the argument by convincing people that religion was more likely to thrive with no state oversight or funding. As a matter of fact, they were correct. The late revolutionary era saw the beginnings of massive new revivals of religion—the Second Great Awakening—which would help transform America into a heavily Christian nation by the time of the Civil War.

CHAPTER 10

"Saving This Land"

Revivals and the Era of American Revolution

O N MAY 19, 1780, New Englanders looked up into the sky and be-held a smoky cloud moving over them, a pall so dark that some said it sent birds back to their roosts as if night had fallen. The smoke came from forest fires roaring through much of the region's backwoods, but the darkened heavens seemed like a sign from an angry God. The effect of the "Dark Day" on New Englanders was electric. An anonymous writer in Massachusetts concluded that the war and the ominous Dark Day presented compelling evidences that "these are the latter days, [and] the scriptures are daily literally fulfilling." The darkness seemingly warned Americans to repent of their sins, or God's gracious protection over America would cease. The following weeks saw frenzied excitement and large numbers of conversions, especially among the Baptists, in what became the climax of the series of wartime religious revivals rumbling through New England, known collectively as the New Light Stir.[1]

The revivals of the revolutionary era were not limited to New England. Baptist itinerant John Leland wrote of a spectacular awakening he witnessed in Virginia in 1785, just as the new nation was coming to terms with its hard-won independence. He witnessed many people overcome with the ecstasies of conversion, scenes in which "a great part of the congregation fall prostrate upon the floor or ground; many of whom entirely lose the use of their limbs for a season." Some penitents cried out for mercy; others praised God for his grace. Ministers and laypeople would exhort simultaneously at all corners of the meetinghouse. People jumped up and down, clapped their hands, and embraced one another, sometimes tumbling together to the floor. This "celestial discord" was criticized by some ministers, but to Leland it signaled the delightful presence of the Holy Spirit. The massive outbreak of conversions reminded old-timers of the Great Awakening of the 1740s.[2]

The distractions and exigencies of war inevitably hindered the activism of evangelical churches, but the conflict hardly sent them into decline. Instead, the period between 1776 and 1783 saw periodic outbursts of revival across North America, with a particularly intense paroxysm engulfing New England in 1780–1782. Then, in 1785, pent-up spiritual energy seemed to discharge under the combined force of the war's end and disestablishment, with Virginia seeing the most spectacular results. Because of the end of the war and the coming of disestablishment, an evangelical empire began to rise in America.

In 1775 and 1776, Virginia experienced the first major Methodist revival effort in America. The Methodists had originated as a renewal movement within the Church of England in the 1730s. Its primary leader, the Anglican John Wesley, had undertaken a mission to the new colony of Georgia in 1735, even though he had not yet experienced the new birth of conversion. While on the ship crossing the Atlantic to Georgia, he had a conversation with a German Moravian pastor who was traveling to the New World from Europe to expand the missionary work of his evangelical church:

"Do you know Jesus Christ?" the missionary inquired.

"I know he is the Savior of the world," Wesley responded.

"True, but do you know he has saved you?"

Wesley said, "I hope he has died to save me."

The conversation stripped away Wesley's facade of formal religiosity and set him on a quest to find what to him would constitute true salvation. A couple of years later in London, as he listened to a reading of

Martin Luther's *Preface to Romans*, his transformation came. "While [Luther] was describing the change which God works in the heart through faith in Christ, I felt my heart strangely warmed. I felt I did trust in Christ, Christ alone, for salvation." Wesley became convinced that the Church of England needed to focus only on the gospel of salvation by faith in Christ. He raised up legions of zealous preachers, who often were not ordained in the Anglican Church and had little formal training, and who would eventually split from the established church to form their own denomination. The Methodists continued to grow quickly in England through the mid-eighteenth century.[3]

Methodists had been late in coming to America, but starting in the 1770s, their hard-working itinerants quickly made up ground. In south-central Virginia, Methodist preachers witnessed hosts of conversions and dramatic revivals. "It was quite common," one Methodist reported, "for sinners to be seized with a trembling and shaking, and from that to fall down on the floor as if they were dead: and many of them have been con-vulsed from head to foot, while others have retained the use of their tongues so as to pray for mercy, while they were lying helpless on the ground." Often these boisterous meetings included both black and white Virginians. Even though the Revolutionary War had already begun, the Methodists' numbers swelled in one year in Virginia from about 2,600 to about 4,400.[4]

No denomination was hurt more by the war than the Methodists, laboring as they did under suspicions of loyalty to the British king. Back in England, John Wesley had denounced the American rebellion, and many of his American preachers fled the country during the war. Francis Asbury, Wesley's key organizer in America, went into hiding in Delaware. Methodists were subjected to persecution, and some preachers were jailed because of their purported support for Britain. Although periodic Methodist revivals transpired in Loyalist areas such as the Eastern Shore of Maryland, the Methodist network languished during the war. But at the war's conclusion, Methodists resumed preaching in force. Their postwar expansion was aided in part by the 1784 organization of an American Methodist Episcopal Church, independent of England's Methodist Church; the new denomination ordained its own ministers, which allowed it to operate more efficiently and disassociate itself from the specter of loyalty to Britain.[5]

Although the Methodist movement was thwarted and oppressed in wartime, not all evangelical churches suffered. Some thrived as shelters for the war's refugees and troubled souls; the radical evangelical churches of Nova Scotia experienced dramatic growth during the Revolution, for instance, fed by the arrival of people displaced by the war in the thirteen rebellious colonies. With no national border separating the Canadian from the American colonies prior to the war, religious trends flowed between them, especially between New England and Nova Scotia. There, with the outbreak of war, the New England–born evangelist Henry Alline led massive revivals. Unlike most of his New England evangelical counterparts, Alline maintained neutrality during the war and helped keep Nova Scotia in the British camp. Alline saw Nova Scotia as uniquely favored because of its preservation from the battles of the war, and he thanked God that although the American colonies had been "involved in the dreadful calamity, we have been blessed with that unparallel blessing, the moving work of the Spirit of God." Alline's neutrality represented the dominant evangelical position in Nova Scotia. Some African American evangelicals, who often supported the British side, fled to Nova Scotia during the war and became involved in Alline's revivals, too.[6]

The Nova Scotia revivals formed part of the larger New Light Stir, a series of revivals that occurred over the entire course of the American Revolution. The New Light Stir particularly energized the Separate Baptist churches of New England. Baptist leader Isaac Backus would chronicle the revivals as beginning in 1779 and increasing dramatically in 1780, becoming the most significant religious excitement there since the 1740s. He estimated that in Massachusetts and New Hampshire about 2,000 people had been baptized by immersion in 1780 alone. He went on to call the revival "a great means of saving this land from foreign invasion, and from ruin by internal corruption." Backus was one of the many Patriots who believed that public morality would preserve the American Republic, and he held that the best means of fostering public morality was through the salvation of sinners. The new revivals, in his estimation, played a direct role in delivering the Americans from the British.[7]

The Dark Day emboldened radical sects already appearing in New England. A couple of the most prominent sects featured bold female leaders. Jemima Wilkinson, a Rhode Island preacher who called herself the "Public Universal Friend," or the "P.U.F.," assumed her ministry after a near-death experience in 1776: as she lay hovering between life and death, she saw a vision of angels who told her that God had chosen her as an earthly tabernacle for the Holy Spirit. Wilkinson claimed that she had actually died and that the Spirit himself had taken command of her body. She pointed to prophecies in the book of Revelation about the "woman in the wilderness" and said they applied to her; she began predicting the imminence of the day of judgment. Rejecting her former identity as a woman, however, Wilkinson began dressing and wearing her hair in the style of a man; she had become a transgendered vessel of the Spirit. The P.U.F. taught that the Dark Day proved the validity of her predictions and that her followers should shortly expect the inauguration of the millennium.[8]

Similarly, the Shakers' messianic leader Mother Ann Lee dated that group's first public witness in America to the Dark Day. Lee had begun her preaching career in England; her followers called her "the true mother of all living in the new creation." Lee believed in celibacy, seeing sex as the foundation of sin. Indeed, to the Shakers, only the celibate could be saved. These "Shaking Quakers" danced, trembled, hopped, and laughed in their uproarious worship meetings. In the mid-1770s they relocated to New York, fleeing terrible persecution in England, but the weary group remained largely passive until the Dark Day, which for them signaled the "first opening of the gospel in America." They quickly gathered a number of converts from evangelical congregations in New York and New England. In the years before Lee's death in 1784, rumors swirled of the Shakers dancing naked in their services, speaking in tongues, and performing exorcisms of demons.[9]

Beyond the spiritual drama that defined the revivals of the Dark Day, the New Light Stir itself fueled a dizzying variety of evangelical sects. Back in the 1740s, the Separate Baptists had represented a radical evangelical challenge to the established order, but they were moderate in tone and theology compared with the groups that broke away from them during the revolutionary era. The new radicals embraced the ideal of individual conversions and intense spiritual experiences, but they challenged common Calvinist beliefs such as predestination (the belief that God alone chose who would be saved from hell). Among the most influential challengers to the Calvinistic Baptists in New England were the appropriately named Freewill Baptists.

Benjamin Randel, one of George Whitefield's very last converts, was the foremost organizer of the Freewill Baptists. Randel had grown up in a Congregationalist family opposed to evangelical principles, but he reluctantly went to hear Whitefield preach in Portsmouth, New Hampshire, shortly before the revivalist's death in 1770. Although Randel initially mocked Whitefield, the news of Whitefield's death shocked him; he was tormented by the thought that "Whitefield is now in heaven, and I am [on] the road to hell." Three weeks of spiritual struggling finally brought him through to conversion and assurance of God's forgiveness. Randel soon came to doubt whether the common Congregationalist practice of infant baptism was really a biblical dictate, and he agreed to be rebaptized by immersion as a believer, joining an evangelical Baptist church in Madbury, New Hampshire. During the war he began itinerating as a Baptist preacher, generating an intense local revival in New Hampshire in 1777. His emotional meetings also generated violent opposition from pro-Patriot locals who saw the revivals as frivolous distractions or Loyalist plots. Mobs threatened to tar and feather him, and he once narrowly avoided death by stoning.[10]

Thanks to his compelling doubts about predestination, Randel would come to challenge prevailing Baptist doctrine. In 1779, he took a pastoral position in New Durham, New Hampshire, but he was forced out after he ran afoul of Separate Baptist officials because of his questioning of Calvinism. Distraught, Randel retired to a secluded cornfield where, as he would testify, he encountered God: "I had no feeling of any thing, but the great and awful, terrible and dreadful majesty of God, which sunk me, as it were, into nothing." He envisioned a white robe being placed on him, and a Bible set before his eyes. A voice told him to look within the sacred text, and for the first time he saw the whole Bible in perfect harmony. In recounting the story, Randel could not say whether he remained in his body or not during this mystical experience, but as it continued he became utterly convinced that Jesus had died for all people and that anyone could freely accept God's offer of salvation. No longer would he preach that God had chosen only the elect for salvation and that the rest of humanity were consigned inevitably to hell. Randel began recruiting followers and establishing new churches that were soon competing with the Separate Baptists for adherents. By 1810 there were about a hundred Freewill Baptist churches in New England.[11]

Scots-Irish Presbyterian churches experienced significant revivals during the Revolutionary era, too, especially in Pennsylvania, where some of these awakenings were stoked by fears of Indian attacks and atrocities. A number of Native Americans had allied with the British during the war, and the American press stoked terror with reports of Native Americans launching brutal raids against the vulnerable frontier settlers. One newspaper letter writer from Fort Pitt (Pittsburgh) lamented that "our situation is more alarming than you have ever seen it" and that the western forts were becoming death traps. Many settlers in western Pennsylvania and Virginia had retreated to forts, but when the Natives attacked the forts became scenes of vicious hand-to-hand combat. Both sides took scalps and dismembered the deceased, even women and children. At the western Pennsylvania settlement of Vance's Fort in 1778, the preaching of a Presbyterian layman named Joseph Patterson precipitated a significant stir among Scots-Irish frontiersmen terrified from fighting with local Native Americans. Patterson spoke to his fellow settlers of "an enemy [the devil] more to be dreaded than the Indian, and a death more terrible than by the scalping-knife." The edgy Presbyterians reportedly attended the revival services with guns in hand. The awakening resulted in the formation of the Cross Creek Presbyterian Church.[12]

In the 1780s, revivals across western and south-central Pennsylvania led to more than 1,000 new members in rural Presbyterian churches. One of the largest awakenings happened in the western Pennsylvania church of Presbyterian pastor John McMillan, beginning in 1781. A revival broke out at the thanksgiving service appointed by Congress to celebrate the American victory at the Battle of Yorktown. "McMillan and his people were patriots," a local historian wrote, "and they mingled their thanksgivings for national blessings with earnest supplications for the presence of the Holy Spirit, now so much needed in order to lift up a standard against the floods of infidelity and irreligion which had come in during the war of the Revolution. While they were yet speaking, God heard them." Special prayer meetings often continued all night at the church, and large numbers joined the congregation in the coming years.[13]

Even though the conditions of war did not halt evangelism in America, many pastors and itinerants did testify that the conflict brought unprecedented difficulties and distracted many people from spiritual matters. "True religion is directly opposite to wars," Isaac Backus wrote of the revolutionary period. Pastors often had to flee the advancing British army, and many congregations and missions were broken up. A fledgling Baptist congregation in Cambridge, New York, was wrecked when the Battle of Bennington, a key conflict in the British campaign in upstate New York in 1777, turned to civil war within the church. A Baptist historian recounted that a number of men in the church, afraid that the Patriots would lose, went over to British general John Burgoyne's army the night before the battle. "During the bloody conflict the heavens and the earth witnessed the shocking spectacle of brethren, who, but a few days before had set together at the table of the Lord, arranged in direful hostility against each other, amidst the clangor of arms and the rage of battle. Brother fighting against brother! Such are the horrors and unnatural effects of war!" The church's pastor fled the area, and when he returned the next year, he could only gather three remaining members of his congregation. But out of suffering came a new revival, so that by 1780 the membership had grown again to 140 people.[14]

The end of the war opened new opportunities for revival. It also enabled the return of many Methodists, including Thomas Coke, who arrived from Britain in 1784 with a commission from John Wesley to create the independent American Methodist Episcopal Church. Within a year the Methodists began to expand their work into South Carolina, Georgia, the West Indies, and Nova Scotia.[15]

In 1785 signs of major new revivals began to appear within the Methodist preaching circuits, particularly in Virginia and Maryland. Soon new circuits were added in New Jersey, New York, and Kentucky, and the Methodist churches ballooned with new preachers and members. The postrevolutionary revival among the Virginia Methodists peaked in the summer of 1787, when thousands of whites and blacks attended fervent meetings. The spiritual power present in these assemblies was overwhelming. An early Methodist recalled that "some were lying and struggling as if they were in the agonies of death, others lay as if they were dead. Hundreds of the believers were so overcome with the power of God that they fell down, and lay helpless on the floor, or on the ground; and some of them continued in that helpless condition for a considerable time, and were happy in God beyond description." Congregants interrupted preachers with roars and screams. Even wealthy attendees fell down and soiled their fine clothes in sweat and dirt. People could hear the noise of the meetings from half a mile away. Thousands were converted in south-central Virginia in 1787, and before long the Methodist circuits spread throughout most of the rest of eastern North America.[16]

The Methodist revival continued in 1788, with particularly remarkable results in Baltimore, which then was the nation's fifth-largest and fastest-growing city, with about 13,000 residents. In 1788 the Methodists began preaching on Baltimore's town common on Sunday afternoons, attracting large audiences of non-Methodists. Methodist bishop Francis Asbury led a number of revival meetings in Baltimore, which were marked by an explosion of spiritual fervor in mid-September at the German Evangelical Reformed Church led by Philip Otterbein. The packed assembly became so overcome with emotion that while many were crying out for God's mercy, others became frightened and wanted to leave. The aisle was blocked with people, however, causing some to climb out the church windows. A number of attendees fell immobile in ecstasy to the church floor, later to rise up weeping for joy that their sins had been forgiven. The Methodists continued preaching to thousands in friendly Baltimore churches like Otterbein's, and hundreds of people experienced salvation.[17]

The Baltimore revival expanded in early 1789 in noisy, emotional meetings centered in the Fell's Point neighborhood on the waterfront. Methodist preacher Ezekiel Cooper, who led the meetings, recalled that the "heart rending cries and throbbing lamentations were truly awful to hear. In one circle on the floor thirty or forty at one time, besides many others in various parts of the house, lifting up their voices in penitential invocations: 'Save, Lord, save or we perish!' their gushing tears, like fountains flowing, and writhing agitations, like convulsive throes on the human frame, were enough to make the stoutest heart feel and tremble." Cooper estimated that at one meeting alone, thirty or forty people were converted. Meetings ran late into the night, and thousands of people swarmed around the meetinghouse trying to get in. Those who scorned the revivals said that these Methodists "worshiped God as if the devil was in us," Cooper wrote. Despite the growing opposition to the work, revival meetings like these continued in Baltimore and Fell's Point through most of 1789.[18]

The Methodists endured a great deal of contempt because their emotional piety attracted so many away from the older denominations. The Episcopal Church was still formally established by law in Maryland, but the 1776 state constitution had extended religious liberty to all Christians and had functionally de-funded the Anglican Church in the state. Ezekiel Cooper pointed to Maryland's protection of religious liberty as essential to the success of the 1789 revival; the Methodists' opponents were thwarted by state provision for civil and religious freedom. Cooper wrote, "We, feeling the benefits of a deliverance from this oppression, and seeking the blessed effects of a free, unshackled toleration in giving truth every advantage to defend its cause and gain the hearts of men, we most certainly should feel grateful, and ever praise the hand of Providence for knocking off every human compulsion over the conscience of men in our government." Cooper and the Methodists relished the opportunities presented by a free market of religion.[19]

The revolutionary-era Methodists embodied a new version of radical evangelical faith that had first emerged in the Great Awakening. Radical evangelicals were distinguished by aggressive evangelism and Spirit-filled religious experiences, including divine dreams, trances, and visions of spiritual beings, an ecstatic style that resonated with many common people. More moderate evangelicals were delighted to see sinners experience salvation, but they worried that radicals like the Methodists were breeding religious chaos. For Methodists, however, preaching up revival was not enough. They wanted to see the power of God manifested in the bodies, voices, and actions of ordinary people. The radicals' critics lamented the frenzied style of their preachers and exhorters, calling the Methodists everything from false prophets to secret agents of the British government. Methodist preachers like Freeborn Garrettson thought the critics were just envious of the Methodists' successes and frightened by the outbreaks of "wild-fire among the people." Garrettson frankly admitted that he did not mind hearing the calls, laments, and joyous shouts of repentant sinners and liberated saints; to him, they were the sounds of the Spirit.[20]

The radical style of the Methodists also appealed to a number of African Americans. Many blacks had resisted conversion because Christianity was the faith of their white oppressors, but evangelicals like the Methodists presented a more attractive kind of Christianity, thanks in part to their reputation at the time for being antislavery. In Delaware, the Methodists won one of their most influential converts, the slave Richard Allen, on a farm near Dover in 1777. Methodist preachers, led by Freeborn Garrettson, helped convert Allen's master, who then agreed to allow Allen to purchase his freedom for $2,000. Working at a host of jobs, Allen paid his master for his freedom in 1783 and immediately began itinerating as a Methodist preacher. Allen liked the Methodists' preaching style and quickly discovered that he himself could exhort successfully before not just blacks but whites too. In 1784 Allen preached for weeks in Radnor, Pennsylvania, to mostly white audiences. He recalled hearing them say that "this man must be a man of God; I never heard such preaching before." Allen said the extemporaneous style of the radical evangelicals was a mode of public speech accessible to poor whites and blacks: "There was no religious sect or denomination would suit the capacity of the colored people as well as the Methodists, for the plain and simple gospel suits best for any people, for the unlearned can understand, and the learned are sure to understand."[21]

Over time, the radicalism of the white Methodists inevitably waned, a situation that led Allen to found a new separate black denomination, the African Methodist Episcopal Church. Although Allen and other black Philadelphia pastors, such as Absalom Jones, had already begun to see the need for an independent African American congregation, an incident involving Jones at Philadelphia's St. George's Methodist Church confirmed their separatist inclinations. With the opening of a renovated sanctuary in 1792, black members of the church were expected to sit in a segregated section of the gallery. Absalom Jones tried to sit in the white section. As Allen memorably recalled, he and other African American members

expected to take the seats over the ones we formerly occupied below, not knowing any better. We took those seats. Meeting had begun, and they were nearly done singing, and just as we got to the seats, the elder said, "let us pray." We had not been long upon our knees before I heard considerable scuffling and low talking. I raised my head up and saw one of the trustees, H—— M——, having hold of the Rev. Absalom Jones, pulling him up off of his knees, and saying, "You must get up—you must not kneel here." Mr. Jones replied, "wait until prayer is over." Mr. H—— M—— said "no, you must get up now, or I will call for aid and force you away." Mr. Jones said, "wait until prayer is over, and I will get up and trouble you no more." With that he beckoned to one of the other trustees, Mr. L—— S—— to come to his assistance. He came, and went to William White to pull him up. By this time prayer was over, and we all went out of the church in a body, and they were no more plagued with us in the church.

Jones, cast out, went on to found the separate St. Thomas's African Episcopal Church, and Allen the Bethel Methodist Church, both of which became very popular among Philadelphia's African Americans. By 1800, about 40 percent of Philadelphia's blacks belonged to one of these churches. Even when their white brethren wavered in their commitment to racial equality before God, black evangelicals like Allen preserved the egalitarianism of their gospel in the new African American churches.[22]

The radical piety of the Methodists threatened the Congregationalist establishment of New England. Methodist itinerants began to appear in the region in the late 1780s. Congregationalists were wary of the work of radical evangelical preachers, just as they had feared the incursions of the

Separates and Baptists of the 1740s. Sometimes critics explicitly compared the Methodists to the enthusiasts of the Great Awakening. Methodist itinerant Jesse Lee met a man in Stratford, Connecticut, in 1789 who told Lee that he knew little about the Methodists but feared they might be like the New Lights of the 1740s. The man recalled how James Davenport, the radical leader of the Great Awakening, would scream at his congregations, beating the pulpit and foaming at the mouth, until the crowd would erupt into a chaos of shouts, tears, and extemporaneous prayers. Lee told the man that he actually hoped the Methodists could re-create such Spirit-filled scenes in Connecticut.[23]

The resistance of New England Congregationalists was not merely a matter of ecclesiastical style or even theological discord. For more mainstream denominations, the Methodists' brand of evangelism suggested disconcerting political implications. Old-line New Englanders worried that the Methodists represented a democratic Spirit-filled religion that would threaten the stability of church and state. After the war concluded, the democratic results of the American Revolution in politics and religion were nowhere less firmly established than in New England. Although the Congregationalist leadership supported the Revolution, they shrank from the prospect of republican government and disestablishment unleashing a populist free-for-all. The often uneducated and enthusiastic Methodists would not only fail to buttress public morality, in their view, but would also undermine the authority of the established churches.

A 1793 sermon by Congregationalist pastor Nathan Williams of Tolland, Connecticut, illustrated the established ministers' fears about the Methodists. In language reminiscent of the antiradical rhetoric of the Great Awakening, Williams warned of strange preachers who claimed immediate inspiration from the Holy Spirit and an apostolic right to preach whatever they wanted, wherever the Spirit led them. The local Congregationalist association encouraged Williams to publish his sermon "to suppress the confusions and disorders of late years occasioned in some parts of this country, by some strangers and transient persons who have assumed the appellation or style of *Methodists*." In an acerbic reply, Methodist itinerant George Roberts called Williams and the established ministers "wicked, designing men, that most effectually build up and promote the kingdom of Satan." Dissenters like the Methodists saw the establishments in Connecticut and Massachusetts as antichristian, while the established clergy and their supporters saw the state churches as essential for preserving public morality.[24]

In spite of the resistance they met from established churches and other institutions that favored the emerging nation's elite and its prosperous classes, the Methodists persisted in winning the allegiance of the common people, and their growth was stunning. Between 1781 and 1791 the American Methodists grew from about 10,500 members to 76,150. Not surprisingly, Methodist membership declined briefly in the mid-1790s, as the denomination faced internal squabbling over slavery and church leadership, and a reorientation toward the frontier West. But the Methodists had successfully transformed themselves from a small, struggling sect into an evangelical juggernaut, positioned to make even greater advances on the western frontier of a rapidly expanding young nation.[25]

Baptists and Presbyterians joined the Methodists in the revival movement of the 1780s. As was the case with the Methodists, many of their revivals were centered in Virginia, with some preachers spreading their influence into Kentucky and Tennessee. Hampden-Sydney College, a Presbyterian school in Virginia, experienced a major awakening in 1787. A small student prayer meeting faced threats from a student mob that complained that the pious students were "singing and praying and carrying on like the Methodists, and they were determined to break it up." Seizing on the spiritual interest shown by the students, college president John Blair Smith began preaching fervently at the school and in neighboring churches. About 225 people, primarily youths, became members at churches that Smith served. Within a year, the surrounding area had seen a great number of conversions. Older visitors to the region said they had seen nothing like it since the awakenings of the 1740s.[26]

Participants in the Presbyterian revivals realized that they touched all classes and races. Although the percentage of evangelical blacks remained low in the South in the 1780s, the message of liberation in Christ continued to draw more slaves into the fellowship of Virginia's evangelical churches. John Blair Smith's father Robert observed an African American

assembly at one of the Presbyterian revival meetings, where a black ex-
horter addressed the crowd, saying,

> We poor negroes were miserable, wretched creatures, taken captives
> and brought from our country in bondage here to men, and what was
> worse, slaves to sin and the devil. But oh! the goodness of God to us
> poor black folks. He has made us free men and women in Christ, joint
> heirs with his own Son. He has sent his servant to preach this gospel
> to us, who takes us to the Lord's table with himself, and calls us his
> brothers and sisters in Christ!

Within those words lay a powerful critique of slavery, similar to the one
that was latent in Jefferson's idea of equality by creation. But white southern Presbyterians, and other white evangelicals, usually did not carry these
antislavery implications to their logical conclusion and take on as a Christian mission the abolition of slavery.[27]

The Hampden-Sydney revival influenced a number of future evangelical Presbyterian ministers. James McGready, who would become the
most influential of these clergymen, had been converted at a Presbyterian communion service in Pennsylvania in 1786. In 1788 he traveled
through Virginia on his way to North Carolina, and stayed temporarily
with John Blair Smith to study the ongoing awakening at Hampden-
Sydney. McGready soon developed into an extraordinarily effective gospel
preacher, de-emphasizing peculiar and less appealing Presbyterian doctrines, such as predestination, and focusing only on the prospect of human
salvation and the equally compelling risk of damnation. McGready would
later recommend that preachers use every means possible to convince sinners that they were headed for hell: "Though the world scorn and revile
us, call us low preachers and madmen, Methodists—do this we must, or
we will be the worst murderers." For McGready, salvation was so literally
a do-or-die proposition that evangelical preachers could not worry about
politeness. In 1791 the preacher led a widespread awakening in north-
central North Carolina, while training a number of men to become ministers, some of whom would soon join him for an evangelical crusade
through pioneer Kentucky. McGready's confrontational, enthusiastic style

earned him many enemies. Antievangelical opponents destroyed much of McGready's church at Stoney Creek, North Carolina, and burned the pulpit outside the church. Inside they left a note, written in blood, threatening violence against McGready if he did not leave town. The Sunday after his church was attacked, he provocatively chose to preach on a text from the Gospel of Matthew: "Oh Jerusalem, Jerusalem, thou that killest the prophets and stonest them which are sent unto thee." McGready reconsidered the threat and moved to Kentucky in 1796, where he prepared to lead even greater revivals.[28]

Thanks to evangelicals' resilience during the war and growth during the mid-1780s, by 1796, as America neared the end of the revolutionary era, the country stood at the threshold of what would be called the Second Great Awakening—yet there was no major gap in revivals between 1775 and 1800, even as war and its aftermath fragmented the new nation. The leaders and participants in the revivalist movements self-consciously associated the new religious movement with those that had begun in the 1740s. To them, even with national independence promising a distinctively American manifestation of religious faith, the movement of God through the land persisted from the colonial era through the advent of the new nation.

In the early 1790s, new revivals began to ripple through New England. Chandler Robbins of Plymouth, Massachusetts, knew the New England revival tradition well; he was the son of the prominent Great Awakening revivalist Philemon Robbins. In 1793, with the conversion of scores of people in his Congregationalist church, Chandler Robbins saw his congregation emerge from what he called spiritual "stupidity." The town's character had changed so dramatically that some believed that they might be seeing what Robbins called the "commencement of that joyful period, so often spoken of in promise and prophecy . . . the latter day glory of the church." Expectations for dramatic spiritual change became more heightened, and 1798 saw a spate of awakenings in New England.[29]

The 1798 revivals emanated initially from the West Simsbury, Connecticut, Congregationalist church of Jeremiah Hallock, who, like most of the moderate evangelical pastors of New England, insisted that the new revivals be strictly controlled. "The work was by no means noisy, but rational, deep, and still," Hallock wrote. His attitude marked the tenor of the whole New England Congregationalist awakening. The energy of Congregationalist radicals such as James Davenport had long since been infused into the Baptist, Methodist, and other sectarian movements. The Congregationalist revivals were also self-consciously Calvinist, with Hallock reporting that difficult doctrines like predestination were now not only tolerated but relished among the people. Mainstream evangelicals could have their revivals, Hallock and his colleagues believed, while maintaining decorum at the same time.[30]

Isaac Backus reported that although the new revivals began among the Congregationalists in Connecticut, in Hartford the work of awakening was propagated by the Baptists. But Connecticut was only one state that experienced Baptist-led revivals. Backus noted that the most impressive church growth occurred in the new areas of settlement in upstate New York, Vermont, and Maine. The Bowdoinham Baptist Association of Maine, for example, was founded only in 1784, but by 1799 it encompassed thirty-two churches with almost 1,600 members. Maine saw phenomenal evangelical growth in the 1790s. In that decade, the radical evangelical churches—including Backus's Calvinist Baptists, the Freewill Baptists, and the Methodists—organized congregations in thirty-five Maine communities, even as the Congregationalists set up churches in only five Maine towns. The Congregationalists led revivals in the more established regions of New England, but they could not compete with the populist evangelical sects on the frontier.[31]

The Calvinist Baptists saw similar successes in evangelizing Vermont and western New York in the late 1790s. Tiny Shaftsbury, Vermont, saw 259 members added to its three Baptist churches in 1798 and 1799. The Otsego Baptist Association of western New York was founded only in 1795 with thirteen churches and 424 members, but by 1799 those numbers had risen to twenty-eight churches and 1,292 members. At an awakening in Hamilton, New York, in late 1798, many youths became convinced of the seriousness of their sins, and the "tongues of the saints were loosed" for fervent praying and exhortation. The Baptists boasted that a deistic reader of Thomas Paine's *Age of Reason* was converted in a

Hamilton revival. Fear of deism, the rationalist faith that was perceived by many people as a denial of the Bible and Christianity altogether, augmented the urgency of revivals, even on the frontier, where the fashionable ideas of Enlightenment religion had less currency than in the cosmopolitan cities.[32]

During the late 1790s, as the revolutionary era drew to a close with an effort to establish a firm political and financial basis for the new country, radical sectarians continued to find success in New England and New York. The Freewill Baptists of New Durham, New Hampshire, still led by Benjamin Randel, experienced a powerful awakening in June 1798 that manifested a "diversity of operations" of the Spirit. People cried out for mercy and fell into trances before breaking through to conversion. The revival went on for four days and attracted several thousand people. It energized Freewill evangelism across northern New England and New York, providing the groundwork for a religious movement that would find an even greater number of adherents in the America of the early nineteenth century.[33]

The most remarkable revivals of the 1790s happened in the new states of Tennessee and Kentucky. Most of the pastors in Kentucky in the late 1790s were evangelical Baptists, Methodists, and Presbyterians, many of whom had relocated there from Virginia or the Carolinas. The most influential pastor in summoning the storm of awakenings in Kentucky was James McGready, who had escaped death threats in North Carolina in 1796 and in 1797 became the pastor of three small congregations in south-central Kentucky. McGready and his revivalist Presbyterian colleagues imported into Kentucky the Scots-Irish tradition of the communion festival. These seasonal sacramental meetings sometimes drew crowds in the thousands and lasted for days. Eager attendees would sing, pray, counsel with pastors, and hear sermons, activities that culminated in a great celebration of the Lord's Supper during which believers would ceremonially eat bread and drink wine representing the body and blood of Christ. The combined effects of such occasions led to emotional revivals in Scotland, Northern Ireland, and America in the 1740s, and beginning in 1798, they did so again in Kentucky.[34]

McGready summoned devout followers to pray for revival beginning in 1797. In summer 1798, the prayers bore fruit with an outpouring of the Spirit that brought many to come to terms with their sins. In the summer of 1799, even greater portents of revival began to appear. Then, in August, the movement reached its crescendo at the Gasper River, Kentucky, congregation, pastored by a McGready convert from North Carolina, John Rankin. According to McGready, the day after the celebration of the Lord's Supper at Gasper River, "Many persons were so struck with deep, heart-piercing convictions [of sin], that their bodily strength was quite overcome, so that they fell to the ground, and could not refrain from bitter groans and outcries for mercy. The work was general with old and young, white and black." Many participants lamented their own religious hypocrisy and feared they were going to hell. The church at Muddy River, Kentucky, saw even more intense scenes in September, and in October McGready and Rankin held another ecstatic sacramental celebration at a church in north-central Tennessee.[35]

In 1800, the fervency experienced by the Gasper River evangelicals consumed hosts of Presbyterian congregations in Kentucky and Tennessee. At Red River, Kentucky, in June, many people were "slain in the Spirit," a phenomenon previously witnessed mostly in Methodist meetings: Participants lost their bodily strength, fell to the floor, and sometimes slipped into trances. Such manifestations had happened occasionally in the First Great Awakening, but among the early American Methodists they became common.

Another novel aspect of the Kentucky revivals was the prominent role of children as converts and exhorters. "It was truly affecting," McGready recalled, "to see little boys and girls, of nine, ten, and twelve years of age, and some younger, lying prostrate on the ground, weeping, praying and crying out for mercy, like condemned criminals at the place of execution." Parents considered these children old enough to understand their state before God, and revivalists marveled as the youths responded emotionally to the message of sin, judgment, and salvation.[36]

Revivalists reassembled at Gasper River in July 1800 for an event that became the first camp meeting of the movement that would burgeon into the Second Great Awakening. People traveled from as much as a hundred miles away and stayed through the weekend in the vicinity of the church. The Spirit's presence set in on Saturday evening, with many people staying up all night at the meetinghouse. McGready reported that many who had previously embraced a polite but superficial faith now experienced the power of God for the first time, falling on the ground and crying out for God's grace. Some young people who traveled from distant churches returned home and "attacked their young companions," telling them of the wrath of God against sinners with the kind of fervor that precipitated revivals throughout the Cumberland region of Kentucky and Tennessee.[37]

Revivals in Kentucky culminated in the massive Cane Ridge revival of August 1801. It was the largest revival meeting of the period and gained the most fame across the country. The planned sacramental celebration at Cane Ridge (near Paris, Kentucky) was advertised for more than a month, and evangelicals in central Kentucky had become well conditioned to expect spectacular results. Crowd estimates ranged widely from 10,000 to 25,000. This was at a time when Lexington, Kentucky (a town founded in 1775 and named for Lexington, Massachusetts) numbered only 2,000 residents. It seems unlikely that more than 10,000 people were present at any one time at Cane Ridge, but 20,000 or more might have attended at least one of the days of the camp meeting. The small meetinghouse could accommodate only 500 people when it was packed to capacity, so most of the activity happened outside, where preachers spoke from stumps and under tents. All manner of spiritual phenomena occurred at Cane Ridge, including uncontrollable shaking, laughing, barking, and falling. Critics said this was no way for Christians to behave and pointed to these reactions as signs of the revival's enthusiastic frenzy, but these manifestations only continued trends seen earlier in Kentucky and elsewhere. Meetings lasted well into the night, when the countryside took on an eerie, apocalyptic cast. One participant remembered that

> the ranges of tents, the fires, reflecting light amidst the branches of the towering trees; the candles and lamps illuminating the encampment; hundreds moving to and fro, with lights or torches, like Gideon's army; the preaching, praying, singing and shouting all heard at once,

rushing from different parts of the ground, like the sound of many waters, was enough to swallow up all the powers of contemplation. Sinners falling, and shrieks and cries for mercy awakened in the mind a lively apprehension of that scene, when the awful sound will be heard, "arise ye dead and come to judgment!"[38]

Although the size and intensity of the Cane Ridge meeting made it particularly notable, it was hardly the first or last meeting of its kind. Influences of the frontier revivals swept through the rest of the South in the next few years. The Carolinas saw a number of camp meetings conducted in the "Kentucky style," as Baptist minister Richard Furman put it. Methodists made the camp meeting central to their efforts at reaching rural populations.[39]

Over the next decades, as the Revolution became a memory and the American nation took on new dimension and character, the religious revivals of the 1780s and 1790s would prove themselves the prelude to a greater and even more pervasive and transformative religious movement. Baptists and Methodists continued to make enormous gains across the country as part of the broad and loosely connected Second Great Awakening. By 1850, the two denominations, which only eighty years earlier had been rather marginal sects on the American landscape, would hold more than 50 percent of the country's church memberships.

Although religious skepticism and deism retained influential advocates in America, critics of traditional Christianity simply could not compete with evangelicals for adherents. The revolutionary period presented logistical challenges to the evangelical movement, but evangelicals nevertheless came into the postwar period ready to expand far beyond the initial growth that had begun during the First Great Awakening. By 1800 evangelical fervor was sweeping both established and frontier regions of the country, transforming the lives of thousands and shaping America into a heavily evangelical nation in both style and numbers.

If the aging Thomas Jefferson was serious in 1822 when he predicted that antievangelical Unitarianism, with its ethical focus and liberal doctrine, would dominate American religion within a generation, he simply was not paying attention. Evangelicals such as Jefferson's friend John Leland had seized the momentum created by disestablishment and the cessation of war to conclude the revolutionary era with a surge of massive revivals. In 1819 Leland (with an obvious knack for religious statistics) recorded that in addition to preaching 8,000 sermons in his career, he had baptized 1,278 converts and itinerated distances across America that together would add up to three trips around the Earth. In American religion, Leland, not Jefferson, represented the wave of the future.[40]

CHAPTER 11

"If Men Were Angels"

Virtue, Freedom, and the Constitution

THE U.S. CONSTITUTION emerged from a crisis of virtue. By 1785 many political leaders had become alarmed about the ineffectiveness of the Articles of Confederation, the system of government that perpetuated the work of the Continental Congress after independence: an intentionally weak government made up of a national legislature. George Washington, for one, told John Jay, "We have probably had too good an opinion of human nature in forming our confederation. Experience has taught us, that men will not adopt and carry into execution, measures the best calculated for their own good without the intervention of a coercive power. . . . We must take human nature as we find it. Perfection falls not to the share of mortals." During the Revolutionary War and into the 1780s, many of the founders discovered that although consolidated political power jeopardized freedom, weak government could not make people act to serve the common good, even in times of national emergency. The best kind of government balanced power and freedom, and the Articles of Confederation, to Washington, erred too much on the side of freedom.[1]

Early in his tenure as general of the Continental Army, Washington grew personally and bitterly aware of the absence of coercive power under the Articles of Confederation. The army's persistently paltry supplies resulted from the Confederation Congress's lack of taxing power and authority to enforce laws. When General Washington needed more funds for the army, all he could do was ask nicely. The states often failed to respond. Soldiers suffered from a lack of adequate clothing and food and went months without pay. The darkest times came during the winter, when the armies temporarily stopped fighting and hunkered down in camp. Americans today remember the winter of 1777–1778 at Valley Forge as one of the army's bleakest moments, but the frigid winter of 1779–1780 at Morristown, New Jersey, was even worse. One American soldier remembered that during those months,

> we were absolutely, literally starved—I do solemnly declare that I did not put a single morsel of victuals into my mouth for four days and as many nights, except a little black birch bark which I gnawed off a stick of wood, if that can be called victuals. I saw several of the men roast their old shoes and eat them, and I was afterwards informed by one of the officer's waiters, that some of the officers killed and ate a favorite little dog that belonged to one of them.

Washington watched and fumed, unable to help.[2]

Even American merchants defrauded the Continental soldiers, selling them rancid beef and barrels of flour with the middle scooped out. Poorly paid teamsters, hired by the army to deliver supplies to the troops, were notorious for embezzling goods, wasting time, drinking heavily, and dumping their loads when roads became impassable. Farmers refused to comply with state price controls and sold their crops to merchant speculators instead of the army. The speculators then held out for the highest prices possible. American soldiers, too, engaged in rampant theft and fraud.[3]

The problems caused by this kind of avarice and ineptitude continued into the postwar period, aggravated by the crushing debts incurred by the national government during the war. Economically, the country became caught in a cruel standoff between creditors and debtors. The claims of domestic and foreign creditors, the debts of Congress and the states, and the debts of individuals all clashed, and there was no obvious means of resolution. The states sometimes found themselves faced with a choice between providing tax relief, or paying bills and inciting rebellion among desperate citizens. When some states tried to comply with congressional requisitions by taxing their citizens, indebted farmers in the states revolted, threatening law enforcement officials and shutting down county courts. By 1786 George Washington feared that if the nation went too long without a new federal form of government, some Americans would seek a return to monarchy.[4]

The postwar American government struggled badly with its inability to react to several other pressing issues as well. These included organizing western lands, securing fair international commercial arrangements from European powers, and confronting military threats from Britain, Spain, and the Barbary pirates of North Africa. The Muslim corsairs seized upon the new American vulnerability at the war's end and began capturing American merchant ships and imprisoning sailors. Americans were forced to choose between waging a naval war in the Mediterranean, which they were unprepared to fight, and enduring years of humiliating bribery to ensure the release of the American prisoners. They chose the latter option, and by the late 1790s the total American payoffs to the North African states would reach $1.25 million, or about 20 percent of the federal budget. All these problems required congressional leadership, but the preponderance of state power under the Articles of Confederation prevented decisive national action. Individual states could easily stall action on any issue.[5]

Washington, John Jay, Alexander Hamilton, James Madison, and other leaders all viewed these difficulties not only as political problems but also as issues of public virtue. The current government system, they concluded, failed to restrain the people's vices. Washington argued in 1786 that the success of the articles depended on unselfish behavior, but said, "Virtue, I fear, has, in a great degree, taken its departure from our land." Thus, in his view, the articles had to be revised. Yet practically speaking, they were almost unrevisable, because any amendment had to be ratified by a unanimous vote by the states. Because of the nearly impossible logistics of changing the articles, the crisis of the document's systemic inefficiencies grew intractable.[6]

Shays's Rebellion of 1786 and 1787 in Massachusetts confirmed many leaders' worst fears about the moral character of the people and the inability of the articles to ensure domestic order. The revolt began when debt-ridden farmers led by Revolutionary War veteran Daniel Shays tried to prevent the legal seizure of farmers' property by forcibly closing courts in western Massachusetts. In a showdown at the federal armory at Springfield, Massachusetts, in January 1787, the Massachusetts militia easily dispersed Shays's rebel army. The Shaysites remained angry, but they were overmatched by state power. Even though the rebellion was put down by March, advocates for stronger central government believed that the uprising proved their argument. These nationalists maintained that the country's government needed the power to tax and the power to suppress domestic rebellion; otherwise, America would remain at risk from the forces of populist tyranny. All that the Massachusetts farmers lacked for success, according to Alexander Hamilton, was effective leadership. "Who can determine," he wrote in Federalist No. 21, "what might have been the issue of [Massachusetts's] late convulsions, if the malcontents had been headed by a Caesar or by a Cromwell?" Episodes like Shays's Rebellion confirmed the nationalists' doubts about the people's ability to act benevolently, resist the siren song of demagogues, and pay the debts they owed. The crisis of virtue required decisive action.[7]

Fifty-five delegates assembled at the Constitutional Convention in Philadelphia in the summer of 1787. One-third of them, including Washington and Hamilton, were veterans of the Continental Army and were thus well familiar with the weaknesses of the Confederation government. The convention had been commissioned to propose changes to the Articles of Confederation, but it quickly became apparent that the delegates intended to do much more. Led by James Madison, they set out to transform the government from a confederacy of states into a national republic. By no means did they represent a unanimous opinion, even among the war's Patriots. Some leaders of the Revolution refused to participate in the convention. Patrick Henry, chosen to represent Virginia, told Hampden-Sydney College's John Blair Smith that he declined to attend the convention because he "smelt a rat."[8]

At a time when public support for religion was an open issue in an America that contained increasing religious diversity within its borders and that had just fought off the domination of a country with one established religious denomination, the very place of religion in the convention's deliberations became a matter of controversy. Most delegates at the convention wanted to carry on the proceedings in as nonsectarian a fashion as possible—a desire that resulted in the most remarkable episode related to religion to occur at the Philadelphia meetings: Benjamin Franklin's failed attempt to get the convention to open its sessions with prayer. As the delegates struggled to agree on the various powers of the government and an equitable system of representation, Franklin told delegates that their difficulties revealed the limits of human understanding. "In this situation of this assembly," he declared, "groping, as it were, in the dark, to find political truth, and scarce able to distinguish it when presented to us, how has it happened, sir, that we have not hitherto once thought of humbly applying to the Father of Lights to illuminate our understandings?" Nearing the end of his life, Franklin privately expressed doubts about Jesus's divinity, but he believed in Christ's ethical teachings and a God who answered human prayers. He reminded the convention that Americans had prayed persistently for divine protection during the Revolution and God had responded; they should do likewise in this moment of national import. But the delegates were unwilling to engage the thorny issues related to a choice of chaplain—what denomination would the pastor represent, for instance?—and Hamilton expressed concern that bringing in a chaplain might suggest that the delegates had reached a point of desperation in resolving the differences among them. The convention debated Franklin's request but failed to act upon it.[9]

Even without prayer, the delegates were able to cut through the most difficult problems at the convention, producing a final draft of the new Constitution in September. Congress under the new Constitution had the power to tax, to borrow money, and to regulate commerce. A powerful new president (the articles government had no executive branch) would serve as the commander in chief of the armed forces. Over the protests of some northern delegates, the convention agreed to count each slave as three-fifths of a person for the purposes of representation, which meant that white southerners would enjoy proportionately greater political power in Congress and in presidential elections through the beginning of the Civil War.

In one of its most notable omissions, the text of the U.S. Constitution contained no reference to God, a silence that scared critics. At least the Articles of Confederation had made an obligatory nod toward "the Great Governor of the World." Luther Martin, a Maryland delegate to the Constitutional Convention who opposed ratification, lamented the document's failure to mention God or to impose a basic theological test for officeholders. His argument was based less on articles of faith than on the necessity of encouraging moral rectitude in leaders. A minority of the convention's delegates believed, according to Martin, that "a belief in the existence of a deity, and of a state of future rewards and punishments would be some security for the good conduct of our rulers, and that in a Christian country it would be at least decent to hold out some distinction between the professors of Christianity and downright infidelity or paganism." The only direct reference to religion in the Constitution was a negative one related to religious tests. Unlike most of the state constitutions, the federal Constitution ensured that "no religious test shall ever be required as a qualification to any office or public trust under the United States." The Constitution took no positive notice of religion, except for guaranteeing free exercise in the First Amendment.[10]

Did such a Constitution represent a triumph of secularism, as Martin believed? It did not. Even though, more than two hundred years after the fact, polemical interpretations of the founding period by Christian conservatives and secular liberals have claimed otherwise, the framers of the Constitution intended to create neither a specifically Christian government nor a "godless Constitution." Instead, led by James Madison, they established a new government committed to maintaining public virtue. Encouraging that standard of rectitude began by diffusing power among political leaders and preventing the establishment of a national religion that could breed spiritual coercion and hypocrisy. Supporters of the Constitution—Christian evangelicals, Christian liberals, deists, and skeptics—all shared these goals. Yet the framers went further. They designed the Constitution with structures to prevent vice and to promote morality in the public sphere and in the actions of the government itself. The Philadelphia delegates sought to give the new national government enough power to overcome the self-ishness of the people, who seemed unwilling to support causes for the general good. At the same time, they feared giving the national government so much power that its leaders would become tyrannical. Some of the most contentious debates in the making of the Constitution centered on the balance of popular and political power. These included arguments about whether consolidated national power jeopardized religious freedom, whether "the people" had sufficient virtue to maintain a republic, and whether Americans needed a national government that extracted "from the mass of the society the purest and noblest characters which it contains," in Madison's words. These noble characters would lead the country in the equitable and righteous path, according to the defenders of the Constitution. No one doubted that only virtuous people could successfully govern the new nation.[11]

The Constitution's framers feared that any Christian or theistic language would provoke paralyzing sectarian arguments. William Williams, a delegate to the Connecticut ratifying convention, advocated for a much longer theistic preamble to the Constitution. His proposed new clause would have read,

> We the people of the United States, in a firm belief of the being and perfections of the one living and true God, the creator and supreme governor of the world, in his universal providence and the authority of his laws: that he will require of all moral agents an account of their conduct, that all rightful powers among men are ordained of, and immediately derived from God, therefore in a dependence on his blessing and acknowledgement of his efficient protection in establishing our independence . . .

Williams's language would have also served as a religious test for officials under the Constitution. The Connecticut ratifying convention did not recommend the preamble be added.[12]

Many evangelicals, deists, and Jews united in their opposition to religious tests like Williams's. One critic using the name "Elihu" denounced Williams's new preamble as a "Pharisaical harangue." Elihu, marshaling the still-powerful ideology of anti-Catholicism, argued that theological support for government was a trick of monks and priests to win converts, support, and money. Commonsense government needed no such sanction; it was the invention of human wisdom and experience. "No deity comes down to dictate it, not even a God appears in a dream to propose any part of it," Elihu wrote, and only religious fanatics wanted to mar the Constitution's brilliance with an inauthentic divine endorsement.[13]

Many American Christians opposed a religious test on more moderate grounds. An exchange in 1789 between George Washington and a group of New England Presbyterians revealed the common opposition of many conservative and liberal Christians to religious tests. The presbytery commended Washington for his ecumenical spirit and resistance to religious tests and establishments. They did express concern, however, that the newly enacted Constitution made no reference to God or Jesus. Washington replied that

> the path of true piety is so plain as to require but little political direction. To this consideration we ought to ascribe the absence of any regulation, respecting religion, from the Magna Carta of our country. To the guidance of the ministers of the gospel this important object is, perhaps, more properly committed—it will be your care to instruct the ignorant, and to reclaim the devious—and, in the progress of morality and science, to which our government will give every furtherance, we may confidently expect the advancement of true religion, and the completion of our happiness.

Washington advanced a positive but discrete relationship between church and state, in which clergy would steward the spiritual lives of Americans and the government would encourage moral public behavior. The "completion of our happiness" depended on both sides working together to promote the interests of religion and virtue, but government should avoid involvement with specific theological matters, according to Washington. His was an amicable separation of church and state.[14]

American Jews also opposed religious tests in the Constitution, especially tests that required assent to Christian doctrine. With some state constitutions mandating that politicians avow faith in the New Testament or in the divinity of Jesus, for instance, Jews understandably sought to exclude such standards from the Constitution. Jewish Revolutionary War veteran Jonas Phillips of Philadelphia wrote to the convention lamenting Pennsylvania's requirement that officeholders affirm the inspiration of the New Testament. Even as he urged that the convention include no such test, Phillips did not shy away from using the language of civil spirituality that both Jews and Christians could affirm. He prayed, he said, that God would "prolong his days among us in this land of liberty" and that the deity would continue to fight against America's enemies. Phillips and his fellow American Jews faced considerable resistance. Some Christians were alarmed that, in their view, the Constitution swung open the door for "Jews and pagans of every kind" to become officeholders, as one evangelical North Carolinian, David Caldwell, put it.[15]

If the Constitution, then, included no overtly Christian language and banned religious tests, and if the delegates declined to hire a chaplain to mark the proceedings with Christian piety, is the Constitution a secular document? Some of its framers said no. James Madison, the Constitution's chief architect, believed that God had helped the convention achieve unanimity. He thought it was "impossible, for the man of pious reflection, not to perceive in [the outcome of the convention] a finger of that almighty hand, which has been so frequently and signally extended to our relief in the critical stages of the revolution." To Madison and the Federalists, the Constitution represented America's greatest providential deliverance since the military victory over Britain.[16]

Subtler ethical and religious concerns also shaped the Constitution. Hamilton, Madison, and other defenders of the Constitution believed that its brilliance lay in its predisposition to empower educated, refined, and independent men—in other words, men of virtue. Their assumption that the elite were the most virtuous people may seem surprising to modern sensibilities, but the founders did not believe in populist democracy as today's Americans do. Most of them did not believe in pure government by the people, and the Federalists in particular feared that the circumstances of the poor and middling classes prevented them from acting out of public-spiritedness. A nationalized republic would mitigate the unruly democracy of the states through the "substitution of representatives, whose enlightened views and virtuous sentiments render them superior to local prejudices, and to schemes of injustice," Madison wrote. The Constitution, by limiting the number of national offices, particularly in the presidency and the Senate, would structurally favor American elites, men who could afford (literally) to distance themselves from selfish concerns and act on behalf of the country as a whole. Madison argued that the tension between good and evil in human nature required a republican system. He knew that human depravity required checks against political power, but he rejected the fatalism of those who believed that any centralized government would eventually become tyrannical. Madison believed that there was "sufficient virtue among men for self-government," but that virtue was not to be taken for granted.[17]

The Antifederalists, who opposed the ratification of the Constitution, also believed that a healthy republic needed virtuous men in positions of leadership, but they simply disagreed with the Federalists about how to ensure ethical, public-minded leadership and about how to thwart tyranny. They had less confidence in the inherent goodness of aristocrats. For them, diffusing power throughout the Republic, particularly among the people of the states, offered the best chance of preserving virtue. Patrick Henry, who became the leading opponent of the Constitution in Virginia, ridiculed the notion that taking power away from the states would promote more virtuous leadership. "The Constitution reflects in the most degrading and mortifying manner on the virtue, integrity, and wisdom of the state legislatures," he argued at the Virginia ratifying convention. "It presupposes that the chosen few who go to Congress will have more upright hearts, and more enlightened minds, than those who are members of the individual legislatures." If one followed Madison's logic of increasing virtue by narrowing the focus of power, Henry asked, then why not entrust all power to one man, a king? All politicians faced the temptation to put personal interest before public good, he said.

Spreading power among many people, legislatures, and states best maintained the ethical boundaries of governments. Under the new constitution, the people's rights rested on whether politicians were good or evil, Henry asserted. An evil president, controlling the armed forces, could easily become a tyrannical king.[18]

Madison and the Federalists shared Henry's worry about the dangers of consolidated power. But they balanced those concerns with a conviction that the national government needed more power to act in the public interest. In framing effective government, Madison argued, "you must first enable the government to control the governed; and in the next place oblige it to control itself." If a people gave the government too much power, it would become tyrannical, but if they gave it too little power, they would render it unable to act on the public's behalf. To Madison, the answer to this conundrum was to create a truly national republic in which substantial checks and balances among governmental power remained. Distributing power among the executive, legislative, and judicial branches addressed the natural human tendency toward corruption. Flawed politicians would counteract one another's worst intentions, but they would still be able to take positive and virtuous action. What more was government, Madison asked, than "the greatest of all reflections on human nature? If men were angels, no government would be necessary." For the Federalists, the fear of human sinfulness did not mean that people should accept utterly ineffective government.[19]

It was by no means guaranteed that Americans would ratify the Constitution. Once the debates began in the states in late 1787, America's religious denominations split within themselves over the Constitution. Some evidence suggests that evangelicals of the backcountry tended to oppose the Constitution, whereas more liberal or established Christians of the East Coast were more likely to support it. In New England, the widespread support of Congregationalist clergy helped secure ratification. Samuel Langdon, a Congregationalist minister of Hampton Falls, New Hampshire, participated in the New Hampshire ratifying convention and, like James Madison, celebrated the Constitution as the latest in a line of providential blessings on America. In 1788, when his state's decision on ratification remained in doubt, Langdon noted, "Only one thing remains to complete [God's] favor toward us; which is, the establishment of a general government. . . . If it passes the scrutiny of the whole . . . we shall have abundant reason to offer elevated thanksgivings to the supreme ruler of the universe for a government completed under his direction." Langdon still believed, however, that the best system of government could be ruined by selfish or impious people. Even government favored by God demanded people of virtue.[20]

Other American Christians believed that the Constitution was a fatally flawed document that put too much power in the hands of a few. Some said it threatened the nation's commitment to Christianity. Many dissenting evangelicals opposed the Constitution out of fear of consolidated national power, making their positions clear in the ratification debates, with a large number of ministers—about one hundred of all denominations—participating in the state conventions.[21]

One leading Antifederalist, the well-known Presbyterian minister David Caldwell of Alamance, North Carolina, opposed the Constitution because of the framers' presumption to speak for the entire populace. To him, the forceful new Constitution seemed like a dangerous usurpation of the power of the American people by the secret meeting of politicians at the Philadelphia convention. Caldwell repeatedly asked the convention how the framers could justify their opening phrase, "We the people," when they did not represent the people. At the outset of the North Carolina convention, he outlined what he called the "fundamental principles of every safe and free government," which included a compact between rulers and people, the retention of unalienable rights, and transparency of law. Like many Antifederalists, evangelical or not, Caldwell found the new Constitution wanting in these precepts.[22]

Caldwell also expressed concerns about the lack of a religious test for officeholders, fearing this omission would open the door to non-Christian politicians. He saw this not as an exclusively religious issue but as a political one as well, and he based his argument on familiar ethical grounds. Even those Americans who were not personally pious, he asserted, acknowledged that the Christian religion represented the best support for public virtue. For him, other religions, including Judaism, were not comparable substitutes for Christianity because they could not maintain moral behavior with the same effectiveness. He pointedly noted that real Christians should not welcome non-Christian immigrants from the "eastern hemisphere," because of their deleterious effects on the Republic; Christians should especially desire to keep these religious outsiders away if the Constitution might allow them to serve in office.[23]

On the issue of religious tests, the evangelicals hardly acted as a bloc. Caldwell's sort of views did not motivate even most evangelical Antifederalists. Baptist Antifederalists lauded the lack of religious tests and hardly believed that the lack of an establishment or a religious test would foster immorality or skepticism. Virginia's John Leland noted that the southern states, where disestablishment proceeded most quickly, had seen the greatest religious revivals in the late 1780s. He anticipated that disestablishment on the national level would lead to similar results. David Caldwell's fellow Presbyterian Antifederalist, the North Carolina judge Samuel Spencer, also disagreed with Caldwell on the religious test issue. Spencer came from an illustrious family of evangelicals; his mother was the sister of David Brainerd, a celebrated missionary to the Indians, and his uncle Elihu Spencer was a Presbyterian minister who had toured backcountry North Carolina in 1775 rousing support for the Revolution. Samuel Spencer, although opposed to the Constitution generally, agreed with the framers' decision to omit theological standards. He asserted that freedom of conscience was an unalienable right and that the nation should establish no religion, much less a denomination. The lack of a religious test, he declared, "leaves religion on the solid foundation of its own inherent validity, without any connection with temporal authority; and no kind of oppression can take place."[24]

Even though leading Antifederalists like Caldwell and Luther Martin pushed for the inclusion of a religious test, there was no consensus among the Constitution's critics on that matter. More typically, Antifederalists' concerns about religion revolved around the reduction of the states' power, the maintenance of public virtue, the guarantee of free exercise of religion, and the absence of a Bill of Rights. Antifederalists widely assumed that the promotion of religious and moral interests could happen effectively only on the state level. If the new, nation-centered Constitution made no positive commentary on religion, they reasoned, it might then bode ill for the public role of religion in the states.

Antifederalists commonly called for a religious freedom amendment to be included in the prospective Bill of Rights that many delegates to the state conventions were demanding. The Constitutional Convention had failed to include a Bill of Rights in the September 1787 draft. Madison had originally not put a Bill of Rights in the Constitution, believing that it raised unnecessary problems for ratification. He and Hamilton also believed that the Constitution should simply not comment on fundamental rights, in order to avoid giving the impression that a single document could comprehensively list all the rights that the government was bound to protect. Some future leader might construe a list of rights as the only rights the government should preserve and hold that all others could be sacrificed. But during the state convention debates Madison realized that popular support for a Bill of Rights was so strong that he had to promise to deliver one in order to win ratification. Many Antifederalists feared that in the absence of a religious freedom amendment the national government might give preference to a specific denomination over others. As the Antifederalist "Federal Farmer" wrote, Americans might not disagree much about the public role of religion in 1788, but "when we are making a constitution, it is to be hoped, for ages and millions yet unborn, why not establish the free exercise of religion, as a part of the national compact." Many Antifederalists, especially evangelical Baptists, agreed.[25]

One of the Federalists' most important tasks was to convince Baptists to support the Constitution. John Leland originally opposed the Constitution because of fears that it left open the door to religious oppression without an explicit statement of freedom of conscience. The Virginia Baptist General Committee agreed with Leland and declared unanimously in March 1788 that the Constitution did not do enough to ensure religious liberty. Leland, campaigning on behalf of an Antifederalist running to be elected delegate to the Virginia ratifying convention, publicized a list of objections to the Constitution. Among them were the lack of a Bill of Rights, insufficient safeguards against national tyranny, and, most especially, the failure to secure religious liberty. Leland did commend the absence of a religious test, but he envisioned a scenario in which a majority in Congress and the president might favor one denomination and force taxpayers to support it. If the Constitution did not lead immediately to religious oppression, it would only be because of the fair-mindedness of officials, not because of any constitutional safeguards. "If the manners of people are so far corrupted," Leland argued, "that they cannot live by republican principles, it is very dangerous leaving religious liberty at their mercy." Like Patrick Henry, Leland expressed serious doubts about trusting in the perpetual good will of politicians to maintain liberty.[26]

Yet Leland eventually became convinced to support the Constitution. He was confident that James Madison and George Washington would support passage of a religious freedom amendment. Baptist tradition holds that Madison and Leland actually met in March 1788, prior to the Virginia ratifying convention, and that Madison prevailed upon the minister to support the Constitution.

Madison's overtures to the Baptists helped bring about a significant turn toward the Constitution in their opinions. Madison himself was narrowly elected to the Virginia ratifying convention upon the promise that he would promote a religious freedom provision and other constitutional amendments. By January 1789 some Baptist ministers in Virginia had begun campaigning for Madison for Congress, and Madison personally contacted Baptist minister George Eve in January 1789 to assure him of his support for an amendment guaranteeing "the rights of conscience in the fullest latitude." Within weeks, Eve reportedly defended Madison's candidacy at a meeting at Blue Run Baptist Church and "spoke long" on Madison's commitment to religious freedom, reminding the Baptists of Madison's sponsorship of the Bill for Establishing Religious Freedom in 1786.[27]

By mid-1789 the Virginia Baptists had come full circle on the Constitution. They wrote to George Washington, saying that though they had initially felt doubts about the Constitution's protection of religious liberty, they believed that Washington's administration would secure their rights. Washington assured them that "no one would be more zealous than myself to establish effectual barriers against the horrors of spiritual tyranny, and every species of religious persecution—For you, doubtless, remember that I have often expressed my sentiment, that every man, conducting himself as a good citizen, and being accountable to God alone for his religious opinions, ought to be protected in worshipping the deity according to the dictates of his own conscience." Their views of religious liberty had made the Virginia Baptists reluctant supporters of the Constitution, but the leadership of rationalist Christians like Washington and Madison helped cement these evangelicals' devotion to the new national Republic.[28]

The New England Baptists also wrestled over whether they should back the Constitution. Although many of his fellow New England Baptists opposed the Constitution because of its centralization of power, Isaac Backus joined Leland in supporting the new system of government, and at the Massachusetts ratifying convention, he commended the absence of a religious standard for officeholders because "no man or men can impose any religious test, without invading the essential prerogatives of our Lord Jesus Christ." Imposing theological tests led inexorably to tyranny, he believed. He noted that some were concerned that the lack of a religious test might open the door to a non-Protestant establishment of religion. Backus reckoned, based on the struggle against the Congregationalist establishments of New England, that the imposition of a Protestant establishment by means of a religious requirement was a much greater risk.[29]

The Baptists were a small but critical constituency in gaining ratification. The dynamics of ratification proceeded differently in each state, but the Federalists' successful courtship of Baptist leaders like Leland and Backus helped secure approval for the Constitution in Virginia and Massachusetts—where ratification passed by only small majority votes. By taming evangelical hostility toward the Constitution, Madison and his allies undercut the dissent of this frequently unruly cohort.

The promise of a religious liberty amendment calmed many evangelicals' fears about the nature and intentions of their new federal government. Several of the ratifying conventions had specifically requested such an amendment. Patrick Henry pushed for and won a recommendation in Virginia that the national government would not establish or prefer any religious group. True to his word, Madison championed the Bill of Rights in the first Congress in 1789. He faced opposition from some staunch Federalists, as well as from some Antifederalists who knew that including the bill would preclude their efforts to hold a second constitutional convention to overhaul the document. Nevertheless, Madison took the recommendations of the several states and boiled them down to a slate of amendments on issues including trial by jury, the right to bear arms, freedom of speech and the press, and freedom of religion. The ensuing congressional debate on the religious freedom or establishment clauses proceeded along the same lines as had the state debates over religion. Peter Sylvester of New York objected to a no-establishment clause because he feared it might "have a tendency to abolish religion altogether"; Roger Sherman of Connecticut reprised the Federalists' argument that the amendment was unnecessary because the Constitution granted the new government no authority regarding religion. Madison and others, however, saw the religious freedom and establishment clauses as ways to reconcile disaffected Antifederalists to the new government. Following debate in the House and Senate over the amendment's language, Congress agreed to the principle that they would "make no law respecting an establishment of religion, or prohibiting the free exercise thereof." These clauses formed part of the first amendment of the ten in the Bill of Rights, which were formally added to the Constitution in late 1791.[30]

The First Amendment was a triumph for both the dissenting evangelicals and the Enlightenment rationalists. The two socially and theologically disparate groups each did its part to prevent America's national government from practicing religious persecution or giving preference to one religious group at the expense of others. The focus of the First Amendment was on restricting the power of the government from enforcing certain beliefs or favoring a specific church. More liberal champions of religious freedom, such as Madison, played essential roles as political leaders, but the popular momentum for religious freedom and disestablishment came primarily from rank-and-file evangelicals, especially Baptists. Some opponents of the Constitution still wondered if the new government might prove hostile to the interests of Christianity, but evangelicals widely believed that disestablishment and free exercise would create an environment suited for the flourishing of true religion, not the growth of secularism.

The ratification process produced as many rifts in America's public religious consensus as any moment in the revolutionary era. Nevertheless, when Americans celebrated the adoption of the new Constitution, they did not hesitate to proclaim its religious significance. At a massive parade in Philadelphia on the Fourth of July, 1788, clergymen were centrally positioned in the festivities. Patriot leader Benjamin Rush commented that the clergy "manifested by their attendance their sense of the connection between religion and good government." Seventeen clergymen, including one rabbi, marched together, and organizers sought to have the most dissimilar clerics walk together arm in arm. "There could not have been a more happy emblem," Rush believed, "contrived of that section of the new Constitution which opens all its power and offices alike not only to every sect of Christians but to worthy men of *every* religion." For Rush, the banning of religious tests was an endorsement of authentic religious pluralism and of a positive role for all religious communities in the new nation.[31]

Even the Enlightenment rationalists saw the hand of God in the adoption of the Constitution. Like Madison, Rush (a Presbyterian, and later a Universalist who believed all people would be saved) was convinced that Providence had intervened in the framing and ratification of the Constitution, even to the point of supplying favorable weather for that Philadelphia parade. Many at the parade half-jokingly remarked that "heaven was on the federal side of the question." Despite local conflict and very close votes in some conventions, the Constitution had been ratified in ten months. Rush did not believe that God had inspired the language of the Constitution, but he did avow that the document was "as much the work of divine providence as any of the miracles recorded in the Old and New Testament." A centralized national government committed to public virtue, disestablishment, and free exercise of religion had been successfully created. "'Tis done!" Rush exulted: "We have become a nation."[32]

The Constitution did not endorse secularism. It erected a shelter for free religious practice and at the same time responded to the need for public virtue. It did not seek to promote any particular denomination. By refusing to do so, it made Christianity in America stronger than ever. Evangelicals pounced on the opportunities created by disestablishment to spread the gospel of the new birth throughout the country, with no fear of persecution from the national government or from most of the states.

The First Amendment hardly ended controversies over the public role of religion in America. In the early national period, Americans who agreed on the need for public morality began to feud over the legal details involved in propagating virtue. In the absence of state churches, many traditional Christians still defended ceremonial and legal connections between church and state, including public days of prayer and fasting and laws requiring observance of the Sabbath. Conservative Christians encouraged public virtue by campaigning against social ills such as dueling, alcohol abuse, and Sunday delivery of mail. Sometimes they also fought for the rights of Native Americans and enslaved African Americans. But the most fascinating test of the revolutionary-era synthesis between evangelicals and deists would come at the end of that era, during the 1800 presidential election, when the "infidel" Jefferson was poised to become the nation's leader.[33]

CHAPTER 12

"Jefferson—and No God!"

The Election of 1800 and the Triumph of Religious Liberty

THOMAS JEFFERSON'S victory over John Adams in the election of 1800, and the peaceful transfer of power that followed, was the final act of the American Revolution. Jefferson himself later termed it the "Revolution of 1800," calling it "as real a revolution in the principles of our government as that of 1776 was in its form." He believed that Adams and his Federalist Party had led the new nation astray, back toward monarchy and an overly friendly relationship with Britain. They had also curtailed America's most prized possession, its liberty, through the Alien and Sedition Acts (1798). Jefferson's presidency was hard-won, his election a trying experience for the new Republic. A very close result in the Electoral College threw the contest into the House of Representatives, which voted thirty-five times without achieving the required majority to elect the president. Finally, a deal with moderate Federalists broke the impasse, and Jefferson was elected. It was the first time that Americans experienced the trauma of a closely contested national election, and it ended without bloodshed. A Jeffersonian newspaper exulted that "the Revolution of 1776, is now, and for the first time arrived at its completion."[1]

Americans drew diametrically opposed conclusions about the religious significance of Jefferson's election. Some Federalists saw his victory as portending apocalypse. The *Gazette of the United States* (Philadelphia), the nation's leading Federalist newspaper, repeatedly printed a notice in the fall of 1800 that instructed Americans to ask themselves, "Shall I continue in allegiance to GOD—AND A RELIGIOUS PRESIDENT; or impiously declare for JEFFERSON—AND NO GOD!!!" Certain New England Federalists reportedly hid their Bibles when they learned that Jefferson had been elected, fearing that Jefferson's minions would come to confiscate them. Other American Christians saw Jefferson's election in an entirely different light. The Danbury Baptist Association wrote to Jefferson in 1801 congratulating him on the election. "We have reason to believe," the Baptists told him, "that America's God has raised you up to fill the chair of state out of that good will which he bears to the millions which you preside over." They prayed that God would keep Jefferson safe and bring him "at last to his heavenly Kingdom through Jesus Christ our glorious mediator." For many Baptists and other Jeffersonian Republican evangelicals, Jefferson's election did not represent the triumph of infidelity—the era's popular term for godlessness and atheism—but a great providential victory for religious freedom.[2]

The campaign of 1800 between Jefferson and John Adams tested the fragile consensus regarding the requirements for personal faith of officeholders in America. In the name of religious freedom, the Constitution had banned religious tests, which left many religious Americans worried that the provision would allow skeptics and non-Christians to assume places in the national government. In the election of 1800, those fears were central to the presidential contest and to America's unfolding definition of the place of faith in its government and in the lives of its leaders.[3]

Jefferson's own distinctive religious beliefs were an incitement to controversy in a way that the faiths of his predecessors had not been. Few Americans had raised questions about the personal beliefs of George Washington or John Adams, the first two presidents under the Constitution, even though neither man was known to profess particularly traditional Christianity. Washington commanded so much reverence and spoke so highly of public religion that no one would presume to criticize his personal piety or theology. He was probably a rationalist but orthodox Episcopalian, but he hardly ever spoke of his personal faith. Most Americans agreed with evangelical Baptist minister Richard Furman of Charleston, South Carolina, who extolled Washington's belief in "God's superintending providence; his special interposition in favor of the just and innocent; his attention to the prayers of his supplicating people; and the necessity of religion, for the support of morality, virtue, and the true interests of society." Without doubt, Washington believed in Providence, prayer, and public religion. As for John Adams, although he was personally inclined toward Unitarianism (which denied the traditional Christian doctrine of the Trinity), he also affirmed the public value of religion. Adams used Christian language in official proclamations, as in a 1798 announcement of a national day of prayer and fasting, when he summoned Americans to ask God "of his infinite grace, through the Redeemer of the world, freely to remit all our offences, and to incline us, by his Holy Spirit, to that sincere repentance and reformation" that would elicit God's favor. Although some of his Republican opponents tried to accuse Adams of holding unorthodox beliefs, Adams's willingness to employ Christian rhetoric on such occasions largely shielded him from questions about his own faith.[4]

Jefferson's personal religious views became a political problem largely because of events outside his control, especially the violent anti-Christian actions of the French Revolution. Inspired in part by ideals of the American Revolution, the French Revolution had begun in July 1789 when rebels stormed the Bastille, a fortress-prison in Paris, setting off a surge of popular unrest across France. By the early 1790s France's revolutionaries had targeted both the monarchy and the established Catholic Church, murdering hundreds of priests and forcing tens of thousands more clergy into exile. King Louis XVI was executed by guillotine in January 1793. Jefferson would be broadly associated with the French Revolution and its brutal assault on religion and state institutions. As Americans grew more alarmed about its implications for faith and democracy in their own country, he would be implicated by their fears.[5]

In spite of its extraordinary assault on Christianity and tradition, most Americans responded positively to the early stages of the French Revolution, with many interpreting news of the Catholic Church's troubles through the persistent ideology of anti-Catholicism. Baptist Elias Lee of

Connecticut spoke for many in America when he presented the French Revolution as the latest providential victory for liberty and republicanism: "The horn of Antichrist is broken amongst [the French], civil and religious monarchy expires, and true liberty and freedom, wafted on the wings of providence, in defiance of millions of enemies, hail a general revolution." To Christians like Lee, the revolutions in America and France possibly portended the beginning of a global campaign against civil and religious tyranny and the imminent arrival of the millennium.[6]

Views of the French Revolution changed dramatically when the anticlericalism in France seemed to threaten traditional faith in America as well—a threat aggravated by the 1794 American publication of Thomas Paine's *The Age of Reason*. Paine, the great pamphleteer of the American Revolution, avidly supported the rebellion by the French against the monarchy. He traveled to France in 1791 and joined the French National Convention, where he voted to convict Louis XVI for crimes against the state, though he opposed the decision to execute him. The relatively moderate Paine ran afoul of radicals, the Jacobins, who imprisoned and nearly executed him during the Reign of Terror of 1794. Only a clerical error at the jail saved him from the guillotine.[7]

The Age of Reason launched a scathing attack on traditional Christian faith. Paine was no atheist, and he did not accept the radical French revolutionaries' rejection of any belief in the divine. Nevertheless, his attack on institutional Christianity fell just short of French revolutionary atheism. Paine pronounced his own simple, individualistic faith: "I believe in one God, and no more. . . . I do not believe in the creed professed by . . . any church that I know of. My own mind is my own church." He excoriated the Bible as full of fables and immoral violence and explicitly denied the most basic tenets of Christianity, including Jesus's divinity, virgin birth, and resurrection. His shocking claims found an eager audience in America, where seventeen editions of *The Age of Reason* appeared between 1794 and 1796. Understandably, *The Age of Reason* precipitated a heated response from Christian critics in America. The Episcopal priest Uzal Ogden of Newark, New Jersey, furiously wondered which of Paine's qualities was most conspicuous in the despicable book: "the weakness of his intellects, the depravity of his mind, or the impertinence of his conduct!"

The pamphlet provoked numerous rebuttals, including a screed by David Nelson with the self-explanatory title *An Investigation of That False, Fabulous and Blasphemous Misrepresentation of Truth, Set Forth by Thomas Paine* (1800).[8]

Opponents of Paine not only attacked him for his openly espoused antichurch deism but also associated it directly with Thomas Jefferson. Jefferson indeed shared many of Paine's doubts about Christianity, although he had been reticent about expressing them. His most provocative comments on religion would come well after his tenure as president when, in personal correspondence written mostly in the 1820s, he attacked the Bible and evangelical theology in the most vicious terms, while disavowing belief in the divinity of Jesus, the miracles of the Bible, and the Trinity. But if he held those incendiary views earlier in his political career, he mostly kept them to himself.[9]

Jefferson nevertheless had a connection with Paine, an association for which his opponents reviled him. In 1791, when he was secretary of state, he had unintentionally endorsed Paine's *The Rights of Man*, a defense of the French Revolution. Upon the book's publication, Jefferson had written to a Philadelphia printer that he was pleased with Paine's stance against "political heresies which have sprung up among us." His remark was a not-too-subtle reference to Vice President John Adams's public criticism of the French Revolution. To Jefferson's surprise, printers began using his comment as a headnote for future printings of *The Rights of Man*.[10]

Growing fears about the supposed atheism of Paine and Jefferson spilled into the American political arena in 1796 during the first American presidential election to have two serious candidates: Adams and Jefferson. The framers of the Constitution had not anticipated the forming of political parties, nor did they envision public election campaigns, but George Washington's retirement unleashed unprecedented political partisanship. Neither Adams, the victor, nor Jefferson, the runner-up (and thus vice president under the Constitution's original rules) campaigned openly for the office. Others did campaign for—and against—the leading candidates, however, employing the sort of personal attacks that would fully emerge in the 1800 election. Jefferson's Federalist opponents painted him as an unbelieving friend of Paine and the French. A writer in New

York's *Minerva* newspaper asserted, "We are not Frenchmen, thank God that made us—we are not like them. And until Mr. Bache's [a Philadelphia publisher's] sale of his twenty thousand copies of the second part of Paine's *Age of Reason* shall be finished, and until the atheistical philosophy of a certain great Virginian shall become the fashion (which God of his mercy forbid) we shall never be." Federalist leaders William Smith and Oliver Wolcott blamed Jefferson's supporters for circulating *The Age of Reason*, speculating that, as president, Jefferson would invite Paine into his administration, and "this enlightened pair of philosophers would fraternize, and philosophize against the Christian religion."[11]

Even some of Jefferson's supporters regretted his attachment to French atheism. Samuel Adams wrote to Paine accusing him of turning against the tradition of the American Revolution. No two people could take more credit for starting the American Revolution than Samuel Adams and Tom Paine, but now Adams asked him, "Do you think that your pen, or the pen of any other man, can unchristianize the mass of our citizens?"[12]

After 1796, during John Adams's tenure as president, the fear of French military power and atheism escalated. Adams inherited from the Washington administration an undeclared naval war with France. Once Louis XVI was deposed and executed in 1793, the United States had also reneged on debts to France, arguing that its loans were owed to the French monarchy, not the new French Republic. The French retaliated by seizing American ships in the Atlantic Ocean. Tensions between the two former allies grew worse in 1797 when American peace negotiators in Paris faced demands from French diplomats (identified by Adams as "X," "Y," and "Z") for bribes in return for continuing the negotiations. An outraged public called for war with France. In the midst of the war fervor, the Federalist-controlled Congress passed the Alien and Sedition Acts. The Alien Acts empowered Adams to take action against resident aliens in America, and the Sedition Act—an incredible assault on freedom of speech—made it a crime to publish anything of a "false, scandalous and malicious" nature against the government. A number of Jeffersonian editors and politicians were arrested under the Sedition Act.

In this tense environment, anti-Jefferson clergymen proclaimed that America was in imminent danger of a French-instigated atheistic assault.

In a Fourth of July sermon in 1798, Yale College's evangelical president, Timothy Dwight, declared that the French Revolution and the expansion of infidelity represented the fulfillment of biblical prophecy, asserting that events described in the book of Revelation, particularly the pouring out of the sixth vial of wrath described in Revelation 16, were unfolding before their eyes. He believed that the sixth vial forecast the destruction of the Roman Catholic Church and the rise of anti-Christian philosophy in the lands where Catholicism once dominated. In this time of surging atheism abroad, Dwight argued that Americans' only hope of survival lay in maintaining traditional Christianity while avoiding alliances with the agents of godlessness. Although he did not mention Jefferson specifically, his listeners could not fail to see the implication of his words. Dalliance with the friends of France risked the imposition of atheist tyranny in America, which would, he predicted, result in "the conflagration of churches and dwellings, the total ruin of families, the butchery of great multitudes of fathers and sons, and the most deplorable dishonor of wives and daughters." The Second Coming of Christ was at hand. Only those who stood firm against the forces of infidelity would survive. To combat these enemies, America presumably needed a leader not only of public virtue but orthodox personal faith.[13]

During the 1800 election, Jefferson's purported penchant for French atheism became one of the issues that most divided the populace. Many critics seized on the provocative statement in Jefferson's book *Notes on the State of Virginia* that "it does me no injury for my neighbor to say there are twenty Gods, or no God. It neither picks my pocket nor breaks my leg." Jefferson argued that the government should never prosecute people for their beliefs, including deism or atheism, but should take steps only against injurious actions, and John Leland and other evangelical Christians made identical arguments. But Federalists believed that such notions neglected the essential role of religion in public life. Quoting this passage, the *Gazette of the United States* wondered who would vote for "this audacious howling atheist?" In one of the most aggressive attacks on Jefferson's religion, prominent Presbyterian pastor John Mason of New York City used *Notes on the State of Virginia* to prove Jefferson's atheism. Mason, who would go on to become Columbia College's first provost, asserted in *The Voice of Warning to Christians, on the Ensuing Election* that Jefferson had denied Noah's flood, the account in Genesis of the origins of the human race, and the religious foundation of civil society. In *Notes* Jefferson had indeed expressed doubt about whether the presence of seashells on mountaintops (a conventional piece of evidence used to prove the historicity of the Great Flood of Noah's time) actually confirmed the ancient deluge. Likewise, Jefferson had postulated that African Americans and whites might have had separate origins, instead of common parentage in Adam and Eve. These two examples, according to Mason, showed Jefferson's open contempt for the Bible.[14]

Worst of all, to critics like Mason, was Jefferson's claim that atheism did no harm to a republic. Quoting the "twenty Gods" passage from *Notes*, Mason instructed his readers to "ponder well this paragraph. Ten thousand impieties and mischiefs lurk in its womb." Mason asserted that if atheism did no damage in civil society, "then religion is not one of the constituent principles of society, and consequently society is perfect without it; that is, perfect in atheism." Along with John Adams, Patrick Henry, and hosts of other revolutionary-era Americans, Mason argued that Christianity was the vital source of the Republic's virtue. The state should support it. To Mason, anyone who doubted the authority of the Bible could not be a Christian. Indeed, such a person actually demonstrated nothing but "hatred to Christ." Electing such a person president would be an abominable mistake. America had already made a grievous error by failing to acknowledge God in the Constitution, Mason believed, and electing Jefferson would be an act that "amounts to nothing less than a deliberate surrender of the cause of Jesus Christ into the hands of his enemies."[15]

Many agreed with Mason that a heretic like Jefferson should never be president. Dutch Reformed minister William Linn, a former Continental Army chaplain, maintained that although the government could impose no religious test on officeholders, the people could perform such an examination when they chose a candidate—a test under which Christian Americans would find Jefferson wanting. In his *Serious Considerations on the Election of a President*, Linn opposed Jefferson because, he said, the Virginian was a deist and did not believe in the Bible. Pointing to the controversial comments in *Notes on the State of Virginia*, Linn argued that

Jefferson's positions all led inexorably toward atheism. Linn conceded that the government should not persecute anyone for their private opinions, but he asserted that beliefs about God shaped a person's conduct. Playing off Jefferson's "twenty Gods" statement, Linn wrote, "Let my neighbor once persuade himself that there is no God, and he will soon pick my pocket, and break not only my leg but my neck." If Jefferson became president, Linn said, his tolerance of atheism would create moral chaos.[16]

Jefferson did not personally attempt to answer the charges about his theological beliefs, but he privately expressed disgust at his opponents' attacks. "What an effort . . . of bigotry in politics and religion have we gone through!" he exclaimed after he had taken office. In a letter to a friend, he wrote that the Federalists meant to take America back to a barbarian age when rulers ruled by power and superstition alone. He believed that the New England Federalists wanted to forge a federal union of church and state. Jefferson had confidence in a better outcome: the establishment of full religious freedom and the cultivation of his own enlightened version of Christianity. "The Christian religion when divested of the rags in which they have enveloped it, and brought to the original purity and simplicity of its benevolent institutor, is a religion of all others most friendly to liberty, science, and the freest expansions of the human mind." That kind of pure Christianity, Jefferson felt, could only be fostered under the canopy of legal freedom of conscience.[17]

Some of Jefferson's supporters did defend him on religious grounds. They emphasized that Jefferson was the candidate of religious freedom and was an enemy to religious establishments, but not to Christianity generally. One editorial averred that Jefferson was "entitled to the applause of every sect of Christians throughout the United States." Jefferson did not wish to preference any denomination or creed, but was a friend to the whole Christian church, his supporters argued. Other advocates for Jefferson tried, implausibly, to present him as a devout Christian. In the widely distributed *Address to the People of the United States*, John Beckley, a Pennsylvania congressman, reminded Americans of Jefferson's Bill for Establishing Religious Freedom, in which he proclaimed that "Almighty God hath created the mind free." His record demonstrated that Jefferson was no heretic, Beckley said, but "a man of pure, ardent and unaffected piety;

of sincere and genuine virtue; of an enlightened mind and superior wisdom; the adorer of our God; the patriot of his country; and the friend and benefactor of the whole human race." New York's DeWitt Clinton likewise called Jefferson a "real Christian" and excoriated William Linn for hypocritically using religion for malicious political aims.[18]

Some of Jefferson's supporters conceded that even if Jefferson was a deist, Adams was worse religiously because he was a hypocrite: The charlatan Adams did not actually believe in traditional Christianity but advocated state support for religion nonetheless, whereas the deist Jefferson would work along with true believers and Patriots for religious freedom. This argument seems to have persuaded many Baptists and other religious minorities, who did not share Jefferson's personal skepticism but delighted in his defense of religious freedom.[19]

Jefferson's supporters, traditional Christians or not, cared less about his personal theology than about his public views on religion. With the Alien and Sedition Acts, President Adams had authorized the stifling of political dissent, and he had also supported the establishment of religion in Massachusetts. Adams even gave signs—unintentionally—that he might support a national establishment of a denomination, perhaps the Presbyterian Church. Critics pointed to the fact that even though Adams was a Congregationalist, in his proclamation of a 1799 national day of prayer he had used language supplied by the Presbyterian General Assembly. Anti-Adams foes spread rumors that he secretly desired a national establishment. The incumbent president could not shake this accusation. Adams later wrote that the opponents of religious establishments—especially the evangelicals—had whispered against him, "Let us have Jefferson, Madison, Burr, anybody, whether they be philosophers, deists, or even atheists, rather than a Presbyterian President." Although the election did not turn on religion alone, the campaign of 1800 pitted those who favored a strong public role for religion against those who feared a religious establishment. Jefferson's victory in 1800 was the era's final triumph of the evangelical-deist political alliance.[20]

Many traditional and evangelical believers regarded Jefferson's election as a victory not for irreligion but for religious freedom. One revealing scene transpired at Philadelphia's German Reformed Church on the new president's inauguration day. There congregants sang a celebratory chorus with this verse:

Rejoice, ye states, rejoice,
And spread the patriot flame;
Culled by a nation's voice,
To save his country's fame,
And dissipate increasing fears,
Our favorite JEFFERSON appears.

These believers, like many other religious minorities in America, saw the new president as their deliverer from oppression, his personal beliefs notwithstanding.[21]

Others saw the hand of Providence at work in Jefferson's election. Samuel Adams wrote to Jefferson that politics in the 1790s had clouded the judgment of many virtuous men, but "providence, who rules the world, seems now to be rapidly changing the sentiments of mankind." The aging Boston patriot considered Jefferson's election a possible step toward the coming of the millennium, when tyranny would be destroyed and the people would "enjoy perfect peace and safety till time shall be no more." To Adams and many of Jefferson's traditional Christian supporters, Jefferson could promote a godly public agenda without sharing their personal beliefs. As shown in the letter from the Danbury churches that rejoiced at his victory, Baptists in America received Jefferson's election enthusiastically. Not surprisingly, John Leland was his most outspoken Baptist supporter. He perceived Jefferson's victory as a providential deliverance from tyranny. To him, Jefferson was a "mound of our liberties, who snatched the constitution from the talons of its enemies, and turned the government into its natural channel." For years, many Baptists and other Jeffersonians celebrated March 4, Jefferson's inauguration day, as a holiday almost religious in its import.[22]

Other evangelicals saw in Jefferson's election apocalyptic significance, but of a beneficent kind. Elias Smith, an eccentric Massachusetts Baptist, actually portrayed Jefferson as the sixth angel of the apocalypse, referenced in the book of Revelation. The radical Smith had experienced conversion when he received a luminous vision of the Lamb of God (representing Jesus) on Mount Zion. Smith and his fellow evangelicals endured a great deal of ridicule and persecution in New England, which helped convince him of God's preference for Jefferson and the Democratic-Republicans. He saw the president as a savior come to destroy the antidemocratic powers of state churches, tyranny, and oppression: "Thomas Jefferson is the angel who poured out his vial upon the river Euphrates, that the way of the kings of the east might be prepared." As one of Smith's critics noted, he forged a "strict union of republican opinions with his doctrines." Smith taunted Federalists who viewed Jefferson's election as the triumph of irreligion. The situation for Christianity was quite the opposite, he wrote in 1805; the years since Jefferson's victory had seen a great new outpouring of the Holy Spirit for revival—evidence, according to Smith, that "Jesus Christ can, and does manage his own cause without human aid." Where Timothy Dwight and others had seen Jefferson as representing the prophetic tide of anti-Christian hatred, Smith believed the president was fulfilling the divine mandate of democracy. The coming of Jeffersonian equality, to him, could herald the Second Coming of Christ.[23]

Although some evangelicals, such as Leland and Smith, spoke out for Jefferson, many did not publicly register their opinion of him. In the South, many Baptists and other evangelicals simply failed to participate in electoral politics in the early national period, but those southerners who did participate, regardless of religion, were overwhelmingly Jeffersonian. The pamphlet wars of the 1800 election raged almost entirely in the North alone. Nevertheless, some direct evidence pointed to evangelical southerners' rejection of the critique of Jefferson as a heretic. An 1804 letter in a Raleigh, North Carolina, newspaper chastised Jefferson's opponents for claiming that his presidency would lead to an anti-Christian crusade. The writer noted that the early years of Jefferson's administration had seen the outbreak of nearly unprecedented revivals of religion, particularly in the South. American evangelicals who believed the Federalist attacks had "treated their best friend Jefferson with ingratitude."[24]

In general, it seemed that most Baptists and other sectarian evangelicals welcomed Jefferson's presidency. Jefferson, in turn, appreciated his base of evangelical support, especially among the Baptists, and cultivated connections with them. In a letter to the Baltimore Baptist Association written while he was president, he cited their common commitment to religious liberty and returned their prayers for him with "supplications to the same almighty being for your future welfare and that of our beloved country." Jefferson routinely implied that he and his evangelical supporters served the same God. To a group of Virginia Baptists, he wrote that together the president and the evangelicals had resolved the great question of whether freedom of religion undermined obedience to the moral law. It did not.[25]

Critics found little evidence of anti-Christian agitation from Jefferson once he gained office. He maintained friendly correspondence with evangelical Democratic-Republicans and a positive stance toward the public role of religion. His first term also coincided with the advent of the Second Great Awakening. Unlike Washington and Adams, Jefferson did not call for national days of prayer, but otherwise his administration did not make any dramatic changes with regard to the government's position on religion. President Jefferson displayed surprising comfort with a public role for the practice of faith, despite his talk of a "wall of separation" between church and state. His positive policy began with the tone of his first inaugural speech, in which he praised America's "benign religion, professed indeed and practiced in various forms, yet all of them inculcating honesty, truth, temperance, gratitude and the love of man, acknowledging and adoring an overruling providence, which by all its dispensations proves that it delights in the happiness of man here, and his greater happiness hereafter." Although he defended freedom of religion, Jefferson still believed that Christianity undergirded American virtues and liberty. Even though he himself felt little spiritual affinity for Christianity's theological tradition, he saw its public effects as essential to the life of the Republic.[26]

For Americans of modern times who are familiar with Jefferson only as the advocate of a "wall of separation" between church and state, his sympathy toward many evangelicals might seem strange. Jefferson showed few signs of what we would now call a "strict separationist" position on church-state issues. Federalists may have charged Jefferson with atheism, but in fact he showed a consistent willingness to use the agencies and property of government as venues for wide-ranging religious expression. He saw religion as an indispensable bulwark of the Republic, and he would never have entertained the idea that government should be hostile to religious exercise in general. He simply believed that the government should never preference any denomination, persecute anyone for his or her beliefs, or coerce anyone into religious observance.

Jefferson routinely permitted worship in federal buildings, and he attended a number of religious services himself on government property—including on the occasion when Leland delivered the mammoth cheese. During his presidency, church services were regularly held in the Treasury Building, the War Office, and the Supreme Court. A variety of clerics, including some evangelicals, spoke to church services in the House of Representatives. Federalist congressman Manasseh Cutler, who also served as a Revolutionary War chaplain and a Congregationalist pastor, thought that Jefferson's attendance at services in the House did not give any evidence that Jefferson had become a sincere believer. Cutler did concede that whatever intentions the president may once have held, Jefferson's "idea of bearing down and overturning our religious institutions . . . is now given up." Even some Federalists were realizing that Jefferson did not intend to initiate a campaign against Christianity in America akin to the one ignited by the French Revolution. In 1802, John Leland went so far as to argue that the success of recent revivals indicated God's approval of Jefferson's election; these awakenings were centered on the firmly Jeffersonian state of Kentucky. Leland scolded the Federalists for claiming that Jefferson and his followers championed irreligion. The revivals showed, he said, that "democrats can be religious," and he noted that no Federalist-dominated areas were seeing any comparable outpourings of the Spirit. For Leland, the fate of revival hinged not upon the personal beliefs of political leaders but on their commitment to religious freedom. In freedom, the pure gospel could go forth unfettered.[27]

What, then, did Jefferson's election in 1800 represent? If we focus only on Federalists' attacks on him as an infidel, then we might conclude that when faced with a choice between a religious and a secular republic in 1800, Americans chose a secular one. But this interpretation appears doubtful in light of Jefferson's promotion of a public role for religion and his deep connections with many American evangelicals, especially Baptists. Neither the Danbury Baptists nor Thomas Jefferson entertained the notion that religion should have no place in the political life of the Republic. The experience of both Jefferson and evangelicals during the revolutionary era had taught them that great danger to liberty arose when governments created or sponsored religious establishments or prevented the free exercise of religion. But they hardly envisioned a secular republic; such a concept was almost incomprehensible in the mental world of the founders. This is not to suggest that Jefferson himself secretly held some kind of traditional Christian faith. He did not. Instead, in spite of his own doubts about God, he fostered a generosity toward the role of religion in the public life of his people. In the final act of the Revolution and its pursuit of liberty, Jefferson and the evangelicals had established an American model of church and state: a combination of public religion and religious freedom.

EPILOGUE

"Freedom Sees Religion as Its Companion"

Faith and American Civil Society

O N MAY 9, 1831, the young Frenchman Alexis de Tocqueville disembarked in Newport, Rhode Island, to begin a nine-month tour of America. Commissioned to study America's prison system, Tocqueville would actually extend his investigation to the nature of America itself. Journeying more than 7,000 miles across North America, from New England to New Orleans, the budding twenty-five-year-old political thinker and historian sought to comprehend the surprising stability of America's republican experiment. In his brilliant *Democracy in America*, published in two parts in 1835 and 1840, Tocqueville explained why American democracy did not degenerate into a vicious tyranny of the majority. Among the most critical reasons, he believed, was the public role of religion in American society. "The religious atmosphere of the country was the first thing that struck me on arrival in the United States," he wrote. In profound contrast to the French experience of revolution, American Patriot leaders had not attacked religious institutions, and traditional Christians had widely supported the Revolution. The partnership of religion and liberty lay at the heart of America's political success. To Tocqueville, the Americans' Christian ethos kept democracy's worst features in check. Their faith sustained their conviction about the equality of all people. The religious aspect of civil society was essential to the survival of the Republic, Tocqueville believed. "Despotism may be able to do without faith," he concluded, "but freedom cannot."[1]

The America Tocqueville explored in 1831 was more heavily evangelical and more religiously diverse than the one of the revolutionary period, but it shared an essentially similar religious culture with that first generation of independence. Most Americans believed in both maintaining religious freedom and fostering the vitality of religious institutions. Their public principles of religion, including disestablishment, providentialism, equality by creation, the importance of virtue, and the dangers of vice, continued to define the American Republic. From observations of the French example, Americans knew that revolutions could become barbarous, assaulting the very religious institutions that prevented the worst tendencies of popular rule. The leaders of the American Revolution, then, endorsed not unfettered individualism but a freedom to do good.

Tocqueville traced the origins of this ethical freedom to the Puritan heritage of New England. There, the deep sense of social responsibility and the widespread participation in church and township governments tutored the people in the principles of moral liberty. Tocqueville readily conceded the extremism of the Puritans' laws against blasphemy, Sabbath-breaking, and other vices, but he believed that the essence of what they practiced had birthed a distinctly American alliance of religion and freedom.

Freedom by itself would inexorably degenerate into rabid selfishness, but religion nurtured the purposefulness of freedom. In the American model, according to Tocqueville, "freedom sees religion as the companion of its struggles and triumphs, the cradle of its infancy, and the divine source of its rights." Because of natural human tendencies toward oppression and selfishness, religion was essential to the preservation of a healthy republic.[2]

Tocqueville contrasted the vital union of religion and liberty with the chaos of amoral freedom. He believed that people's actions resulted, fundamentally, from ideas—or a lack thereof—about God and about divine expectations for moral behavior. An absence of fixed ideas about God would condemn people to anarchy, which would inevitably lead to the rise of a despot, Tocqueville believed. Those who abandoned their core religious convictions would be unable to prioritize and defend their most important values; society would degenerate into the survival of the fittest, a condition under which the majority of people would not wish to live for long. At that point, a strong leader who promised law and order would be able to seize control of a rapidly degenerating and aimless society.

Tocqueville asserted that more than any other political systems, egalitarian democracies needed the ballast of religion. Equality of condition and opportunity, which was more evident in America than anywhere else in the world, tended "to isolate men from each other so that each thinks only of himself." People in an egalitarian democracy naturally became consumed with selfish lusts and desires, exhibiting a greater willingness to harm those who stood in the way of their advancement. Religion, teaching the obligation of love toward God and man, created motivations essential to healthy democracy. In Tocqueville's view, liberty and religion together held the possibility of engendering a benevolent republic in which the public good remained a serious priority in competition with private gain.[3]

According to Tocqueville, the essential factor contributing to the health of religion in America, as compared to Europe, was disestablishment. He believed that faith best influenced culture by remaining separate from government. Religion had political consequences in America—it helped maintain America's focus on ethical responsibilities in law and society—but not because government directly promoted particular denominations. Tocqueville, a Catholic, knew well the European system of established churches, yet he found that the Christian influence over American society was much stronger than in Europe. He asked many priests and pastors about this apparent paradox, and he found that "all thought that the main reason for the quiet sway of religion over their country was the complete separation of church and state." Although Tocqueville undoubtedly underestimated the political activism of churches and pastors in the early Republic, he nevertheless recognized the brilliance of the American religious compromise. When government did not try to fund or promote particular denominations, and when people were free to practice religion without state interference, religion flourished. State religion would inevitably become impure and unsound, whereas religion freely exercised would focus on the essential principles of faith, affect far more people, and maintain the vigor of the Republic.[4]

Despite his sanguine view of American religion, Tocqueville was personally skeptical about Christianity. Early in life he became a deist, and for most of his life he did not receive communion as a Catholic. Nevertheless, he always maintained a general belief in God, Providence, and an afterlife. In this combination of personal doubt but public support for religion, Tocqueville manifested a view of religion not unlike that of several prominent founding fathers, including Jefferson. Jefferson and Tocqueville personally abandoned traditional orthodoxy, while maintaining that it was essential for the masses to keep believing in Christianity—or at least in good and evil—and in eternal rewards in the afterlife.

For Tocqueville, the public, political effects of faith were everything. He made a sharp distinction between private belief, which was between a person and God, and public doctrine, which tempered democracy's excesses. In some passages of *Democracy in America*, Tocqueville seemed utterly pragmatic about the role of religion in society, writing that it did not matter whether a society accepted the true religion, as long as it accepted a publicly useful one. Similarly, he recommended that politicians act as if they believed in the doctrine of the immortality of the soul, whether or not they actually did. He also had no patience for the evangelical faith surging on the frontier, seeing it as a mystical overreaction to the pervasive worldliness of American society.[5]

We can see in hindsight that Tocqueville's and Jefferson's combination of public piety and personal skepticism was not likely to maintain the power of religion in an entire society. For most believers, the efficacy of faith begins with personal conviction and emanates out to inform their actions and beliefs in the public world.

Despite Tocqueville's personal spiritual leanings, it would be a mistake to see him, or the more deistic founders, as politically utilitarian or Machiavellian in their approach to religion. Christianity for them was not just a prop or an enabler of democracy. Tocqueville sincerely believed that Christianity taught people values essential to their moral survival under democracy. Amoral democracy could not last, but democracy chastened by religion would allow people to enjoy the fruits of freedom, while remembering their moral obligations and the state of their souls before God. Tocqueville and founders like Jefferson did not embrace the traditional doctrines of Christianity, but they knew that a republic could not maintain its freedoms without the ennobling principles of religion.[6]

Tocqueville showed that the revolutionary era sealed a nexus between religion and freedom in America. The most salient political accomplishments resulting from that nexus were disestablishment in the states and the no-establishment clause of the First Amendment. Led by evangelicals who had long suffered under the state establishments, and by Enlightenment rationalists like Jefferson who feared government persecution of the evangelical and heterodox alike, the United States became committed to the free practice of religion with no government preferences or funding for denominations.

Disestablishment hardly reflected government hostility to religion, however. Under the canopy of disestablishment and religious freedom, the churches of America flourished in astounding ways. Whatever Jefferson meant by his "wall of separation," hardly anyone across the religious spectrum in America believed that separation should entail government antagonism toward religion or the elimination of religious rhetoric or symbols from the political sphere.

Whatever their personal convictions about religion, Patriots typically believed that virtue sustained a republic and that religion was the most common resource that trained people in virtue. As John Adams wrote to his wife Abigail, religion was humanity's "most awful sanction of morality." Believing in the importance of religion and virtue did not solve all ethical questions in politics, of course. The revolutionary generation struggled to settle the great moral issues of their day, just as modern Americans do. For example, it would take a devastating Civil War, not Bible reading alone, to convince Americans that slavery was immoral. Nevertheless, revolutionary Americans realized that the individual "pursuit of happiness" could degenerate into irresponsibility and viciousness if not checked by some sense of moral obligation. If people were entrusted with the governance of a republic, then they had to maintain a sense of responsibility for the well-being of others. There was no need to invent a wellspring of public-spiritedness, for religion already taught people, as Jesus said in the Gospels, to "do unto others as you would have them do unto you."[7]

The fear of vice profoundly shaped the Revolution and the new Republic as well. Revolutionary Americans' dim view of human nature had Christian as well as classical republican origins, and it convinced Americans that power centralized in too few hands was dangerous. The British monarchical system was replaced originally with a radically decentralized association of states under the Articles of Confederation. Reform leaders like Madison and Hamilton felt that a constitutional compromise was needed between the dangers of centralized government power and the inefficiencies and institutional selfishness of confederation. Ultimately, the Federalist leaders were able to convince the ratification conventions that the new Constitution did not centralize power in ways that would invite corruption and oppression. The Federalists and Antifederalists debated the point at which government vigor became an invitation for sinful men to become tyrants. Madison emphasized that internal checks and balances in the Constitution would play politicians' aggrandizing motivations off one another.

Providentialism also heavily colored the revolutionary era, as Patriot and religious leaders pointed to the power of God's transcendent purposes to inspire confidence during America's struggle against Britain. Americans paid a high price for their liberty, and the Patriots constantly assured themselves that if God was on their side, and if they acted morally and retained God's favor, they could not fail. Benjamin Franklin had major doubts about Christianity, but he had no question about God's providential role in the Revolution; he wrote in 1784, "If it had not been for the justice of our cause, and the consequent interposition of providence, in which we had faith, we must have been ruined" in the Revolution.[8]

In time, as America crafted the narrative of its Revolution, Franklin and the other major founders became civil saints, paragons of right action, bravery, and public virtue. No one held a more exalted place in this pantheon of American heroes than George Washington. In a Fourth of July oration just seven months after Washington's death in December 1799, the Massachusetts lawyer Luther Richardson evinced the heightened reverence Americans held for their victorious general and first president. Richardson reminded his audience of the dark times of the Revolution, in 1776, when it looked as if all might be lost. Then, providentially, "the God of Liberty proclaimed aloud 'what men can do, has already been done; I have found a patriot worthy to rule a nation of freemen.' A flood of glory burst from heaven, and encircled Washington. At the boldness of his achievements the ministers of Britain stood appalled, their monarch trembled upon his throne, and despotism himself, blinded by the blaze of his fame, threw down his chains." God had raised Washington up at just the right time, a Moses of the New World, to win the nation's freedom from political bondage.[9]

Americans have repeatedly returned to this kind of providential rhetoric and veneration of popular leaders, especially in times of war. The enormous, bloody sacrifices required by war seem to require providential justifications. If people do not believe that a war has transcendent significance, it is much more difficult to motivate them to keep fighting. But providentialism has always been dangerous, to Americans and to other peoples, because it has a singular capacity for obfuscating injustice in war. If God is on your side, then how can you do wrong? In the colonial period, horrific wars against Native Americans were routinely rationalized in providential language; during the Revolution, the episodes of vicious treatment they endured were justified by the rhetoric of divine purpose. In the antebellum period, America's unilateral expansion into Mexican territory was framed in the language of "manifest destiny," which posited that it was God's plan for America to expand into the southwest and to the Pacific. Abraham Lincoln noted in his 1865 second inaugural address that both North and South read the same Bible and prayed to the same God, yet he still saw the Civil War as fulfilling divine purposes.

Providential interpretations of war are not easily abandoned by Americans, but wise leaders will employ them with extreme care, remaining keenly attentive to the power of perceived righteousness. Providentialist rhetoric might work in times of overwhelming moral consensus about war, but not as a means to justify or rouse support for morally dubious or ill-conceived military actions. President George W. Bush famously insisted in 2003 that democracy is God's gift to humanity, issuing a moral call to justify the invasion of Iraq. But poor postinvasion planning and failure to find the weapons of mass destruction whose existence had been the motive for invasion turned his providentialist rhetoric into a farce. By contrast, General Dwight D. Eisenhower used providential rhetoric in his message to Allied troops before the D-day invasion, speaking of the attack as a "crusade" to end Nazi tyranny. He ended the message with a prayer for "the blessings of Almighty God upon this great and noble undertaking." This sentiment rang (and still rings) true for most Americans, but an exhortation to Providence remains a problematic endeavor.[10]

Far above providentialism, the most dynamic product of the nexus between religion and freedom in America was a national belief in equality by creation. With a century of political philosophy crystallized in the Declaration of Independence's soaring claim of human equality, revolutionary Americans came to the conviction that because God created everyone, all persons were fundamentally equal before him. This belief immediately threw the legitimacy of slavery into a state of profound moral doubt. The founders, especially Jefferson, remained largely inactive against slavery, but even Jefferson recognized the implications of equality by creation. Reflecting on the political effects of slavery, Jefferson asked, "Can the liberties of a nation be thought secure when we have removed their only firm basis, a conviction in the minds of the people that these liberties are of the gift of God?" Slavery, to Jefferson, removed that core conviction.[11]

By making equality by creation a central tenet of the revolutionary cause, Jefferson handed the weapon of egalitarianism to those of his adversaries who rightfully condemned him for owning slaves. In the ninety years between the Revolution and the Civil War, African American leaders used Jefferson's religious language against him. As early as 1791, Benjamin Banneker, a free black leader in Maryland, excoriated Jefferson for his failure to live up to the principles of the Declaration. "How pitiable it is to reflect," he told Jefferson, "that although you were so fully convinced

of the benevolence of the Father of mankind, and of his equal and impartial distribution of these rights and privileges, which he hath conferred
upon them, that you should at the same time counteract his mercies, in
detaining by fraud and violence so numerous a part of my brethren, under
groaning captivity and cruel oppression."[12]

Banneker and other antislavery activists were sorely disappointed with
the Revolution's limited progress against slavery. But the doctrine of
equality by creation gave a robust theological basis for antislavery ideas, as
well as for later movements for civil rights. Most of America's early antislavery advocates were black and white northern evangelicals. Even some
radical southern white evangelicals continued to speak out against slavery
into the 1790s, and even later. By making equality a transcendent American principle, Jefferson unwittingly made an unassailable religious case
for equality and freedom. Activists have used his logic for centuries. For
Martin Luther King Jr., equality by creation was not simply a political
principle but America's "creed." In 1963 King was still dreaming of the
day in which Americans would live out the true meaning of that belief.

Whether by emphasizing the need for virtue, claiming God's providential blessings, or articulating equality by creation, clearly, religion
played an indispensable role in shaping the origins of the American Republic. Although leaders from Thomas Jefferson to John Leland held
highly dissimilar personal beliefs, Americans united around public religious principles to inspire the Revolution and to articulate the basis for
American rights. Of course, religious hypocrisy abounded in America
then, just as it does now, as was abundantly demonstrated in the keeping
of slaves and the abuse of Native Americans by white American Christians. But we cannot underestimate the great good that public religious
values served in the revolutionary period, particularly by securing disestablishment and building an inalienable religious basis for human equality. Americans' faith allowed them to articulate why oppression was wrong
in the eyes of God, and it helped them envision a republic where individual freedom could be guided by ancient ideals of the Scriptures: charity, justice, and protection for the weak and poor.

Does the national significance of these precepts mean that America
was founded as a Christian nation? Yes, in the sense that believers—the

majority of whom were Christians of some kind, with an important minority of Jews—played a formative role in the creation of the American Republic. But today's advocates of a "Christian America" tend to misunderstand or underestimate the extent to which Americans already held widely varying religious beliefs at the time of the founding. The founders' religious agreement was on public values, not private doctrines. By 1776 religious coercion could no longer garner consensus in America, but giving an honored place to the free exercise of religion did bring people together and help ensure their independence.

A religious history of the American Revolution raises a few final cautionary notes for understanding our own time. First, despite the prominence of providentialism in the founding era, religious believers should remain very careful about claiming that a position or policy is God's preference. Few issues possess the moral and religious clarity to warrant such claims. More often, the complexities of politics and the limits of our vision disallow total confidence that we are following God's will. Believers will often find themselves on the other side of political debates from other, equally sincere believers, or from people who do not share their religious beliefs at all. If we are to maintain the vitality and cohesion of American civil society, we need to be able to appreciate different opinions and largely forego conversation-stopping assertions that "we are on God's side of an issue and you are not."

The alliances of the founding period also offer lessons for politically conservative believers. As we have seen in the relationship between Jefferson and Leland, evangelicals in the founding era often cooperated with people who held personal beliefs that were very different from their own. The Baptist Leland worked with the deist Jefferson because the two men shared a vision of the role of religion in public life. They both wanted no direct government support for religion, but they did not want religion removed from public discourse. Evangelicals such as Leland did not have to agree with Jefferson's personal theology to work with him in politics.

Skeptics or secularists might also learn from Jefferson's example. We should never try to eliminate religious principles from the American political arena, for there are times when the challenges facing us require transcendent justification and moral courage beyond mere pragmatism or political preference. During the Revolution, the appeal to God-given human equality placed the war with Britain on a far higher plane, showing that the war was more than a squabble over tax policy. More recently, Martin Luther King Jr. cited God's will for racial equality not simply because he was a Baptist minister, but because he knew that the argument would mobilize a largely religious nation to look beyond the technicalities of voting rights and segregation to confront the great religious principle of justice.

If America were populated largely by skeptics and atheists, then perhaps there would be no point in appeals to greater theological truths. But from the Revolution to today, many Americans cannot make sense of equality and justice as rootless human preferences. To most believers, these are values that originated in the mind of God.

The vast majority of Americans today profess to believe in God. Around half attend worship services at least occasionally, and as many as 40 percent even claim to be "born again," or to have a personal relationship with Jesus Christ. If anything, America is more religious and evangelical now than it was in the revolutionary era. If a large number of Americans come to believe American governments are hostile to religion in general, we risk alienating them from civic life. Believers should not seek to use government to coerce anyone into religious practice (such as by mandating school prayer for all), but the government and its judges in particular need to think carefully before seeking to diminish religion's influence in American public life.

The religious symbols and practices that American courts and secularist groups have challenged since the 1960s—Ten Commandments monuments, manger scenes, and crosses; prayer at events from football games to presidential inaugurations; the use of schools and government buildings by religious groups—all acknowledge historical and present reality: the importance of religion in American public life. Recalling Tocqueville, it is still difficult to imagine a better source than religion for channeling American freedom toward benevolent ends. Freedom disengaged from morality can bear bitter fruit, indeed. We could point to countless examples in modern American society; perhaps the most obvious recent example is the rampant greed and deception that helped cause the deep economic recession that began in late 2007. Of course, religious hypocrisy abounds in our era as it has in previous times, but religion also retains unmatched power to motivate believers to do good. Fear of religious coercion by government, as justified as it is, must be balanced with a healthy respect for the value of religion in fostering the best aspects of American republicanism. As Tocqueville recognized, one of the greatest accomplishments of the American Revolution was the ingenious balance between religious freedom and religious strength.

ACKNOWLEDGMENTS

My thanks go to the friends and family who helped me write this book: David Bebbington, Barry Hankins, Mark Noll, and the readers for Basic Books, who gave a host of excellent suggestions; my agent extraordinaire, Giles Anderson; friends and colleagues in Baylor University's history department and Institute for Studies of Religion, including Jeff Hamilton, Byron Johnson, Philip Jenkins, and Rodney Stark; and research assistants at Baylor, including Michael Sturdy, Holly Young, and Jonathan Reid. At Basic Books, I am very grateful to Lara Heimert, Michele Jacob, Alex Littlefield, Mary McCue, Kay Mariea, Kathy Delfosse, Ross Curley, Brandon Proia, and the many others who worked on the project. David Groff edited the book with thoroughness and verve. I am thankful most of all for my wife, Ruby, and my boys, Jonathan and Josh.

NOTES

INTRODUCTION

1. John Ferling, *Almost a Miracle: The American Victory in the War of Independence* (New York, 2007), 48–60.

2. David Avery, *The Lord Is to Be Praised for the Triumphs of His Power* (Norwich, CT, 1778), 14; J. T. Headley, *The Chaplains and Clergy of the Revolution* (New York, 1864), 295.

3. Headley, *Chaplains and Clergy*, 287–288; Alan Heimert, *Religion and the American Mind: From the Great Awakening to the Revolution* (Cambridge, MA, 1966), 475.

4. Thomas Allen to David Avery, June 23, 1775, in David Avery Papers, Princeton Theological Seminary.

5. Diary of David Avery, December 26, 1776, in David Avery Papers; Avery, *Lord Is to Be Praised*, 24; David Hackett Fischer, *Washington's Crossing* (New York, 2004), 257.

6. David Avery diary, October 17, 1777; Avery, *Lord Is to Be Praised*, 30.

7. In the eighteenth century, deism referred to a philosophical movement advocating natural religion, or a nonsectarian faith based primarily on ethics rather than theology. Deists often believed that God had created the natural world but did not now interfere in the affairs of men. They were often skeptical about traditional Christian doctrines such as the divinity of Christ or his resurrection.

8. Daniel L. Dreisbach, "Mr. Jefferson, a Mammoth Cheese, and the 'Wall of Separation Between Church and State': A Bicentennial Commemoration," *Journal of Church and State* 43, no. 4 (2001): 725, 742.

9. William B. Sprague, *Annals of the American Pulpit* (New York, 1969), 6:176; Thomas Jefferson, in *The Founders on Religion: A Book of Quotations*, ed. James H. Hutson (Princeton, NJ, 2005), 123, 218.

10. *Gazette of the United States*, May 3, 1800, 3.

11. Thomas Paine, *Common Sense and Related Writings*, ed. Thomas P. Slaughter (Boston, 2001), 113.

12. I have silently modernized capitalization and spelling in quotations.

13. Adams quoted in Gordon S. Wood, *The Creation of the American Republic, 1776–1787* (Chapel Hill, NC, 1969), 118.

14. Backus and Manning in Warren Association, *Minutes of the Warren Association* ([Boston? 1784]), 6–7; George Washington, in Hutson, *Founders on Religion*,

19; "the cause of America," Robert Smith quoted in Mark A. Noll, *America's God: From Jonathan Edwards to Abraham Lincoln* (New York, 2002), 206.

CHAPTER 1

1. John Adams, "Instructions of the Town of Braintree" (1765), in *The Revolutionary Writings of John Adams*, ed. C. Bradley Thompson (Indianapolis, IN, 2000), 41.

2. Diary of John Adams, December 18, 1765, in Adams Family Papers: An Electronic Archive, Massachusetts Historical Society, http://www.masshist.org/digital adams/.

3. John Adams, *A Dissertation on the Canon and Feudal Law* (1765), in Thompson, *Revolutionary Writings of John Adams*, 28.

4. John Adams diary, December 29, 1765.

5. John Adams diary, August 22, 1756; David McCullough, *John Adams* (New York, 2001), 37, 42.

6. Adams, *Dissertation on the Canon and Feudal Law*, 25.

7. Ibid., 34.

8. Thomas Bernard, *A Sermon Preached Before His Excellency Francis Bernard* (Boston, 1763), 44.

9. *A Discourse, Addressed to the Sons of Liberty* (Providence, 1766), 6; cited in Ruth H. Bloch, *Visionary Republic: Millennial Themes in American Thought, 1756–1800* (New York, 1985), 54.

10. Theodorus Frelinghuysen, *Wars and Rumors of Wars* (New York, 1755), 36.

11. Burt and Davies quoted in Nathan O. Hatch, "The Origins of Civil Millennialism in America: New England Clergymen, War with France, and the Revolution," *William and Mary Quarterly*, 3d ser., 31, no. 3 (July 1974): 419–420; also Samuel Davies, *Religion and Patriotism the Constituents of a Good Soldier* (Philadelphia, 1755), 22.

12. Quoted in Thomas S. Kidd, ed., *The Great Awakening: A Brief History with Documents* (Boston, 2007), 98.

13. Dr. Alexander Hamilton quoted in Robert Brockway, *A Wonderful Work of God: Puritanism and the Great Awakening* (Bethlehem, PA, 2003), 149.

14. Kidd, *Great Awakening: Brief History*, 54.

15. Josiah Smith, *The Character, Preaching, &c. of the Reverend Mr. George Whitefield* (Boston, 1740), 19–20; Thomas S. Kidd, *The Great Awakening: The Roots of Evangelical Christianity in Colonial America* (New Haven, CT, 2007), 95.

16. Howard H. Peckham, *The Colonial Wars, 1689–1762* (Chicago, 1964), 102–104.

17. Jonathan Edwards to a Correspondent in Scotland, November 1745, in Jonathan Edwards, *Letters and Personal Writings*, ed. George S. Claghorn, vol. 16 of *The Works of Jonathan Edwards* (New Haven, CT, 1998), 185; Benjamin Franklin to John Franklin, 1745, in *The Papers of Benjamin Franklin*, ed. Leonard W. Labaree (New Haven, CT, 1961), 3:26–27; George M. Marsden, *Jonathan Edwards: A Life* (New Haven, CT, 2003), 310–312.

18. Thomas Prince, *Extraordinary Events the Doings of God* (Boston, 1747), 34–35.

19. Samuel Davies, *Virginia's Danger and Remedy* (Williamsburg, VA, 1756), 45.

20. Thaddeus Maccarty, *The Advice of Joab to the Host of Israel* (Boston, 1759), 21.

21. Samuel Langdon, *Joy and Gratitude to God* (Portsmouth, NH, 1760), 42–43; Amos Adams, *Songs of Victory Directed by Human Compassion* (Boston, 1759), 26; poem in *Canada Subjected: A New Song* ([Unknown, 1760?]); Hatch, "Origins," 421.

22. Fred Anderson, *Crucible of War: The Seven Years' War and the Fate of Empire in British North America* (New York, 2000), 499–501; Joseph Sewall, *A Sermon Preached at the Thursday-Lecture in Boston* (Boston, 1762), 28; North Carolina Governor Dobbs quoted in Nelson Vance Russell, "The Reaction in England and America to the Capture of Havana, 1762," *Hispanic American Historical Review* 9, no. 3 (August 1929): 314.

23. Jonathan Mayhew, *Two Discourses Delivered October 25, 1759* (Boston, 1759), 60, 61.

24. Amos Adams, *A Concise, Historical View of the Perils* (Boston, 1769), 26.

25. Edmund Burke quoted in David Womersley, "Introduction: A Conservative Revolution," in *Liberty and American Experience in the Eighteenth Century*, ed. David Womersley (Indianapolis, IN, 2006), 6; George Whitefield quoted in Carl Bridenbaugh, *The Spirit of '76: The Growth of American Patriotism Before Independence* (New York, 1975), 118.

26. Edmund S. Morgan and Helen M. Morgan, *The Stamp Act Crisis: Prologue to Revolution*, rev. ed. (New York, 1962), 52.

27. James Otis, *The Rights of the British Colonies Asserted and Proved* (Boston, 1764), 18.

28. Franklin and Hughes quoted in Morgan and Morgan, *Stamp Act Crisis*, 203, 321; *Boston Gazette*, April 21, 1766.

29. Samuel Peters, *A General History of Connecticut* (New Haven, CT, 1829), 256–58; Alan Heimert, *Religion and the American Mind: From the Great Awakening to the Revolution* (Cambridge, MA, 1966), 346; Joseph Emerson, *A Thanksgiving-Sermon Preach'd at Pepperrell* (Boston, 1766), 12; Brendan McConville, *The King's Three Faces: The Rise and Fall of Royal America, 1688–1776* (Chapel Hill, NC, 2006), 261–262.

30. Nathaniel Whitaker, *A Funeral Sermon, on the Death of the Reverend George Whitefield* (Salem, MA, 1770), 34.

31. Jonathan Mayhew, *The Snare Broken* (1766), in *Political Sermons of the Founding Era, 1730–1805*, ed. Ellis Sandoz, 2d ed. (Indianapolis, IN, 1998), 1:258; Benjamin Throop, *A Thanksgiving Sermon* (New London, CT, 1766), 12.

32. John J. Zubly, *The Stamp-Act Repealed* (1766), in *"A Warm and Zealous Spirit": John J. Zubly and the American Revolution, a Selection of His Writings*, ed. Randall M. Miller (Macon, GA, 1982), 47.

33. John Adams, "Governor Winthrop to Governor Bradford," February 9 and 16, 1767, in Thompson, *Revolutionary Writings of John Adams*, 63.

CHAPTER 2

1. James Madison to William Bradford Jr., January 24, 1774, in *The Writings of James Madison*, ed. Gaillard Hunt (New York, 1900), 1:21.

2. James Madison to William Bradford Jr., April 1, 1774, in Hunt, *Writings of James Madison*, 1:22–23.

3. Ibid., 1:23.

4. Frank Lambert, *The Founding Fathers and the Place of Religion in America* (Princeton, NJ, 2003), 68–69; Joseph Conforti, *Saints and Strangers: New England in British North America* (Baltimore, MD, 2006), 95.

5. Thomas Welde in John Winthrop, *A Short History of the Rise, Reign, and Ruin of the Antinomians* (London, 1692), preface.

6. Roger Williams, *The Bloody Tenent of Persecution* (1643), in *The Puritans in America: A Narrative Anthology*, ed. Alan Heimert and Andrew Delbanco (Cambridge, MA, 1985), 198.

7. *Boston Gazette*, December 16, 1742, quoted in C. C. Goen, *Revivalism and Separatism in New England, 1740–1800: Strict Congregationalists and Separate Baptists in the Great Awakening*, rev. ed. (Middletown, CT, 1987), 71.

8. Elisha Paine quoted in Goen, *Revivalism and Separatism*, 120.

9. Solomon Paine, *A Short View of the Difference* (Newport, RI, 1752), 9.

10. Richard L. Bushman, ed., *The Great Awakening: Documents on the Revival of Religion, 1740–1745* (Chapel Hill, NC, 1969), 103.

11. George W. Paschal, *History of North Carolina Baptists* (Raleigh, NC, 1930), 1:287.

12. Charles Woodmason, *The Carolina Backcountry on the Eve of the Revolution: The Journal and Other Writings of Charles Woodmason, Anglican Itinerant*, ed. Richard J. Hooker (Chapel Hill, NC, 1953), 240–241; Herman Husband, *A Continuation of the Impartial Relation* ([New Bern, NC?], 1770), 15.

13. Patrick Henry to William Dawson, February 13, 1745, in William Dawson Papers, Library of Congress.

14. Samuel Davies quoted in Timothy D. Hall, *Contested Boundaries: Itinerancy and the Reshaping of the Colonial American Religious World* (Durham, NC, 1994), 120.

15. Patrick Henry quoted in Robert Middlekauff, *The Glorious Cause: The American Revolution, 1763–1789* (New York, 1982), 79.

16. James Ireland, *The Life of the Rev. James Ireland* (Winchester, VA, 1819), 165–166.

17. Timoleon [pseud.], *Virginia Gazette*, August 22, 1771.

18. Edwin S. Gaustad, *Neither King nor Prelate: Religion and the New Nation, 1776–1826*, rev. ed. (Grand Rapids, MI, 1993), 174; Thomas E. Buckley, S.J., *Church and State in Revolutionary Virginia, 1776–1787* (Charlottesville, VA, 1977), 18; Rhys Isaac, *The Transformation of Virginia, 1740–1790* (Chapel Hill, NC, 1982), 279; Thomas J. Curry, *The First Freedoms: Church and State in America to the Passage of the First Amendment* (New York, 1986), 135.

19. Isaac, *Transformation of Virginia*, 279–280; Buckley, *Church and State*, 18–19; Curry, *First Freedoms*, 135.

20. Thomas Jefferson, *Autobiography*, ed. Frank E. Grizzard Jr., http://etext.lib.virginia.edu/jefferson/grizzard/autobiography/.

CHAPTER 3

1. A Puritan [Samuel Adams], *Boston Gazette*, April 4, 11, 1768, in *The Writings of Samuel Adams,* ed. Harry Alonzo Cushing (reprint, New York, 1968), 1:201, 203; John C. Miller, *Sam Adams: Pioneer in Propaganda* (Palo Alto, CA, 1936), 129–130.

2. John Adams to Jedidiah Morse, December 2, 1815, in *The Works of John Adams,* ed. Charles Francis Adams (Boston, 1850–1856), 10:185.

3. Jonathan Mayhew, *A Discourse Concerning Unlimited Submission* (1750), in *The Pulpit of the American Revolution,* ed. John Wingate Thornton (reprint, New York, 1970), 50.

4. Mayhew, *Discourse Concerning Unlimited Submission,* 94, 104; Adams quoted in Thornton, *Pulpit of the American Revolution,* 45.

5. *Boston Gazette,* January 2, 1761; East Apthorp, *Considerations on the Institution and Conduct of the Society for the Propagation of the Gospel* (Boston, 1763), 17; Jonathan Mayhew, *Observations on the Charter and Conduct of the Society* (Boston, 1763), 107, 175.

6. Jonathan Mayhew, *Remarks on an Anonymous Tract* (Boston, 1764), 58, 62.

7. John Adams to H. Niles, February 13, 1818, in *Works of John Adams* 10:288; Carl Bridenbaugh, *Mitre and Sceptre: Transatlantic Faiths, Ideas, Personalities, and Politics, 1689–1775* (New York, 1962), 226; Bernard Bailyn, *The Ideological Origins of the American Revolution,* enlarged ed. (Cambridge, MA, 1992), 254–257.

8. John Ewer, *A Sermon Preached Before the Incorporated Society* (New York, 1768), 5, 8; Bridenbaugh, *Mitre and Sceptre,* 289–292.

9. Charles Chauncy, *A Letter to a Friend* (Boston, 1767), 51; William Livingston, *A Letter to the Right Reverend Father in God* (New York, 1768), 3; John Rodgers to ?, March 29, 1768, Gratz Collection, Historical Society of Pennsylvania; Bridenbaugh, *Mitre and Sceptre,* 313; Andrew Eliot to Thomas Hollis, February 1, 1770, in Massachusetts Historical Society, *Collections,* 4th ser., 34, no. 4 (1858): 448.

10. Quoted in Richard R. Beeman, *Patrick Henry: A Biography* (New York, 1974), 13–22.

11. Thomas Gwatkin, *A Letter to the Clergy of New York and New Jersey* (Williamsburg, VA, 1772), 7; *To the Public* (New York, 1771), 1.

12. Richard Bland to Thomas Adams, August 1, 1771, in *William and Mary College Quarterly Historical Magazine* 5, no. 3 (January 1897): 153–154; Rhys Isaac, *The Transformation of Virginia, 1740–1790* (Chapel Hill, NC, 1982), 183–189.

13. Charles Woodmason, *The Carolina Backcountry on the Eve of Revolution: The Journal and Other Writings of Charles Woodmason, Anglican Itinerant,* ed. Richard J. Hooker (Chapel Hill, NC, 1953), 240–241.

14. William Tennent III to Ezra Stiles, August 18, 1774, in the Papers of Ezra Stiles, Beinecke Library, Yale University; Bridenbaugh, *Mitre and Sceptre,* 322–323; Marjoleine Kars, *Breaking Loose Together: The Regulator Rebellion in Pre-Revolutionary North Carolina* (Chapel Hill, NC, 2002), 108–109.

15. Samuel Cooper, *A Discourse on the Man of Sin,* 2d ed. (Boston, 1774), 57–58; *Connecticut Courant,* January 26, 1773, 4; Samuel Langdon, *A Rational Explication of*

St. John's Vision of the Two Beasts (Portsmouth, NH, 1774); Charles H. Metzger, *The Quebec Act: A Primary Cause of the American Revolution* (New York, 1936), 30–31.

16. *Connecticut Courant*, July 5, 1774, 3.

17. *Massachusetts Spy*, September 8, 1774, 3.

18. Joseph Lyman, *A Sermon Preached at Hatfield* (Boston, 1775), 30–31.

19. *Extracts from the Votes and Proceedings of the American Continental Congress* (New York, 1774), 32–33; Francis D. Cogliano, *No King, No Popery: Anti-Catholicism in Revolutionary New England* (Westport, CT, 1995), 48–49.

20. Richard Furman, "An Address to the Residents Between the Broad and Saluda Rivers Concerning the American War for Independence, November, 1775," in James Rogers, *Richard Furman: Life and Legacy* (Macon, GA, 2001), 269; John J. Zubly, *The Law of Liberty* (1775), in *"A Warm and Zealous Spirit": John J. Zubly and the American Revolution, a Selection of His Writings*, ed. Randall M. Miller (Macon, GA, 1982), 125.

21. Alexander Hamilton, "Remarks on the Quebec Bill," June 15 and 22, 1775, in *The Papers of Alexander Hamilton*, ed. Harold C. Syrett, vol. 1, *1768–1778* (New York, 1961), 166, 173, 175; Alexander Hamilton, *A Full Vindication of the Measures of the Congress* (New York, 1774), 26.

22. Scipio [pseud.], in the *Pennsylvania Journal*, printed in the *Connecticut Courant*, October 24, 1774; A Scotchman [pseud.], *Connecticut Courant*, November 14, 1774; Pauline Maier, *From Resistance to Revolution: Colonial Radicals and the Development of American Opposition to Britain, 1765–1776*, rev. ed. (New York, 1991), 238; Brendan McConville, *The King's Three Faces: The Rise and Fall of Royal America, 1688–1776* (Chapel Hill, NC, 2006), 288–290.

23. *The Diary of Isaac Backus*, ed. William G. McLoughlin, vol. 2, *1765–1785* (Providence, RI, 1979), 938–939.

24. Thomas Gage to the Earl of Dartmouth, September 12, 1774, in *The Correspondence of General Thomas Gage with the Secretaries of State, 1763–1775*, ed. Clarence E. Carter (reprint, New York, 1969), 1:374.

25. Samuel Sherwood, *The Church's Flight into the Wilderness* (1776), in *Political Sermons of the American Founding Era, 1730–1805*, ed. Ellis Sandoz, 2d ed. (Indianapolis, IN, 1998), 1:503, 514, 524.

26. Henry Cumings, *A Sermon, Preached in Billerica* (Worcester, MA, 1776), 12n, 15, 23.

27. Philip Livingston, *To the Inhabitants of the City and County of New-York* (New York, 1775), 1; Arthur Lee, *An Appeal to the Justice and Interests of the People of Great Britain*, 4th ed. (New York, 1775), 29; *Address to the British Soldiery* (Salem, MA, 1775), 1.

28. George Washington, in *The Founders on Religion: A Book of Quotations*, ed. James H. Hutson (Princeton, NJ, 2005), 43.

29. Thomas Paine, *Common Sense and Related Writings*, ed. Thomas P. Slaughter (Boston, 2001), 65, 82.

30. *Pennsylvania Ledger*, May 13, 1778.

31. John Murray, *Nehemiah; or, The Struggle for Liberty Never in Vain* (Newbury, MA, 1779), 50; Alan Heimert, *Religion and the American Mind: From the Great Awakening to the Revolution* (Cambridge, MA, 1966), 394.

CHAPTER 4

1. Edmund Burke, *The Speech of Edmund Burke, Esq.; On Moving His Resolution for Conciliation with the Colonies* (London, 1775), 15–17.

2. Ibid., 18.

3. William Wirt Henry, *Patrick Henry: Life, Correspondence, and Speeches* (New York, 1891), 1:265–266; Rhys Isaac, *The Transformation of Virginia, 1740–1790* (Chapel Hill, NC, 1982), 267–269.

4. Israel Holly, *A Word in Zion's Behalf* (Hartford, CT, 1765), 5–7.

5. Israel Holly, *God Brings About His Holy and Wise Purpose* (Hartford, CT, 1774), 19, 21–22.

6. Ibid., 17.

7. [Elisha Williams], *The Essential Rights and Liberties of Protestants* (Boston, 1744), in *Political Sermons of the American Founding Era, 1730–1805*, ed. Ellis Sandoz, 2d ed. (Indianapolis, IN, 1998): 1:61, 76, 83, 93, 117–118.

8. William Hooper, *The Apostles Neither Impostors nor Enthusiasts* (Boston, 1742), 9; Jonathan Todd, *Civil Rulers the Ministers of God* (New London, CT, 1749), 2.

9. Solomon Paine, *A Short View of the Difference* (Newport, RI, 1752), 44.

10. *An Answer to a Letter of December 26, 1763* (Boston, 1764), 5; John Cleaveland, *A Short and Plain Narrative of the Late Work of God's Spirit* (Boston, 1767), 38–40.

11. *Essex Gazette*, October 25, 1768.

12. *Essex Gazette*, May 31, 1774.

13. *Essex Gazette*, April 18, 1775, and July 6, 1775.

14. Continental Congress, *In Congress, Monday, June 12, 1775* (Watertown, MA, 1775), broadside; Jefferson quoted in Emory Elliot, "The Dove and the Serpent: The Clergy in the American Revolution," *American Quarterly* 31, no. 2 (Summer 1979): 188.

15. William Tennent III, *An Address, Occasioned by the Late Invasion of the Liberties of the American Colonies* (Philadelphia, 1774), 6, 8.

16. William Tennent III, "Fragment of a Journal Kept by the Rev. William Tennent," *Charleston Year Book* (Charleston, SC, 1894): 302–303.

17. Walter Edgar, *Partisans and Redcoats: The Southern Conflict That Turned the Tide of the American Revolution* (New York, 2001), 33.

18. Richard Furman, "An Address to the Residents Between the Broad and Saluda Rivers Concerning the American War for Independence" (November 1775), in James A. Rogers, *Richard Furman: Life and Legacy* (Macon, GA, 2001), 29–30, 272.

19. John Zubly to John Dickinson, n.d., Logan Papers 12/118, Historical Society of Pennsylvania.

20. John J. Zubly, *The Law of Liberty* (1775), in *"A Warm and Zealous Spirit": John J. Zubly and the American Revolution, a Selection of His Writings,* ed. Randall M. Miller (Macon, GA, 1982), 126.

21. Thomas Paine, *Common Sense,* in *Common Sense and Related Writings,* ed. Thomas P. Slaughter (Boston, 2001), 82, 98; Nathan R. Perl-Rosenthal, "The 'Divine Right of Republics': Hebraic Republicanism and the Debate over Kingless Government in Revolutionary America," *William and Mary Quarterly,* 3d ser., 66, no. 3 (July 2009): 535–537.

22. Paine, *Common Sense,* 113–114.

23. Eric Foner, *Tom Paine and Revolutionary America* (New York, 1976), 80–81; Harvey J. Kaye, *Thomas Paine and the Promise of America* (New York, 2005), 50.

24. John M. Bumsted and Charles E. Clark, "New England's Tom Paine: John Allen and the Spirit of Liberty," *William and Mary Quarterly,* 3d ser., 21, no. 4 (October 1964): 562–565.

25. [John Allen], *An Oration upon the Beauties of Liberty* (Boston, 1773), xiii, 11; Harry S. Stout, "Religion, Communications, and the Ideological Origins of the American Revolution," *William and Mary Quarterly,* 3d ser., 34, no. 4 (October 1977): 537.

26. Jonathan Parsons, *Freedom from Civil and Ecclesiastical Slavery* (Newburyport, MA, 1774), 5, 11, 16.

27. Nathaniel Niles, *Two Discourses on Liberty* (Newburyport, MA, 1774), 15n, 38, 59.

28. J. P., *Concerning the Number of the Beast* ([Unknown], 1777), 2; Samuel West, *A Sermon Preached Before the Honorable Council* (Boston, 1776), 67; Ebenezer Baldwin, *The Duty of Rejoicing Under Calamities and Afflictions* (New York, 1776), 38–39.

29. Samuel Clarke, *The American Wonder; or, The Strange and Remarkable Cape-Ann Dream* (Salem, MA, 1776), 14, 21.

30. Publicola [pseud.], introduction to Clarke, *American Wonder,* 9, 18.

31. [Samuel Clarke?], *The Strange and Remarkable Swansey Vision* (Salem, MA, 1776), 5, 7.

32. Samuel Sherwood, *Scriptural Instructions to Civil Rulers* (1774), in Sandoz, *Political Sermons* 1:377, 395.

33. Samuel Sherwood, *The Church's Flight into the Wilderness* (1776), in Sandoz, *Political Sermons* 1:501–502, 1:523.

35. Jonathan Sewall to Frederick Haldimand, May 30, 1775, in *Colonies to Nation, 1763–1789: A Documentary History of the American Revolution,* ed. Jack Greene (New York, 1975), 266–267.

CHAPTER 5

1. *Massachusetts Spy,* November 9, 1780.

2. John Ferling, *Almost a Miracle: The American Victory in the War of Independence* (New York, 2007), 439–442.

3. Samuel Adams to John Scollay, December 30, 1780, in *The Writings of Samuel Adams*, ed. Harry Alonzo Cushing (reprint, New York, 1968), 4:237–238.

4. Hugh Henry Brackenridge, *Six Political Discourses Founded on the Scripture* (Lancaster, PA, 1778), 30.

5. A Lover and Friend of Mankind, *An Affectionate Address to the Inhabitants of the British Colonies in America* (Philadelphia, 1776), iv.

6. *A Proclamation for a Continental Fast*, March 16, 1776 [Philadelphia], broadside.

7. Mark A. Noll, *America's God: From Jonathan Edwards to Abraham Lincoln* (New York, 2002), 107–113.

8. Franklin quoted in "Papers of Dr. James McHenry on the Federal Convention of 1787," *American Historical Review* 11, no. 3 (April 1906): 618.

9. Joseph Emerson, *A Thanksgiving-Sermon Preach'd at Pepperell* (Boston, 1766), 35.

10. Stephen Johnson, *Some Important Observations, Occasioned by, and Adapted to, the Publick Fast* (Newport, RI, 1766), 7, 20.

11. Fred Anderson, *A People's Army: Massachusetts Soldiers and Society in the Seven Years' War* (Chapel Hill, NC, 1984), 117–120; Robert Middlekauff, *The Glorious Cause: The American Revolution, 1763–1789* (New York, 1982), 195; John Witherspoon, *The Dominion of Providence over the Passions of Men* (1776), in *Political Sermons of the American Founding Era, 1730–1805*, ed. Ellis Sandoz, 2d ed. (Indianapolis, IN, 1998), 1:556.

12. William Tennent III, *An Address, Occasioned by the Late Invasion of the Liberties of the American Colonies* (Philadelphia, 1774), 15.

13. Montesquieu quoted in Peter Whitney, *The Transgressions of a Land Punished* (Boston, 1774), 69; John Adams, "Novanglus," no. IV, in *The Revolutionary Writings of John Adams*, ed. C. Bradley Thompson (Indianapolis, IN, 2000), 184.

14. William Henry Drayton, *A Charge, on the Rise of the American Empire* (Charlestown, SC, 1776), 3.

15. Valerius Poplicola [Samuel Adams], *Boston Gazette*, October 5, 1772, in Cushing, *Writings of Samuel Adams* 2:336; Samuel Adams to John Scollay, April 30, 1776, in Cushing, *Writings of Samuel Adams* 3:286.

16. Jeffry H. Morrison, *John Witherspoon and the Founding of the American Republic* (Notre Dame, IN, 2005), 130.

17. Continental Congress, *In Congress, Saturday, March 16, 1776* (New London, CT, 1776), 1; Morrison, *John Witherspoon*, 24; Witherspoon, *Dominion of Providence*, 550.

18. Witherspoon, *Dominion of Providence*, 553.

19. Ibid., 556–558.

20. Jonathan Odell quoted in Moses Coit Tyler, *The Literary History of the American Revolution, 1763–1783* (New York, 1897), 2:99–100, 122.

21. Charles Royster, *A Revolutionary People at War: The Continental Army and American Character, 1775–1783* (Chapel Hill, NC, 1979), 269–277.

22. Abraham Keteltas, *God Arising and Pleading His People's Cause* (1777), in Sandoz, *Political Sermons* 1:603; Keteltas, *Reflections on Extortion* (Newburyport, MA, 1778), 30.

23. Keteltas, *Reflections on Extortion*, 33–34, 36.

24. Washington quoted in Gordon S. Wood, *The Creation of the American Republic, 1776–1787* (Chapel Hill, NC, 1969), 132.

25. Thomas Paine, *Common Sense and Related Writings*, ed. Thomas P. Slaughter (Boston, 2001), 86.

26. John Adams, *Thoughts on Government* (1776), in Thompson, *Revolutionary Writings of John Adams*, 288.

27. Donald S. Lutz, "The Relative Influence of European Writers on Late Eighteenth-Century American Political Thought," *American Political Science Review* 78, no. 1 (March 1984): 189–197; Noll, *America's God*, 61.

28. Peter Whitney, *American Independence Vindicated* (Boston, 1777), 51, 54.

29. Benjamin Rush, *A Plan for the Establishment of Public Schools* (Philadelphia, 1786), 15, 27; Noll, *America's God*, 64–65.

30. Rush, *Plan for the Establishment*, 15–16.

31. *The Constitutions of the Several Independent States of America* (Philadelphia, 1781), 36; John Jay quoted in Clinton Rossiter, *Seedtime of the Republic: The Origin of the American Tradition of Political Liberty* (New York, 1953), 373; Wood, *Creation of the American Republic*, 426; Abigail Adams to John Adams, November 11, 1783, in *The Founders on Religion: A Book of Quotations*, ed. James H. Hutson (Princeton, NJ, 2005), 94.

32. George Washington, *Resignation of His Excellency George Washington* (New York, 1796), 17; Noll, *America's God*, 203–204; Vincent Phillip Muñoz, "George Washington on Religious Liberty," *Review of Politics* 65, no. 1 (Winter 2003): 18–20; Jeffry H. Morrison, *The Political Philosophy of George Washington* (Baltimore, MD, 2009), 165.

33. Washington, *Resignation*, 19; George Washington to Moses Seixas, August 17, 1790, in *A Documentary History of Religion in America to the Civil War*, ed. Edwin Gaustad (Grand Rapids, MI, 1982), 279; Muñoz, "George Washington," 20.

34. William Vans Murray, *Political Sketches* (London, 1787), 28; "Answers to Principal Questions That Have Been Raised Against the Proposed Federal Constitution," *Providence Gazette*, December 29, 1787, 1; Wood, *Creation of the American Republic*, 610–611.

35. John Adams to Samuel Adams, October 18, 1790, in *The Political Writings of John Adams*, ed. George W. Carey (Washington, DC, 2001), 665; Philip Greven, *The Protestant Temperament: Patterns of Child-Rearing, Religious Experience, and the Self in Early America* (New York, 1977), 358–359; Gordon S. Wood, *The Radicalism of the American Revolution* (New York, 1991), 252–253.

36. James Madison, "The Federalist No. 51," in *The Federalist*, ed. George W. Carey and James McClellan (Indianapolis, IN, 2001), 269; Jefferson quoted in Noll, *America's God*, 204.

CHAPTER 6

1. Henry A. Muhlenberg, *The Life of Major-General Peter Muhlenberg* (Philadelphia, 1849), 49, 52–53; J. T. Headley, *The Chaplains and Clergy of the Revolution* (New York, 1864), 123–125.

2. "Journal of Rev. William Rogers," in *Journals of the Military Expedition of Major General John Sullivan Against the Six Nations of Indians in 1779*, ed. Frederick Cook (Auburn, NY, 1887), 250; Charles Royster, *A Revolutionary People at War: The Con-*

tinental Army and American Character, 1775–1783 (Chapel Hill, NC, 1979), 18; Colin G. Calloway, *The American Revolution in Indian Country: Crisis and Diversity in Native American Communities* (New York, 1995), 51.

3. Charles Metzger, "Chaplains in the American Revolution," *Catholic Historical Review* 31, no. 1 (1945–1946), 52–53.

4. Nathaniel Taylor, *Praise Due to God for All the Dispensations of His Wise and Holy Providence* (New Haven, CT, 1762), 18.

5. Cleaveland quoted in Fred Anderson, *A People's Army: Massachusetts Soldiers and Society in the Seven Years' War* (Chapel Hill, NC, 1984), 216.

6. David L. Holmes, *The Faiths of the Founding Fathers* (New York, 2006), 67–69.

7. Peter Oliver, *Peter Oliver's Origin and Progress of the American Rebellion*, ed. Douglass Adair and John A. Schutz (Stanford, CA, 1961), 132; George Washington to Governor Jonathan Trumbull, December 15, 1775, in *The Writings of George Washington*, ed. John C. Fitzpatrick (Washington, DC, 1931), 4:164.

8. George Washington, General Orders, July 9, 1776, in Fitzpatrick, *Writings of George Washington* 5:245.

9. George Washington to the President of Congress, June 8, 1777, in Fitzpatrick, *Writings of George Washington* 8:203–204.

10. Hezekiah Smith to Hephzibah Smith, June 21, 1776, Gratz Collection, Historical Society of Pennsylvania.

11. John Witherspoon, *The Dominion of Providence over the Passions of Men* (1776), in *Political Sermons of the American Founding Era, 1730–1805*, ed. Ellis Sandoz, 2d ed. (Indianapolis, IN, 1998), 1:555–556.

12. Abiel Leonard, *A Prayer, Composed for the Benefit of the Soldiery, in the American Army* (Cambridge, MA, 1775), 4–7.

13. Royster, *Revolutionary People at War*, 170–174.

14. William Linn, *A Military Discourse, Delivered in Carlisle* (Philadelphia, 1776), 12, 16, 21, 23.

15. John Hurt, *The Love of Our Country* (Philadelphia, 1777), 14, 18, 21.

16. Ibid., 7, 18.

17. George Washington to Henry Laurens, December 23, 1777, in *The Papers of George Washington Digital Edition,* ed. Theodore J. Crackel (Charlottesville, VA, 2007), http://rotunda.upress.virginia.edu:8080/pgwde.

18. John Hurt, "An Address to the First and Second Virginia Brigades" (1778), *Virginia Magazine of History and Biography* 17, no. 2 (1909): 213–214; Royster, *Revolutionary People at War*, 251.

19. David Avery to Eleazar Wheelock, February 13, 1776, in David Avery Papers, Princeton Theological Seminary; Avery, *The Lord Is to Be Praised for the Triumphs of His Power* (Norwich, CT, 1778), 46.

20. *The Fall of Lucifer* (Hartford, CT, 1781), 11; Royster, *Revolutionary People at War*, 288–294.

21. John Calvin Thorne, *A Monograph on the Rev. Israel Evans, M.A.* (Concord, NH, 1902), 5–6; George Washington to Israel Evans, March 13, 1778, in *Papers of George Washington Digital Edition.*

22. *In Congress, November 1, 1777* ([Boston, 1777]), 1; Israel Evans, *A Discourse Delivered on the 18th Day of December, 1777* (Lancaster, PA, 1778), 17, 24.

23. Israel Evans, *A Discourse, Delivered at Easton* (Philadelphia, [1779]), 38.

24. Ibid., 40.

25. John Ferling, *Almost a Miracle: The American Victory in the War of Independence* (New York, 2007), 530–538.

26. Israel Evans, *A Discourse Delivered Near York in Virginia* (Philadelphia, 1782), 46.

27. Thorne, *Monograph on the Rev. Israel Evans*, 18; Alan Heimert, *Religion and the American Mind: From the Great Awakening to the Revolution* (Cambridge, MA, 1966), 498; Israel Evans, *A Discourse Delivered in New-York* (New York, [1784]), 8; George Duffield, *A Sermon Preached in the Third Presbyterian Church* (Philadelphia, 1784), in Sandoz, *Political Sermons* 1:784.

28. John Adams quoted in Ezra Stiles, *The United States Elevated to Glory and Honor* (New Haven, CT, 1783), in *The Pulpit of the American Revolution*, ed. John W. Thornton (reprint, New York, 1970), 464–465.

29. Samson Occom to the Oneida Tribe, 1775, in *The Collected Writings of Samson Occom, Mohegan: Leadership and Literature in Eighteenth-Century Native America*, ed. Joanna Brooks (New York, 2006), 111–112.

30. Samson Occom to John Bailey, [June or July 1783], in Brooks, *Collected Writings of Samson Occom*, 119; Alan Taylor, *The Divided Ground: Indians, Settlers, and the Northern Borderland of the American Revolution* (New York, 2006), 81–82, 101, 208–213.

31. Oliver, *Origin and Progress*, 132.

CHAPTER 7

1. John Winthrop, *A Model of Christian Charity*, in *The Puritans*, ed. Perry Miller and Thomas H. Johnson (New York, 1963), 1:195.

2. James Forten, *Letters from a Gentleman of Color* (1813), quoted in Gary B. Nash, *The Unknown American Revolution: The Unruly Birth of Democracy and the Struggle to Create America* (New York, 2005), 210.

3. George Fox, *Gospel Family-Order* (Philadelphia, 1701), 14, 17; Winthrop D. Jordan, *White over Black: American Attitudes Toward the Negro, 1550–1812* (reprint, New York, 1977), 194.

4. Samuel Sewall, *The Selling of Joseph* (Boston, 1700), 1.

5. John Wise, *A Vindication of the Government of New-England Churches* (reprint, Boston, 1772), 40.

6. George Whitefield, *Sermons on Various Subjects* (Philadelphia, 1740), 2:206.

7. Jonathan Edwards, *The Nature of True Virtue*, in *Two Dissertations* (Boston, 1765), 140; "Wig" quote in George M. Marsden, *Jonathan Edwards: A Life* (New Haven, CT, 2003), 299.

8. Edwards quoted in Gerald R. McDermott, *One Holy and Happy Society: The Public Theology of Jonathan Edwards* (University Park, PA, 1992), 156.

9. Jonathan Edwards, *The Great Christian Doctrine of Original Sin Defended* (1758), quoted in Rachel Wheeler, "'Friends to Your Souls': Jonathan Edwards' Indian Pas-

torate and the Doctrine of Original Sin," *Church History* 72, no. 4 (December 2003): 737–738; Marsden, *Jonathan Edwards*, 258.

10. William Cooper, *One Shall Be Taken, and Another Left* (Boston, 1741), 12–13.

11. Gordon S. Wood, *The Radicalism of the American Revolution* (New York, 1991), 122–123.

12. Dr. Alexander Hamilton quoted in Alan Heimert, *Religion and the American Mind: From the Great Awakening to the Revolution* (Cambridge, MA, 1966), 170; Anglican parson Jacob Duché quoted in J. R. Pole, "Equality," in *A Companion to the American Revolution*, ed. Jack P. Greene and J. R. Pole (Malden, MA, 2000), 633.

13. John Locke, *An Essay Concerning the True Original Extent and End of Civil Government* (reprint, Boston, 1773), 4, 25, 54; Carl L. Becker, *The Declaration of Independence: A Study in the History of Political Ideas* (reprint, New York, 1958), 26–27; J. R. Pole, *The Pursuit of Equality in American History*, rev. ed. (Berkeley, CA, 1993), 14–15.

14. [Elisha Williams], *The Essential Rights and Liberties of Protestants* (1744), in *Political Sermons of the American Founding Era, 1730–1805*, ed. Ellis Sandoz, 2d ed. (Indianapolis, IN, 1998), 1:56–57.

15. James Otis, *A Vindication of the Conduct of the House of Representatives* (Boston, 1762), 17–18.

16. The Earl of Clarendon [John Adams] to William Pym, *Boston Gazette*, January 27, 1766, in *The Works of John Adams*, ed. Charles Francis Adams (Boston, 1850–1856), 3:480; Wood, *Radicalism of the American Revolution*, 237.

17. Thomas Paine, *Common Sense and Related Writings*, ed. Thomas P. Slaughter (Boston, 2001), 79.

18. "Speech of an Honest, Sensible, and Spirited Farmer of Philadelphia County," in *Principles and Acts of the Revolution in America*, ed. Hezekiah Niles (reprint, New York, 1876), 221.

19. *The People the Best Governors* (1776), reprinted in Frederick Chase, *A History of Dartmouth College* (Cambridge, MA, 1891), 1:654, 661; Bernard Bailyn, *The Ideological Origins of the American Revolution*, enlarged ed. (Cambridge, MA, 1992), 293–294.

20. Pauline Maier, *American Scripture: Making the Declaration of Independence* (New York, 1997), 133–134.

21. Ibid., 134.

22. Thomas Jefferson to Henry Lee, May 8, 1825, in *The Writings of Thomas Jefferson*, ed. Albert E. Bergh (Washington, DC, 1907), 15:118.

23. Edmund Randolph quoted in *The Founders' Constitution*, ed. Philip B. Kurland and Ralph Lerner (Chicago, 1987), 1:522.

24. John C. Calhoun, "Speech on the Oregon Bill [June 27, 1848]," in *Union and Liberty: The Political Philosophy of John C. Calhoun*, ed. Ross M. Lence (Indianapolis, IN, 1992), 566; Maier, *American Scripture*, 199–200.

25. David Ramsay, *An Oration on the Advantages of Independence* (Charleston, SC, 1778), 2.

26. James Madison, *Manifestation of the Beneficence of Divine Providence Towards America* (1795), in Sandoz, *Political Sermons* 2:1311–1312.

27. Samuel Stillman, *A Sermon Preached Before the Honorable Council* (Boston, 1779), 8–10, 29.

28. Samuel Cooper, *A Sermon Preached Before His Excellency John Hancock* (1780), in Sandoz, *Political Sermons* 1:637.

29. Samuel Adams, "To the Legislature of Massachusetts (Jan. 17, 1794)," in *The Writings of Samuel Adams*, ed. Harry Alonzo Cushing (reprint, New York, 1968), 4:356–359.

30. Thomas Jefferson, *Notes on the State of Virginia by Thomas Jefferson with Related Documents*, ed. David Waldstreicher (Boston, 2002), 175–178.

31. Frederick Douglass, "What to the Slave Is the Fourth of July? (1852)," in *Narrative of the Life of Frederick Douglass, an American Slave, Written by Himself with Related Documents*, ed. David W. Blight, 2d ed. (Boston, 2003), 167.

CHAPTER 8

1. Patrick Henry to Robert Pleasants, January 18, 1773, in William Wirt Henry, *Patrick Henry: Life, Correspondence, and Speeches* (New York, 1891), 1:152–153.

2. Ruth Bogin, "'Liberty Further Extended': A 1776 Anti-Slavery Manuscript by Lemuel Haynes," *William and Mary Quarterly*, 3d ser., 40, no. 1 (January 1983): 94–95; John Saillant, *Black Puritan, Black Republican: The Life and Thought of Lemuel Haynes, 1753–1833* (New York, 2003), 1–15.

3. Thomas S. Kidd, ed., *The Great Awakening: A Brief History with Documents* (Boston, 2007), 116; Kidd, *The Great Awakening: The Roots of Evangelical Christianity in Colonial America* (New Haven, CT, 2007), 217–218.

4. David quoted in James Habersham to Robert Keen, May 11, 1775, in "The Letters of Hon. James Habersham, 1756–1775," *Collections of the Georgia Historical Society* (Savannah, GA, 1904), 6:244; George quoted in Robert Olwell, "'Domestick Enemies': Slavery and Political Independence in South Carolina, May 1775–March 1776," *Journal of Southern History* 55, no. 1 (February 1989): 34; Simon Schama, *Rough Crossings: Britain, the Slaves and the American Revolution* (New York, 2006), 69.

5. Woody Holton, *Forced Founders: Indians, Debtors, Slaves, and the Making of the American Revolution in Virginia* (Chapel Hill, NC, 1999), 155–156.

6. John Rippon, ed., "An Account of the Life of Mr. David George," *Baptist Annual Register for 1790, 1791, 1792, and Part of 1793* ([London], [1793]), 476–477; Kidd, *Great Awakening: Roots of Evangelical Christianity*, 225–226.

7. Phillis Wheatley to Samson Occom, February 11, 1774, in *The Collected Works of Phillis Wheatley*, ed. John C. Shields (New York, 1988), 176–177.

8. David Brion Davis, *Inhuman Bondage: The Rise and Fall of Slavery in the New World* (New York, 2006), 234.

9. Tom Paine, "African Slavery in America (1774)," in *Common Sense and Related Writings*, ed. Thomas P. Slaughter (Boston, 2001), 61; Paine quoted in Harvey J. Kaye, *Thomas Paine and the Promise of America* (New York, 2005), 37.

10. Jonathan Edwards Jr. and Ebenezer Baldwin, "Some Thoughts upon the Slavery of Negroes," *Connecticut Journal*, October 8, 1773; Kenneth P. Minkema and

Harry S. Stout, "The Edwardsean Tradition and the Antislavery Debate, 1740–1865," *Journal of American History* 92, no. 1 (June 2005), http://www.historycooperative.org/journals/jah/92.1/minkema.html, para. 16.

11. Samuel Hopkins, *A Dialogue, Concerning the Slavery of the Africans* (Norwich, CT, 1776), 5; Jonathan D. Sassi, ed., "'This Whole Country Have Their Hands Full of Blood This Day': Transcription and Introduction of an Antislavery Sermon Manuscript Attributed to the Reverend Samuel Hopkins," *Proceedings of the American Antiquarian Society* 112, part 1 (2002): 66, 70–71.

12. *A Discourse on the Times* (Norwich, CT, 1776), 4; David Avery, *The Lord Is to Be Praised for the Triumphs of His Power* (Norwich, CT, 1778), 46; Jacob Green, *A Sermon Delivered at Hanover* (Chatham, NJ, 1779), 16.

13. Benjamin Rush, *An Address to the Inhabitants of the British Settlements in America, upon Slave-Keeping* (New York, 1773), 30–31; John Jay to Egbert Benson, September 18, 1780, Papers of John Jay (digital resource), Columbia University Library, http://www.columbia.edu/cu/lweb/digital/jay/.

14. Thomas Jefferson, *Notes on the State of Virginia by Thomas Jefferson with Related Documents*, ed. David Waldstreicher (Boston, 2002), 195–196; Peter S. Onuf, "'To Declare Them a Free and Independant People': Race, Slavery, and National Identity in Jefferson's Thought," *Journal of the Early Republic* 18, no. 1 (Spring 1998): 1–6.

15. George Mason quoted in Philip B. Kurland and Ralph Lerner, eds., *The Founders' Constitution* (Chicago, 1987), http://press-pubs.uchicago.edu/founders/documents/a1_9_1s3.html; Jeff Broadwater, *George Mason: Forgotten Founder* (Chapel Hill, NC, 2006), 191–192.

16. Henry Wiencek, *An Imperfect God: George Washington, His Slaves, and the Creation of America* (New York, 2003), 274.

17. Ibid., 212–213; Jefferson, *Notes on the State of Virginia*, 178.

18. Winthrop D. Jordan, *White over Black: American Attitudes Toward the Negro, 1550–1812* (Chapel Hill, NC, 1968), 345–346.

19. Ibid., 346–348.

20. *Minutes of the Baptist General Committee* (Richmond, VA, 1790), 7.

21. John Poindexter Jr. to Isaac Backus, April 3, 1797, Louisa County, Virginia, photocopy, Virginia Baptist Historical Society; John Leland, *The Writings of the Late Elder John Leland*, ed. L. F. Greene (New York, 1845), 174.

22. Manumission deed quoted in Randolph Ferguson Scully, *Religion and the Making of Nat Turner's Virginia: Baptist Community and Conflict, 1740–1840* (Charlottesville, VA, 2008), 111.

23. Carlos R. Allen Jr., "David Barrow's Circular Letter of 1798," *William and Mary Quarterly*, 3d ser., 20, no. 3 (July 1963): 451; Thomas Jefferson to David Barrow, May 1, 1815, in *The Writings of Thomas Jefferson*, ed. Albert E. Bergh (Washington, DC, 1907), 14:297; James D. Essig, *The Bonds of Wickedness: American Evangelicals Against Slavery, 1770–1808* (Philadelphia, 1982), 76.

24. John Wesley, *Thoughts upon Slavery* (Philadelphia, 1774), 57; Dee E. Andrews, *The Methodists and Revolutionary America, 1760–1800* (Princeton, NJ, 2000), 125; Methodist Episcopal Church, *Minutes of Several Conversations* (Philadelphia, 1785),

15–17; Donald G. Mathews, *Slavery and Methodism: A Chapter in American Morality, 1780–1845* (Princeton, NJ, 1965), 10–11.

25. Andrews, *Methodists*, 126–127; Charles F. Irons, *The Origins of Proslavery Christianity: White and Black Evangelicals in Colonial and Antebellum Virginia* (Chapel Hill, NC, 2008), 68.

26. Grant quoted in Christine Leigh Heyrman, *Southern Cross: The Beginnings of the Bible Belt* (New York, 1997), 138–139; Andrews, *Methodists*, 130.

27. Freeborn Garrettson, *The Experience and Travels of Mr. Freeborn Garrettson* (Philadelphia, 1791), 35, 40, 76; Andrews, *Methodists*, 127–128.

28. O'Kelly quoted in H. Shelton Smith, *In His Image, But . . . Racism in Southern Religion, 1780–1910* (Durham, NC, 1972), 41–42; Irons, *Origins of Proslavery Christianity*, 75–76; Mathews, *Slavery and Methodism*, 21–22.

29. Darien committee quoted in Peter Force, ed., *American Archives: Documents of the American Revolution, 1774–1776*, 4th ser. (Washington, DC, 1837–1846), 1:1136; Jordan, *White over Black*, 301.

30. David Rice, *Slavery Inconsistent with Justice and Good Policy* (Philadelphia, 1792), 36; Essig, *Bonds of Wickedness*, 86–88.

31. Morgan J. Rhees, *Letters on Liberty and Slavery*, 2d ed. (New York, 1798), 6–7. Rhees replied to Lawrence's text. No copy of Lawrence has been discovered.

32. David Barrow, *Involuntary, Unmerited, Perpetual, Absolute, Hereditary Slavery* (Lexington, KY, 1808), 28–29n; Smith, *In His Image, But . . .* , 130–131.

33. Jordan, *White over Black*, 393, 399; Sylvia R. Frey, *Water from the Rock: Black Resistance in a Revolutionary Age* (Princeton, NJ, 1991), 256–258; Irons, *Origins of Proslavery Christianity*, 95.

34. Benjamin Ford quoted in Michael P. Johnson, "Denmark Vesey and His Co-Conspirators," *William and Mary Quarterly*, 3d ser., 58, no. 4 (October 2001): 970; Frey, *Water from the Rock*, 322; Richard Furman, "Exposition of the Views of the Baptists Relative to the Coloured Population of the United States" (1822), in James A. Rogers, *Richard Furman: Life and Legacy* (Macon, GA, 2001), 284–285; Frey, *Water from the Rock*, 264–265.

35. [Frederick Dalcho], *Practical Considerations Founded on the Scriptures* (Charleston, SC, 1823), 34; Mathews, *Slavery and Methodism*, 41.

36. [Dalcho], *Practical Considerations*, 33n.

37. Kenneth S. Greenberg, ed., *The Confessions of Nat Turner and Related Documents* (Boston, 1996), 47–48, 80.

CHAPTER 9

1. William White, *The Case of the Episcopal Churches in the United States Considered* (Philadelphia, 1782), iii.

2. "General Assessment Bill," in *Documentary History of the Struggle for Religious Liberty in Virginia*, comp. Charles F. James (Lynchburg, VA, 1900), 129.

3. Elisha Rich, *The Number of the Beast Found Out by Spiritual Arithmetic* (Chelmsford, MA, 1775), 11.

4. Benjamin Franklin, *The Autobiography of Benjamin Franklin*, ed. Louis P. Masur, 2d ed. (Boston, 2003), 93; Benjamin Franklin to Richard Price, October 9, 1780, in *The Founders' Constitution*, ed. Philip B. Kurland and Ralph Ketcham, vol. 4, article 6, clause 3, document 5, http://press-pubs.uchicago.edu/founders/documents/a6_3s5.html; Colin Kidd, "Civil Theology and Church Establishments in Revolutionary America," *Historical Journal* 42, no. 4 (December 1999): 1019–1020; *The Constitution of the Common-Wealth of Pennsylvania* (Philadelphia, 1776), 13; Thomas J. Curry, *The First Freedoms: Church and State in America to the Passage of the First Amendment* (New York, 1986), 160–161.

5. *In Convention, at New-Castle, for the Delaware State* (Wilmington, DE, 1776), 9; Curry, *First Freedoms*, 161.

6. *The Constitution of the State of New York* (Fishkill, NY, 1777), 30, 33; Curry, *First Freedoms*, 161–162; John Webb Pratt, *Religion, Politics, and Diversity: The Church-State Theme in New York History* (Ithaca, NY, 1967), 90–97; Mark Douglas McGarvie, *One Nation Under Law: America's Early National Struggles to Separate Church and State* (DeKalb, IL, 2005), 109–111.

7. Isaac Backus, *An Appeal to the Public for Religious Liberty* (Boston, 1773), 52.

8. Isaac Backus, *The Diary of Isaac Backus*, ed. William G. McLoughlin (Providence, RI, 1979), 2:917.

9. Baptist petition quoted in Backus, *Diary* 2:995n1; Curry, *First Freedoms*, 163.

10. Phillips Payson, *A Sermon Preached Before the Honourable Council* (Boston, 1778), 19–20; William G. McLoughlin, *Isaac Backus and the American Pietistic Tradition* (Boston, 1967), 140.

11. Isaac Backus, *Government and Liberty Described* (Boston, 1778), 15–18; "Tory plan" quoted in William G. McLoughlin, *Soul Liberty: The Baptists' Struggle in New England, 1630–1833* (Hanover, NH, 1991), 212, see also ibid., 197–200.

12. *A Constitution or Frame of Government* (Boston, 1784), 7–8; John Leland, *The Writings of the Late Elder John Leland*, ed. L. F. Greene (New York, 1845), 118; Curry, *First Freedoms*, 163–164.

13. Return of Granville, May 8, 1780, and Ashby, June 2, 1780, in Oscar Handlin and Mary Handlin, eds., *The Popular Sources of Religious Authority: Documents on the Massachusetts Constitution of 1780* (Cambridge, MA, 1966), 557, 634; Philanthropos [pseud.], *Continental Journal*, April 6, 1780; Samuel Eliot Morison, "The Struggle over the Adoption of the Constitution of Massachusetts, 1780," *Proceedings of the Massachusetts Historical Society* 50 (1917): 378–380; Curry, *First Freedoms*, 169, 171; Irenaeus [pseud.], *Continental Journal*, March 9, 1780.

14. Isaac Backus, *A Door Opened for Equal Christian Liberty* (Boston, 1783), 14–15; William G. McLoughlin, "The Balkcom Case (1782) and the Pietistic Theory of Separation of Church and State," *William and Mary Quarterly*, 3d ser., 24, no. 2 (April 1967): 275–278.

15. McLoughlin, *Soul Liberty*, 299–300.

16. Judah Champion, *Christian and Civil Liberty and Freedom Considered and Recommended* (Hartford, CT, 1776), 10–11; J. T. Headley, *The Chaplains and Clergy of the Revolution* (New York, 1864), 320.

17. Champion, *Christian and Civil Liberty*, 10–11; Curry, *First Freedoms*, 178.

18. Israel Holly, *An Appeal to the Impartial* (Norwich, CT, 1778), 6; Curry, *First Freedoms*, 180.

19. John Leland, *The Rights of Conscience Inalienable* … (New Haven, CT, 1791), 13; Lyman H. Butterfield, "Elder John Leland, Jeffersonian Itinerant," *Proceedings of the American Antiquarian Society* 62, part 2 (1952): 197–199; Curry, *First Freedoms*, 182.

20. Thomas Jefferson to the Danbury Baptist Association, January 1, 1802, http://www.loc.gov/loc/lcib/9806/danpre.html; Daniel L. Dreisbach, "Thomas Jefferson and the Danbury Baptists Revisited," *William and Mary Quarterly*, 3d ser., 56, no. 4 (October 1999): 811–813; Philip Hamburger, *Separation of Church and State* (Cambridge, MA, 2002), 163.

21. Lyman Beecher quoted in Edwin S. Gaustad, *Neither King nor Prelate: Religion and the New Nation, 1776–1826*, rev. ed. (Grand Rapids, MI, 1993), 120; Thomas Jefferson quoted in ibid., 49; McLoughlin, *Soul Liberty*, 290–291.

22. *A Constitution, Containing a Bill of Rights* (Portsmouth, NH, 1783), 4; John M. Murrin, "Religion and Politics in America from the First Settlements to the Civil War," in *Religion and American Politics: From the Colonial Period to the 1980s*, ed. Mark A. Noll (New York, 1990), 29.

23. Junius [pseud.], in *New-Hampshire Patriot*, October 10, 1815; McGarvie, *One Nation Under Law*, 169, 182; McLoughlin, *Soul Liberty*, 292.

24. *The Constitution of the State of Vermont* (Hartford, CT, 1778), 8, 14; Caleb Blood, *A Sermon Preached Before the Honourable Legislature* (Rutland, VT, 1792), 27; Curry, *First Freedoms*, 188–189; McLoughlin, *Soul Liberty*, 290.

25. William Tennent, "Petition of the Dissenters" and "Speech on the Dissenting Petition" (both 1777), in "Writings of the Rev. William Tennent," *South Carolina Historical Magazine* 61, no. 4 (1960): 195, 203.

26. Charlestown Association, *Minutes of the Charlestown Association* (Charleston, SC, 1778), 4; Gaustad, *Neither King nor Prelate*, 170–172; James Lowell Underwood, "The Dawn of Religious Freedom in South Carolina: The Journey from Limited Tolerance to Constitutional Right," in *The Dawn of Religious Freedom in South Carolina*, ed. James Lowell Underwood and Lewis Burke (Columbia, SC, 2006), 31–33; Curry, *First Freedoms*, 149–153.

27. Charles Woodmason, *The Carolina Backcountry on the Eve of the Revolution: The Journal and Other Writings of Charles Woodmason, Anglican Itinerant*, ed. Richard J. Hooker (Chapel Hill, NC, 1953), 80–81; Samuel Rabinove, "How—and Why—American Jews Have Contended for Religious Freedom: The Requirements and Limits of Civility," *Journal of Law and Religion* 8, nos. 1–2 (1990): 137; Curry, *First Freedoms*, 151–152.

28. *A Declaration of Rights, and the Constitution and Form of Government* (Annapolis, MD, 1776), 12; Patrick Allison, *Candid Animadversions* (Baltimore, MD, 1783), iv; Curry, *First Freedoms*, 153–157.

29. Petition of Hanover Presbytery, October 24, 1776, in James, *Documentary History*, 71–72; Rhys Isaac, *The Transformation of Virginia, 1740–1790* (Chapel Hill, NC, 1982), 280.

30. George Washington to George Mason, October 3, 1785, in *The Papers of George Washington Digital Edition,* ed. Theodore J. Crackel (Charlottesville, VA, 2007), http://rotunda.upress.virginia.edu:8080/pgwde; Petition of the Hanover Presbytery, October 1784, in James, *Documentary History,* 231–235; Curry, *First Freedoms,* 135–136, 140–41; Isaac, *Transformation of Virginia,* 280–281.

31. James Madison, *Memorial and Remonstrance* (1785), in James, *Documentary History,* 259; Thomas E. Buckley, S.J., *Church and State in Revolutionary Virginia, 1776–1787* (Charlottesville, VA, 1977), 134–135.

32. Baptist General Committee petition (1785), in James, *Documentary History,* 137–138; Buckley, *Church and State,* 140, 145–147, 175.

33. Thomas Jefferson, *Statute for Establishing Religious Freedom* (1786), in Gaustad, *Neither King nor Prelate,* 149–150; Thomas E. Buckley, S.J., "The Political Theology of Thomas Jefferson," in *The Virginia Statute for Religious Freedom: Its Evolution and Consequences in American History,* ed. Merrill D. Peterson and Robert C. Vaughan (New York, 1988), 93.

34. Jefferson, *Statute for Establishing Religious Freedom,* 151.

35. Buckley, *Church and State,* 171–172.

CHAPTER 10

1. A Farmer, *Some Remarks on the Great and Unusual Darkness* (Danvers, MA, 1780), 6; Susan Juster, "Demagogues or Mystagogues? Gender and the Language of Prophecy in the Age of Democratic Revolutions," *American Historical Review* 104, no. 5 (December 1999): 1560; Stephen Marini, *Radical Sects of Revolutionary New England* (Cambridge, MA, 1982), 47; Thomas S. Kidd, *The Great Awakening: The Roots of Evangelical Christianity in Colonial America* (New Haven, CT, 2007), 313.

2. John Leland, *The Virginia Chronicle* (Norfolk, VA, 1790), 33–34.

3. Stephen Tomkins, *John Wesley: A Biography* (Grand Rapids, MI, 2003), 48, 61.

4. Jesse Lee, *A Short History of the Methodists* (Baltimore, MD, 1810), 53; Kidd, *Great Awakening,* 243–244.

5. Lee, *Short History,* 64, 74–75; Wesley Gewehr, *The Great Awakening in Virginia, 1740–1790* (Durham, NC, 1930), 159.

6. Henry Alline, *A Sermon on a Day of Thanksgiving* (1782), in *Henry Alline: Selected Writings,* ed. George A. Rawlyk (New York, 1987), 125.

7. Isaac Backus, *A History of New England* (Newton, MA, 1871), 264–265.

8. Abner Brownell, *Enthusiastical Errors* (New London, CT, 1783), 13; Ruth Bloch, *Visionary Republic: Millennial Themes in American Thought, 1756–1800* (New York, 1985), 91; Catherine A. Brekus, *Strangers and Pilgrims: Female Preaching in America, 1740–1845* (Chapel Hill, NC, 1998), 80–97.

9. Kidd, *Great Awakening,* 318; Stephen J. Stein, *The Shaker Experience in America: A History of the United Society of Believers* (New Haven, CT, 1992), 11–12; Brekus, *Strangers and Pilgrims,* 97–103.

10. John Buzzell, *Life of Elder Benjamin Randal* (Limerick, ME, 1827), 13; Marini, *Radical Sects,* 64–65.

11. Buzzell, *Life of Elder Benjamin Randal*, 88–89; Isaac Backus, *The Diary of Isaac Backus*, ed. William G. McLoughlin (Providence, RI, 1979), 3:1145n1.

12. *Pennsylvania Evening Post*, May 11, 1779; Peter Silver, *Our Savage Neighbors: How Indian War Transformed Early America* (New York, 2008), 229–230; Frank G. Beardsley, *A History of American Revivals* (New York, 1912), 72–73; Patterson sermon described in Aaron Williams, "The Religious History," in *Centenary Memorial of the Planting and Growth of Presbyterianism in Western Pennsylvania* (Pittsburgh, 1876), 40–41; Heman Humphrey, *Revival Sketches and Manual* (New York, 1859), 189.

13. "McMillan and his people" quotation from Williams, "Religious History," 42; Stephen Marini, "Religion, Politics, and Ratification," in *Religion in a Revolutionary Age*, ed. Ronald Hoffman and Peter J. Albert (Charlottesville, VA, 1994), 198–199.

14. Backus, *History of New England*, 264; David Benedict, *A General History of the Baptist Denomination* (Boston, 1813), 1:551–552.

15. Lee, *Short History*, 119; Douglas H. Sweet, "Church Vitality and the American Revolution: Historiographical Consensus and Thoughts Towards a New Perspective," *Church History* 45, no. 3 (September 1976): 357.

16. Lee, *Short History*, 130–131; Gewehr, *Great Awakening*, 169–170.

17. Lee, *Short History*, 139–140; John H. Wigger, *Taking Heaven by Storm: Methodism and the Rise of Popular Christianity in America* (New York, 1998), 221n63.

18. George A. Phoebus, comp., *Beams of Light on Early Methodism in America. Chiefly Drawn from the Diary, Letters, Manuscripts, Documents, and Original Tracts of the Rev. Ezekiel Cooper* (New York, 1887), 87–89, http://docsouth.unc.edu/church/phoebus/phoebus.html; Terry D. Bilhartz, *Urban Religion and the Second Great Awakening: Church and Society in Early National Baltimore* (Rutherford, NJ, 1986), 85.

19. Phoebus, *Beams of Light*, 89–90.

20. Freeborn Garrettson, *American Methodist Pioneer: The Life and Journals of the Rev. Freeborn Garrettson, 1752–1827*, ed. Robert Drew Simpson (Rutland, VT, 1984), 134–135; Wigger, *Taking Heaven*, 110.

21. Richard Allen, *The Life, Experience, and Gospel Labours of the Right Rev. Richard Allen* (Philadelphia, 1833), 5–8, 10, 16, http://docsouth.unc.edu/neh/allen/allen.html; Gary B. Nash, "New Light on Richard Allen: The Early Years of Freedom," *William and Mary Quarterly*, 3d ser., 46, no. 2 (April 1989): 336–337; Nathan O. Hatch, *The Democratization of American Christianity* (New Haven, CT, 1989), 104.

22. Allen, *Life, Experience*, 13; Hatch, *Democratization*, 107–109; Douglas R. Egerton, *Death or Liberty: African Americans and Revolutionary America* (New York, 2009), 189–191.

23. Jesse Lee, *Memoir of the Rev. Jesse Lee*, ed. Minton Thrift (New York, 1823), 113–114; Eric Baldwin, "'The Devil Begins to Roar': Opposition to Early Methodists in New England," *Church History* 75, no. 1 (March 2006): 99.

24. Nathan Williams, *Order and Harmony in the Churches of Christ, Agreeable to God's Will* (Hartford, CT, 1793), 15–16, 28; George Roberts, *Strictures on a Sermon*

Delivered by Mr. Nathan Williams (Philadelphia, 1794), v; Baldwin, "Devil Begins to Roar," 101, 104.

25. Donald G. Mathews, "The Second Great Awakening as an Organizing Process, 1780–1830: A Hypothesis," *American Quarterly* 21, no. 1 (Spring 1969): 36–37; Richard Carwardine, *Trans-Atlantic Revivalism: Popular Evangelicalism in Britain and America, 1790–1865* (Westport, CT, 1978), 50.

26. Student mob quotation from William H. Foote, *Sketches of Virginia* (Philadelphia, 1850–1855), 417, 422; Gewehr, *Great Awakening*, 178–180.

27. Foote, *Sketches of Virginia*, 423.

28. McGready quoted in John B. Boles, *The Great Revival: Beginnings of the Bible Belt*, rev. ed. (Lexington, KY, 1996), 41, see also 37–38, 42–43; William H. Foote, *Sketches of North Carolina* (New York, 1846), 370.

29. Letter from Chandler Robbins, May 31, 1793, in Peter P. Roots, *A Letter to the First Congregational Paedobaptist Church* (Hartford, CT, 1794), 135–137.

30. Letter of Jeremiah Hallock, in *Connecticut Evangelical Magazine* 1, no 4 (October 1800): 139; David W. Kling, *A Field of Divine Wonders: The New Divinity and Village Revivals in Northwestern Connecticut, 1792–1822* (University Park, PA, 1993), 17–18.

31. Isaac Backus to Timothy Thomas, July 21, 1801, in *The Baptist Annual Register for 1798, 1799, 1800, and Part of 1801*, ed. John Rippon (London, 1801), 611–612; Alan Taylor, *Liberty Men and Great Proprietors: The Revolutionary Settlement on the Maine Frontier, 1760–1820* (Chapel Hill, NC, 1990), 139.

32. Isaac Backus to Timothy Thomas, July 21, 1802, in Rippon, *Baptist Annual Register*, 612; John Peck and John Lawson, *Historical Sketch of the Baptist Missionary Convention of the State of New York* (Utica, NY, 1837), 16, 20.

33. Marini, *Radical Sects*, 120–121.

34. Leigh Eric Schmidt, *Holy Fairs: Scotland and the Making of American Revivalism*, 2d ed. (Grand Rapids, MI, 2001), 63–64.

35. James McGready, "A Short Narrative of the Revival of Religion in Logan County," *New-York Missionary Magazine* (April 1803): 152–153; Boles, *Great Revival*, 49–50.

36. McGready, "Short Narrative of the Revival," 154–155; Boles, *Great Revival*, 57.

37. McGready, "Short Narrative of the Revival," 192–195; Boles, *Great Revival*, 55–57.

38. Revival description from Theophilus Armenius [pseud.], "Account of the Rise and Progress of the Work of God in the Western Country," *Methodist Magazine* 2 (July 1819): 273, quoted in Boles, *Great Revival*, 67; see also 64–65; Paul K. Conkin, *Cane Ridge: America's Pentecost* (Madison, WI, 1990), 88.

39. Boles, *Great Revival*, 77.

40. Stephen Prothero, *American Jesus: How the Son of God Became a National Icon* (New York, 2003), 31; William B. Sprague, *Annals of the American Pulpit* (New York, 1969), 6:176.

CHAPTER 11

1. George Washington to John Jay, August. 15, 1786, in *The Papers of George Washington Digital Edition*, ed. Theodore J. Crackel (Charlottesville, VA, 2007), http://rotunda.upress.virginia.edu:8080/pgwde.

2. Joseph Plumb Martin, *A Narrative of a Revolutionary Soldier* (New York, 2001), 148.

3. Charles Royster, "'The Nature of Treason': Revolutionary Virtue and American Reactions to Benedict Arnold," *William and Mary Quarterly*, 3d ser., 36, no. 2 (April 1979): 177; E. Wayne Carp, *To Starve the Army at Pleasure: Continental Army Administration and American Political Culture, 1775–1783* (Chapel Hill, NC, 1984), 62–67.

4. Gordon S. Wood, *The Creation of the American Republic, 1776–1787* (Chapel Hill, NC, 1969), 472; Woody Holton, *Unruly Americans and the Origins of the Constitution* (New York, 2007), 65–66.

5. Frank Lambert, *The Barbary Wars: American Independence in the Atlantic World* (New York, 2005), 93.

6. George Washington to John Jay, May 18, 1786, in *Papers of George Washington Digital Edition*; Jack N. Rakove, "From One Agenda to Another: The Condition of American Federalism, 1783–1787," in *The American Revolution: Its Character and Limits*, ed. Jack P. Greene (New York, 1987), 92.

7. Alexander Hamilton, "The Federalist No. 21," in *The Federalist*, ed. George W. Carey and James McClellan (Indianapolis, IN, 2001), 100–101; Holton, *Unruly Americans*, 157–158.

8. Hugh Blair Grigsby, *The History of the Virginia Federal Convention of 1788* (Richmond, VA, 1890), 32n36.

9. Benjamin Franklin, *The Works of Benjamin Franklin*, ed. John Bigelow (New York, 1904), 11:376–377; Gordon S. Wood, *The Americanization of Benjamin Franklin* (New York, 2004), 220, 229; Walter Isaacson, *Benjamin Franklin: An American Life* (New York, 2003), 451–452.

10. Articles of Confederation, Article 13, http://avalon.law.yale.edu/18th_century/artconf.asp; Luther Martin, *The Genuine Information* (Philadelphia, 1788), 80; Saul Cornell, *The Other Founders: Anti-Federalism and the Dissenting Tradition in America, 1788–1828* (Chapel Hill, NC, 1999), 57.

11. James Madison, "Vices of the Political System of the United States," in *The Founders' Constitution*, ed. Philip B. Kurland and Ralph Ketcham (Chicago, 2000), ch. 5, doc. 16, http://press-pubs.uchicago.edu/founders/documents/v1ch5s16.html.

12. William Williams to the Landholder, *American Mercury*, February 11, 1788; Isaac Kramnick and R. Laurence Moore, *The Godless Constitution: A Moral Defense of the Secular State*, rev. ed. (New York, 2005), 37.

13. Elihu [pseud.], in *American Mercury*, February 18, 1788.

14. George Washington to the Presbyterian Ministers of Massachusetts and New Hampshire, November 2, 1789, in *Papers of George Washington Digital Edition*; Paul F. Boller Jr., *George Washington and Religion* (Dallas, TX, 1963), 147–148.

15. Jonas Phillips to His Excellency the President and the Honourable Members of the Convention Assembled, September 7, 1787, in *The Records of the Federal Convention of 1787*, ed. Max Farrand (1911), 78–79, http://memory.loc.gov/ammem/amlaw/lwfr.html; David Caldwell speech of July 30, 1788, in *The Debates in the Several State Conventions on the Adoption of the Federal Constitution*, ed. Jonathan Elliot (Philadelphia, 1891), 4:199.

16. James Madison, "The Federalist No. 37," in Carey and McClellan, *The Federalist*, 185.

17. James Madison, "The Federalist No. 10" and "The Federalist No. 55," in Carey and McClellan, *The Federalist*, 48, 291; Wood, *Creation of the American Republic*, 505.

18. Patrick Henry, speeches of June 5 and June 9, 1788, in Elliot, *Debates* 3:59, 167; Wood, *Creation of the American Republic*, 507.

19. James Madison, "The Federalist No. 51," in Carey and McClellan, *The Federalist*, 268–269.

20. Stephen Marini, "Religion, Politics, and Ratification," in *Religion in a Revolutionary Age*, ed. Ronald Hoffman and Peter J. Albert (Charlottesville, VA, 1994), 192–193; Samuel Langdon, *The Republic of the Israelites an Example to the American States* (Exeter, NH, 1788), in *Political Sermons of the American Founding Era, 1730–1805*, ed. Ellis Sandoz, 2d ed. (Indianapolis, IN, 1998), 1:958–959.

21. Marini, "Religion," 189–191.

22. David Caldwell, debate of July 24, 1788, in Elliot, *Debates* 4:9, 23; Marini, "Religion," 205.

23. Caldwell, debate of July 30, 1788, in Elliot, *Debates* 4:199.

24. John Leland, *The Rights of Conscience Inalienable* (1791), in *The Writings of the Late Elder John Leland*, ed. L. F. Greene (New York, 1845), 191–192; Lyman H. Butterfield, "Elder John Leland, Jeffersonian Itinerant," *Proceedings of the American Antiquarian Society* 62, part 2 (1952): 186–189; Samuel Spencer, debate of July 30, 1788, in Elliot, *Debates* 4:200; "Samuel Spencer," in *Princetonians*, ed. James McLachlan (Princeton, NJ, 1976), 1:289–292.

25. Federal Farmer [pseud.], letter no. 4, October 12, 1787, in *The Complete Anti-Federalist*, ed. Herbert J. Storing (Chicago, 1981), 2:249; Herbert J. Storing, "What the Anti-Federalists Were For," in Storing, *Complete Anti-Federalist* 1:22–23.

26. John Leland's Objections to the Federal Constitution (1788), in Butterfield, "Elder John Leland," 187–188.

27. Butterfield, "Elder John Leland," 191–193; James Madison to George Eve, January 2, 1789, and Benjamin Johnson to James Madison, January 19, 1789, both in *The Papers of James Madison*, ed. William T. Hutchinson and William M. E. Rachal (Chicago, 1991), 11:405, 424; Michael W. McConnell, "The Origins and Historical Understanding of Free Exercise of Religion," *Harvard Law Review* 103, no. 7 (May 1990): 1477.

28. "Address of the Committee of the United Baptist Churches of Virginia, August 8, 1789," in *Writings of the Late Elder John Leland*, 53–54; George Washington to the United Baptist Churches of Virginia, [May 1789], in *Papers of George Washington Digital Edition*.

29. Isaac Backus in Elliot, *Debates* 2:148–149; William G. McLoughlin, *Isaac Backus and the American Pietistic Tradition* (Boston, 1967), 196–199.

30. Debate of the House on Amendments, August 1789, in *The Founders' Constitution*, http://press-pubs.uchicago.edu/founders/documents/amendI_religions53.html; Leonard W. Levy, *The Establishment Clause: Religion and the First Amendment* (New York, 1986), 71.

31. Benjamin Rush to [Elias Boudinot?], July 9, 1788, in *Letters of Benjamin Rush*, ed. Lyman H. Butterfield (Princeton, NJ, 1951), 1:474; Chris Beneke, *Beyond Toleration: The Religious Origins of American Pluralism* (New York, 2006), 4.

32. Rush to [Elias Boudinot?], July 9, 1788, 475.

33. John G. West Jr., *The Politics of Revelation and Reason: Religion and Civic Life in the New Nation* (Lawrence, KS, 1996).

CHAPTER 12

1. Thomas Jefferson to Spencer Roane, September 6, 1819, in *The Writings of Thomas Jefferson*, ed. Albert E. Bergh (Washington, DC, 1907), 15:212; Gordon S. Wood, *Empire of Liberty: A History of the Early Republic, 1789–1815* (New York, 2009), 284–285.

2. *Gazette of the United States* (Philadelphia), September 13, 1800; Danbury Baptist Association to Thomas Jefferson, October 7, 1801, reprinted in Daniel L. Dreisbach, *Thomas Jefferson and the Wall of Separation Between Church and State* (New York, 2002), 31–32; Robert M. S. McDonald, "Was There a Religious Revolution of 1800?" in *The Revolution of 1800: Democracy, Race, and the New Republic*, ed. James Horn, Jan Ellen Lewis, and Peter Onuf (Charlottesville, VA, 2002), 173; Edward J. Larson, *A Magnificent Catastrophe: The Tumultuous Election of 1800, America's First Presidential Campaign* (New York, 2007), 173–174.

3. Frank Lambert, *The Founding Fathers and the Place of Religion in America* (Princeton, NJ, 2003), 266.

4. Richard Furman, *Humble Submission to Divine Sovereignty the Duty of a Bereaved Nation* (Charleston, SC, 1800), 13; John Adams, *By the President of the United States of America, a Proclamation* (Philadelphia, 1798), broadside.

5. McDonald, "Was There a Religious Revolution," 175–176.

6. Elias Lee, *The Dissolution of Earthly Monarchies* (Danbury, CT, 1794), 16–17.

7. Harvey J. Kaye, *Thomas Paine and the Promise of America* (New York, 2005), 84–85.

8. Thomas Paine, *The Age of Reason* (Boston, 1794), 4; Uzal Ogden, *Antidote to Deism* (Newark, NJ, 1795), 16; Kaye, *Thomas Paine*, 82–84; Gary B. Nash, "The American Clergy and the French Revolution," *William and Mary Quarterly*, 3d ser., 22, no. 3 (July 1965): 402.

9. John G. West Jr., *The Politics of Revelation and Reason: Religion and the Civic Life in the New Nation* (Lawrence, KS, 1996), 60–61.

10. Noble E. Cunningham Jr., *In Pursuit of Reason: The Life of Thomas Jefferson* (Baton Rouge, LA, 1987), 167–168.

11. *Minerva*, September 3, 1796; William Smith and Oliver Wolcott, *The Pretensions of Thomas Jefferson to the Presidency Examined* (Philadelphia, 1796), 37; McDonald, "Was There a Religious Revolution," 178; Nash, "American Clergy," 409.

12. Samuel Adams to Thomas Paine, November 30, 1802, in *The Writings of Samuel Adams*, ed. Henry Alonzo Cushing (New York, 1968), 4:412–413.

13. Timothy Dwight, *The Duty of Americans, at the Present Crisis* (New Haven, CT, 1798), in *Political Sermons of the American Founding Era, 1730–1805*, ed. Ellis Sandoz, 2d ed. (Indianapolis, IN, 1998), 2:1369–1371, 1386; Larson, *Magnificent Catastrophe*, 167–169.

14. Thomas Jefferson, *Notes on the State of Virginia by Thomas Jefferson with Related Documents*, ed. David Waldstreicher (Boston, 2002), 192; *Gazette of the United States*, May 3, 1800, 3; [John M. Mason], *The Voice of Warning to Christians, on the Ensuing Election* (New York, 1800), in Sandoz, *Political Sermons* 2:1455–1457; Larson, *Magnificent Catastrophe*, 171–172.

15. [Mason], *Voice of Warning*, 1461, 1471–1472, 1475.

16. William Linn, *Serious Considerations on the Election of a President* (New York, 1800), 19; Larson, *Magnificent Catastrophe*, 172.

17. Thomas Jefferson to Joseph Priestley, March 21, 1801, and Thomas Jefferson to Moses Robinson, March 23, 1801, both in *The Papers of Thomas Jefferson*, ed. Barbara B. Oberg, vol. 33, *17 February to 30 April 1801* (Princeton, NJ, 2006), 393–394, 423–424.

18. "For the Chronicle," *Independent Chronicle*, July 21, 1800, 2; [John Beckley], *Address to the People of the United States* (Philadelphia, 1800), 7, 32; Grotius [DeWitt Clinton], *A Vindication of Thomas Jefferson* (New York, 1800); Larson, *Magnificent Catastrophe*, 174; McDonald, "Was There a Religious Revolution," 186.

19. "For the Centinel," *Centinel of Freedom*, November 4, 1800, 2.

20. Edwin S. Gaustad, *Sworn on the Altar of God: A Religious Biography of Thomas Jefferson* (Grand Rapids, MI, 1996), 95–96; Larson, *Magnificent Catastrophe*, 177.

21. Andrew Burstein, *Sentimental Democracy: The Evolution of America's Romantic Self-Image* (New York, 1999), 215–216.

22. Samuel Adams to Thomas Jefferson, April 24, 1801, and November 18, 1801, both in Cushing, *Writings of Samuel Adams* 4:408–411; John Leland, "Address to the Association of the Sons of Liberty, Cheshire, March 4, 1813," in *The Writings of the Late Elder John Leland*, ed. L. F. Greene (New York, 1845), 373.

23. Elias Smith, *The Whole World Governed by a Jew* (Exeter, NH, 1805), 73, 77; *The Diary of William Bentley* (Salem, MA, 1914), 4:386; Michael G. Kenny, *The Perfect Law of Liberty: Elias Smith and the Providential History of America* (Washington, DC, 1994), 24–25; Wood, *Empire of Liberty*, 617.

24. "Old Soldier," *Raleigh Register and North-Carolina Gazette*, October 1, 1804, quoted in John B. Boles, *The Great Revival: Beginnings of the Bible Belt*, rev. ed. (Lexington, KY, 1996), 180.

25. Thomas Jefferson to the Members of the Baltimore Baptist Association, October 17, 1808, and Thomas Jefferson to the General Meeting of Correspondence of Six Baptist Associations Represented at Chesterfield, Virginia, November 21, 1808,

both in *The Writings of Thomas Jefferson*, ed. Albert E. Bergh (Washington, DC, 1907), 16:317–318, 320–321.

26. Thomas Jefferson, "First Inaugural Address," in Oberg, *Papers of Thomas Jefferson* 33:150.

27. Cutler quoted in James H. Hutson, "Thomas Jefferson's Letter to the Danbury Baptists: A Controversy Rejoined," *William and Mary Quarterly*, 3d ser., 56, no. 4 (October 1999): 786, see also 787–789; John Leland, "An Oration Delivered at Cheshire, July 5, 1802," in Greene, *Writings of the Late Elder John Leland*, 264; Nicholas Guyatt, *Providence and the Invention of the United States, 1607–1876* (New York, 2007), 157–158.

EPILOGUE

1. Alexis de Tocqueville, *Democracy in America*, ed. J. P. Mayer (New York, 1969), 294–295.

2. Ibid., 47; Hugh Heclo, *Christianity and American Democracy* (Cambridge, MA, 2007), 10–12.

3. Tocqueville, *Democracy in America*, 444.

4. Ibid., 295, 545.

5. Ibid., 290, 535, 546; Hugh Brogan, *Alexis de Tocqueville: A Life* (New Haven, CT, 2007), 52–53.

6. Heclo, *Christianity and American Democracy*, 17.

7. John Adams to Abigail Adams, November 18, 1775, in *The Founders on Religion: A Book of Quotations*, ed. James H. Hutson (Princeton, NJ, 2005), 146.

8. Benjamin Franklin to William Strahan, August 19, 1784, in Hutson, *Founders on Religion*, 179.

9. Luther Richardson, *An Oration, Pronounced July 4, 1800* (Boston, 1800), 10.

10. General Dwight D. Eisenhower, D-Day Message, June 6, 1944, http://www.army.mil/D-day/message.html.

11. Thomas Jefferson, *Notes on the State of Virginia by Thomas Jefferson with Related Documents*, ed. David Waldstreicher (Boston, 2002), 195.

12. Benjamin Banneker to Thomas Jefferson, August 19, 1791, in Jefferson, *Notes on the State of Virginia*, 211.

INDEX